# THE CONSTITUTION OF MALAYSIA

This is the highly anticipated new edition of the seminal introduction to Malaysia's constitution by the leading expert in the field. Retaining its comprehensive approach, it examines constitutional governance in light of authoritarianism and continuing intercommunal strife, as well as examining the impact of colonisation on Malaysia's legal public law structure.

Updated throughout to include all statutory and case law developments, it also retains its socio-political perspective. It is a must read for all students and scholars of Malaysian law.

## Pictorial Narrative

An imposing colourful juxtaposition of deconstructed imagery provides fragmentary glimpses of the Malaysian constitutional settings.

The top layer framing the composition consists of, from left to right: a red dragon reflecting the Chinese ethnic and cultural influence; the crescent moon and stars symbolising the importance of Islam; the fourteen-pointed federal star with crescent moon on blue with fourteen alternating red and white stripes,[1] referring to the national flag. On the left hand side a ceremonial Iban spear celebrates Sarawak's native peoples.

The central focus of the picture is comprised of emblems from the royal coat of arms. There is a depiction of a pair of imposing, prancing tigers, the five krises[2] just beneath, and an orange hibiscus, the national flower: images that combine to symbolise the power and authority of the monarchs as heads of state.

The interplay of dissonant geometric shapes bottom left stands for recent political turmoil and fragmentation. This bottom layer is another reminder of the federal dimension of the constitution. To the right a swordfish refers to Kota Kinabalu, state capital of Sabah, while the cat represents Kuching, the state capital of Sarawak.

The right-hand bottom corner features open hands reaching out to grab ringgit, alluding to the prevalence of graft and malpractice in the political domain.

*Putachad*
Artist
(Sources of inspiration: Picasso and Popova)

---

[1] Representing the 13 member states and the federal territories.
[2] Ceremonial curved daggers, symbols of authority.

Constitutional Systems of the World
General Editors: Benjamin L Berger, Rosalind Dixon,
Andrew Harding, Heinz Klug, and Peter Leyland

In the era of globalisation, issues of constitutional law and good governance are being seen increasingly as vital issues in all types of society. Since the end of the Cold War, there have been dramatic developments in democratic and legal reform, and post-conflict societies are also in the throes of reconstructing their governance systems. Even societies already firmly based on constitutional governance and the rule of law have undergone constitutional change and experimentation with new forms of governance; and their constitutional systems are increasingly subjected to comparative analysis and transplantation. Constitutional texts for practically every country in the world are now easily available on the internet. However, texts which enable one to understand the true context, purposes, interpretation and incidents of a constitutional system are much harder to locate, and are often extremely detailed and descriptive. This series seeks to provide scholars and students with accessible introductions to the constitutional systems of the world, supplying both a road map for the novice and, at the same time, a deeper understanding of the key historical, political and legal events which have shaped the constitutional landscape of each country. Each book in this series deals with a single country, or a group of countries with a common constitutional history, and each author is an expert in their field.

### Published volumes

*The Constitution of the United Kingdom; The Constitution of the United States; The Constitution of Vietnam; The Constitution of South Africa; The Constitution of Japan; The Constitution of Germany; The Constitution of Finland; The Constitution of Australia; The Constitution of the Republic of Austria; The Constitution of the Russian Federation; The Constitutional System of Thailand; The Constitution of Malaysia; The Constitution of China; The Constitution of Indonesia; The Constitution of France; The Constitution of Spain; The Constitution of Mexico; The Constitution of Israel; The Constitutional Systems of the Commonwealth Caribbean; The Constitution of Canada; The Constitution of Singapore; The Constitution of Belgium; The Constitution of Taiwan; The Constitution of Romania; The Constitutional Systems of the Independent Central Asian States; The Constitution of India; The Constitution of Pakistan; The Constitution of Ireland; The Constitution of Brazil; The Constitution of Myanmar; The Constitution of Czechia; The Constitution of New Zealand; The Constitution of Italy*

### Link to series website

www.bloomsbury.com/uk/series/
constitutional-systems-of-the-world/

# The Constitution of Malaysia

*A Contextual Analysis*

Second Edition

Andrew Harding

·HART·

OXFORD · LONDON · NEW YORK · NEW DELHI · SYDNEY

HART PUBLISHING

Bloomsbury Publishing Plc

Kemp House, Chawley Park, Cumnor Hill, Oxford, OX2 9PH, UK

1385 Broadway, New York, NY 10018, USA

29 Earlsfort Terrace, Dublin 2, Ireland

HART PUBLISHING, the Hart/Stag logo, BLOOMSBURY and the Diana logo are
trademarks of Bloomsbury Publishing Plc

First published in Great Britain 2022

Copyright © Andrew Harding, 2022

A catalogue record for this book is available from the British Library.

Library of Congress Cataloging-in-Publication data

Names: Harding, Andrew, 1950- author.

Title: The Constitution of Malaysia : a contextual analysis / Andrew Harding.

Description: Second edition. | Oxford ; New York : Hart, 2022. | Series: Constitutional systems
of the world | Includes bibliographical references and index.

Identifiers: LCCN 2021059525 (print) | LCCN 2021059526 (ebook) |
ISBN 9781509957859 (hardback) | ISBN 9781509927432 (paperback) |
ISBN 9781509927456 (pdf) | ISBN 9781509927449 (Epub)

Subjects: LCSH: Malaysia. Perlembagaan Persekutuan. | Constitutional law—Malaysia. |
Constitutional history—Malaysia. | Malaysia—Politics and government—20th century. |
Malaysia—Politics and government—21st century.

Classification: LCC KPG1744.51957 .H37 2022 (print) | LCC KPG1744.51957 (ebook) |
DDC 342.59502/3—dc23/eng/20220128

LC record available at https://lccn.loc.gov/2021059525

LC ebook record available at https://lccn.loc.gov/2021059526

ISBN:  PB:  978-1-50992-743-2
       ePDF:  978-1-50992-745-6
       ePub:  978-1-50992-744-9

Typeset by Compuscript Ltd, Shannon
Printed and bound in Great Britain

To find out more about our authors and books visit www.hartpublishing.co.uk.
Here you will find extracts, author information, details of forthcoming events
and the option to sign up for our newsletters.

*The author's efforts in writing this book are dedicated to the blessed memory of his friend,* **Ang Hean Leng,** *who passed away, too young, in 2019.*

# Acknowledgements

THERE ARE TOO many people to thank. Over many years I have derived enormous benefit from the views and encouragement of my fellow scholars in Malaysia, Singapore, Britain, Australia and elsewhere; my students; lawyers; officials; politicians; and so many others. In particular I have to thank Peter and Nong Leyland for their personal support, as well as for Peter's insights and encouragement, and Nong's (Putachad's) wonderfully evocative cover design; and Hart Publishing for their support and sterling efforts in the process of turning the manuscript into a book and these books into a series.

This book could not have been written without the hospitality, guidance, assistance, enthusiasm, and idealism of all of my many Malaysian friends and family members from many sectors, parties and communities. I remain extremely grateful to everybody, and hope that this book is at least a half-adequate return on their generous investment in my efforts and some kind of a contribution to the understanding of a relentlessly fascinating and complex subject.

# Contents

# Table of Cases

# Table of Legislation

# Introduction

'Rambut sama hitam, hati berlain-lain'

(We may all have black hair, but our dispositions are different')[1]

MALAYSIA HAS A population of approximately 33 million people, of whom about 61 per cent are Muslim and 39 per cent are non-Muslim. The group of non-Muslims consists of Buddhists (19 per cent), Christians (9 per cent), Hindus (6 per cent) and Sikhs (2 per cent). The members of the native tribes of East Malaysia (Sabah and Sarawak) and of the *orang asli* (original inhabitants) of West Malaysia profess animistic religions, although large numbers of Dayaks, Ibans and Kadazans in East Malaysia have converted to Christianity. The largest ethnic group in Malaysia is the Malays (50 per cent), followed by the Chinese (24 per cent), the indigenous people (11 per cent), and the Indians (ie those of South Asian heritage, 8 per cent). Bahasa Malaysia is the official language, but English, Chinese (mainly in Cantonese and Hokkien dialect), Tamil, Telugu, Malayalam, Panjabi, Thai and several indigenous languages in Eastern Malaysia are also widely spoken in places. Malaysia has one of the most diverse societies in the world.

The Federation of Malaya became independent in 1957 under a Constitution drafted by Commonwealth jurists. It gathered under its wing the Straits Settlements of Penang and Malacca; and the nine Malay States, Federated[2] and Unfederated.[3] This Constitution became the Federal Constitution of Malaysia when Malaysia was formed with the addition of three new states,[4] making 14 altogether, and the passing of some consequential amendments in 1963. It embodied Westminster-type constitutional ideas and traditions, but also embraced constitutional supremacy, federalism and a constitutional Bill of Rights, as well as

---

[1] Various headings of this book begin with a Malay proverb. The versions quoted are often based on CC Brown, *Malay Sayings* (Graham Brash, Singapore, 1951: 1986). The translations, however, are sometimes my own, or provided by Malay friends, and adapted to their significance for the passage in question.

[2] Negeri Sembilan, Pahang, Perak and Selangor.

[3] Johor, Kedah, Kelantan, Perlis and Terengganu.

[4] Sabah, Sarawak and Singapore. Singapore left the Federation in 1965.

other ideas squarely based on the Indian Constitution of 1950 and its precursors.[5] This structure was also infused with traditional elements and modified according to the perceived needs of a new polity divided by race and religion, and confronted by terrorism. Although amended frequently, and being the site of continual and intense struggle, the Constitution survived to celebrate its 60th anniversary on 31 August 2017. It has achieved, due to its longevity and in spite of its colonial origins, a status quite rare in the contemporary world – that of an autochthonous constitution. It is, in other words, meaningful after more than 60 years to refer to 'Malaysian constitutional traditions'.

It is with this story of constitutional continuity along with continued constitutional struggle that Malaysia offers this series a fascinating microcosm of virtually all the intractable problems of constitutionalism today. In contemporary Malaysia we find a heady mix of a lively democracy in perpetual motion; authoritarian nationalism; rapid economic development and urbanisation; and ethnic tension heightened by religious conflict. All of these elements have deeply affected the contours of the Constitution. More than this, it is the Constitution which has also shaped, as well as providing a battlefield for, continued political struggle.

Ten years after the appearance of the first edition, this second edition involves extensive reconsideration of the constitutional context. In particular, Malaysia has, since 2018, experienced an unprecedented period of political fragmentation that has brought to the fore innumerable constitutional issues that have been debated with increasing ferocity. Contested constitutional ideas dressed in Malaysian garb will be in evidence in all the chapters of this book. In the spirit of this series, the task of this book is thus to uncover, describe, analyse and critique constitutionalism as it is practised in Malaysia, pinpointing those issues, events and landmarks which are either foundational or simply indicative of the way things are. It will be an exercise in what Scheppele calls 'constitutional ethnography'.[6]

The essence of constitutionalism, as the guiding concept of this series, is a system of principles, rules and practices of a legal or quasi-legal, binding, nature that frame political action and public decision-making. Constitutionalism also provides both limits and meaning to such acts and decisions. However, it is not a mere abstraction or a set of ideals. It must

---

[5] The Government of India Act 1935, the British North America Act 1867.

[6] K Scheppele, 'Constitutional Ethnography: An Introduction' (2004) 38 *Law and Society Review* 389.

also become and be seen as an aspect of the lived experience, history and discourse of the nation, and therefore will take on characteristics that are particular to the nation. We can observe that constitutionalism generally takes shape only through struggle, controversy and disagreement, seemingly changing its meaning and appearance over time. Nowhere, perhaps, is this truer than in Malaysia, where it is apparent that public life often resembles a fierce struggle over the Constitution itself; a struggle in which every issue, it seems, is capable of being framed as a constitutional issue. Seen in this light, Malaysian constitutionalism leaps out of the law texts and becomes relevant to the lives of all citizens. It is this living reality of constitutionalism in practice and in context that this book examines. The reader will not find here anything like comprehensive or detailed coverage in the style of a law text or reference work (several of these are listed as 'Further Reading' at the end of Chapter 1). Instead the objective in this series of linked essays is to gain insight into the principal areas of constitutional contention.

The major theme of the book will therefore be the ways in which pluralism (especially ethnic and religious pluralism) has affected, and is affected by, the struggles over constitutional principle. By 'pluralism' is meant here the conscious ways in which the polity, communities and public opinion conceive and address the social facts of diversity. Thus by looking at constitutional problems through the lens of pluralism, and in a society that in some way embodies virtually all of our hopes and fears in this age of what James Tully has called 'strange multiplicity',[7] we can perhaps gain some insight into how constitutional government can play a large part in binding us together and resolving our differences.

Chapter 1 will set out the subject's historical background. We will see a remarkable trajectory from a strange assortment of territories under various forms of colonial rule towards the birth of a modern and successful nation under a constitutional system of government.

Chapter 2 examines the nature and concept of the Malaysian state. The emphasis here will be on aspects of executive power and governmental roles and structures. The chapter will also discuss the principles and practice of Cabinet government; and the public service in the age of privatisation and deregulation.

Chapter 3 is a completely new chapter for this edition. It deals with the social contract, as a critical response to majority–minority relations.

---

[7] J Tully, *Strange Multiplicity: Constitutionalism in an Age of Diversity* (Cambridge, Cambridge University Press, 1995).

This involves discussion of one of the central issues in Malaysian constitutionalism: the issue of special privileges for *bumiputera* citizens (Malays and natives of Sabah and Sarawak).

Chapter 4 deals with the legislative branch, analysing the political party system in the context of electoral coalition politics and parliamentary representation. Here we will discover the nature of Malaysia's evolving democracy in a party system historically dominated by the ruling Barisan Nasional (BN) coalition but now challenged by political fragmentation.

Chapter 5 examines constitutional monarchy; a topic that has become extremely important over the last few years. This chapter looks at the Malaysian constitutional monarchy and its role with regard to constitutional conventions and how these have operated in the Malaysian context.

Chapter 6 focuses on territorial governance, examining federal and state powers in the context of the evolving nature of governance at state and local government levels.

Chapter 7 discusses human rights, examining their constitutional definition, restriction and enforcement. Given the large dimensions of this topic, the approach will be to look at one area of rights (liberty of the person), one institution (Suhakam, the National Human Rights Commission), and one group with human rights issues (the indigenous peoples of Malaysia).

In Chapter 8 we look at the judicial branch. The focus here will be on the threats to, and the defence of, judicial independence and the role of the Malaysian Bar in its struggle to maintain constitutional government.

With this structure the book will, up to this point, not differ greatly from others in this series. But we will also see, in Chapter 9, on religion, how religious considerations cut across, explain, comment on, and also challenge the fundamental principles of the contemporary constitutional order. The chapter will consider in particular the jurisdictional conflicts over the jurisdiction of the civil and Syariah courts and the issue of religious freedom as the leading site of disagreement over the relationship between the state and religion.

Malaysia is a nation of paradoxes, defying attempts to parse its public discourse or indulge in familiar forms of categorisation. Not least of these paradoxes are the constitutional paradoxes explored in this book. This is, as we will see, a nation that embraces democracy but is not comfortably classed as fully democratic. It exhibits fundamental rights mechanisms and rhetoric, but these are sporadically applied and habitually restricted in scope. It relies on the rule of law, but the rule of law is also perpetually compromised. It bases its system of government on constitutionalism, but the Constitution itself is the subject of profound and controversial cleavages in understanding and interpretation. It is rampantly diverse, but the majority asserts its dominance over the rest. These and other Malaysian paradoxes will be examined in this book through the lens of Malaysia's evolving, troubled and contested, but always intriguing, constitutional system.

Note: All references to 'Article' in this book are references to Articles of the Federation Constitution of Malaysia 1957, unless the context indicates otherwise.

# 1

# Historical Background

Pre-colonial Constitutional traditions – Colonial Constitutionalism – Post-war Constitutional Developments – Constitution-drafting and Constitutional Debates – The Creation of Malaysia

## I. SYMBOLIC MALACCA

'Di atas robohan Melaka, Kita dirikan jiwa merdeka, Bersatu padulah segenap baka, Membela hak keadilan pusaka' (Malay pantun by Burhanuddin Al-Helmy)

(On the ruins of Malacca fort, We build the soul of independence, Be united every race, Defend the right of justice inherited)[1]

I N A SMALL area of the city of Malacca[2] one can find nestled closely together a Chinese Buddhist temple, a mosque, the tomb of Malacca's Malay national hero Hang Tuah, a Hindu temple, a Catholic church and a Tamil Wesleyan church. The close proximity of these religious buildings and cultural symbols has never been a source of tension. The author was informed that for several hundred years those responsible for each form of worship or culture have been careful not to harm or irritate the adherents of the others. It would be hard to find a better symbol of the rich and historically deep diversity and mutual tolerance of Malaysian society. These buildings, redolent of several different cultures and religions, have existed in close proximity for centuries, adding colour and variety to a great city where one can also see the beautiful nineteenth-century houses of the culturally mixed Peranakan or

---

[1] Quoted in TN Harper, *The End of Empire and the Making of Malaya* (Cambridge, Cambridge University Press, 1999) 13.

[2] The Malaysian spelling is 'Melaka'. 'Malacca' is used in this book, given its greater familiarity internationally.

'Baba Nyonya' middle class;[3] a Dutch Stadthuys and church; a Portuguese fort, church and village; an ancient Chinese cemetery; and a Chinatown of British colonial design.

The Malacca Empire of the fifteenth century is, even today, symbolic in Malaysia as an ideal and glorious Malay civilisation that continues to stand as the benchmark for the Malay community.[4] It is regarded as an ideal pre-colonial polity for other reasons. It was here that an empire was formed in the fifteenth century that embraced much of what is characteristic of its successor, the Malaysian Federation, in the twenty-first century. Malacca is the Malays' archetypal kingdom, regarded as the historical fount of Malay culture, literature and political thought; a necessary idea perhaps in an age of nationalist sensibility. Malacca was also the first Islamic kingdom (1409) in the territories now forming Malaysia. It had a highly developed legal code, the *Undang-Undang Melaka*,[5] referred to by Winstedt as the first constitution in Malaya of which we have any adequate record.[6] Malacca's constitution influenced the Malay States and the Borneo States in the centuries after Malacca's destruction by the Portuguese in 1511. The Portuguese victory was followed by that of the Dutch over them in 1641 and Malacca's cession by the Dutch to the British in 1824. Malacca presents a remarkable 500-year history of diversity. Even before 1511 Malacca was home to a great mixture of various communities of Malays, Indians and Chinese, and was also a successful and well-run centre for international trade. Its first Ruler, Parameswara, had been a Hindu King from Singapore who married a Muslim woman and converted to Islam, changing his name to Iskandar Shah. Thus the Sultan was 'no longer an incarnate Hindu god but the shadow of Allah upon earth'.[7]

This chapter tracks the emergence of the Malaysian polity over time through an examination of its pre-colonial, colonial and post-colonial history, and the formation of the Constitution of 1957. The emphasis will be not so much on general history as on the origins and development of the institutions and constitutional principles which can be seen in the

---

[3] The Peranakan are descendants of the original Straits Chinese, who sometimes married local Malays and became non-Chinese-speaking stalwarts of the British Empire; they were often British subjects.

[4] Abdul Aziz Bari, *The Malaysian Constitution: A Critical Introduction* (Kuala Lumpur, The Other Press, 2003) 21.

[5] Liaw Yock Fang, *Undang-Undang Melaka: The Laws of Melaka* (The Hague, Martinus Nijhoff, 1976).

[6] R Winstedt, *The Malays: A Cultural History* (6th edn, London, Routledge and Kegan Paul, 1961) 70.

[7] Ibid.

contemporary constitution. It is fitting to begin this history with a reference to the constitution of Malacca, a city that symbolises all the ideas and factors that have influenced the Malaysian Constitution: Malay monarchy, Islam, colonial government, cosmopolitan internationalism, and the diversity of Malaysian society.

## II. THE CONSTITUTION OF MALACCA
## AND THE MALAY CONCEPT OF MONARCHY

'Raja sa-keadilan, Penghulu sa-undang'

(The King is the fount of justice, but the Headman carries out the law)

Constitutional ideas in the Malay world exhibit unobtrusive mingling of various ideas of government drawn from Buddhist, Hindu, Islamic and purely customary roots. These ideas revolved around the person of the *Raja*. *Kerajaan* (strictly, the condition of having a *Raja*) is identical in Malay culture and language with government itself – historically, there simply is no concept of republicanism.[8]

The Malacca constitution was therefore based on the idea of kingship.[9] The *Undang-Undang Melaka* contained a number of clearly constitutional rules, and was directed to the powers of the Sultan and the organisation of government. If one looks closely at the constitutional rules concerning the Sultan, one finds that they are mainly ceremonial (for example, they legislate on issues of language and dress): they give him great dignity but little actual power. Although the *Undang-Undang Melaka* gives the Sultan extensive powers of appointment, this is so that he will not need to be, and indeed should not be, bothered with the trivialities of government. In fact these official positions, associated as they were with rights of revenue, were often appropriated by district chiefs who exercised considerable political power, passing the office on to their descendants. The Sultan's main prerogative was the exercise of judicial powers as a final court of appeal; he had the power to pass a sentence of death, as well as the right to grant honours, concessions and revenue monopolies, which were used by him to some political and fiscal effect. This was also true, later, of the *Rajas* (later usually styled 'Sultans') of the Malay States and the Borneo sultanates that formed what we now

---

[8] A Milner, *Kerajaan: Malay Political Culture on the Eve of Colonial Rule* (Tucson, University of Arizona Press, 1982).

[9] RH Hickling, *Malaysian Law: An Introduction to the Concept of Law in Malaysia* (Petaling Jaya, Pelanduk, 2001) ch 5.

know as Malaysia. The Malacca Sultanate's legacy may be clearly seen in the monarchies of today, as we shall see in Chapter 5.

The Malacca Empire in the sixteenth century dominated the Malay States during Malaya's brief period of unification. The splintering of the empire led to these States following Malaccan ideas of monarchy. Moreover, being riverine States with quite inaccessible interiors, they were very hard to bring under the control of a central power. This not only hindered the unification of Malaya but resulted in the constant assertion of local chiefly power and the elevation of consultation and consensus, which came to be a constitutional matter. The actual political functions of the *Raja* were essentially confined to military, foreign and judicial affairs. This was quite logical in the sense that it was only in these areas that the chiefs really needed a central power. Even here, as with other important matters, the *Raja* had to consult his chiefs and achieve a consensus (*muafakat*) before acting, otherwise his decisions would not be implemented: this was, of course, a useful buttress against erratic or arbitrary acts.[10] When several chiefs of Perak refused to sign the Pangkor Engagement of 1874, which introduced an obligation to follow the advice of a British Resident, its legitimacy was doubtful. This point was brought home even more forcibly when the British Government attempted to unify Malaya in the Malayan Union Plan of 1946, getting the Sultans one by one to sign away their powers. This provoked a dramatic response, with the Malays mobilising as never before to resist unification, citing their ancient governance traditions and the profound unconstitutionality (some even accused the Sultans of *derhaka* – treason) of literally signing away the Malay States without consulting the chiefs.[11] Malay monarchy was fundamental but not absolute: the *Raja* being held in check by the chiefs and by his duty to observe Islam and adhere to *adat* (Malay custom).[12]

We will see in the course of this book, especially in Chapter 5, that the monarchy has been a source of great controversy and its powers, even under a system of constitutional monarchy, have been restricted in some respects but increased in others. Not the least of the restrictions was the abolition of sovereign immunity in 1993;[13] a reform which runs very much counter to Malay tradition in which the *Raja* cannot be questioned.

---

[10] J Gullick, *Indigenous Political Systems of Western Malaya* (London, Athlone, 1988).

[11] A Lau, *The Malayan Union Controversy 1942–1948* (Singapore, Oxford University Press, 1991).

[12] M Hooker (ed), *Readings in Malay Adat Law* (Singapore, Singapore University Press, 1970).

[13] See p 114.

Nonetheless, it is to the continued cultural relevance of Malay constitutional traditions that Malaysia owes its federal structure.[14] Deep disaffection from the Rulers in the 1980s and 1990s, resulting in executive loss of patience, might, all else being equal, have signalled the end of the monarchy: but it did not.[15] The abolition of this ancient institution was unthinkable, even at the institution's lowest ebb. In the twenty-first century the monarchy remains more relevant and influential than at any time since the beginning of the colonial period.

The constitutions of the Malay States, Malacca aside, were unwritten, even though codes of law were not at all unknown before the arrival of the ever-legalistic Europeans.[16] It was not, however, until 1895 that a Malay State (Johor under Sultan Abu Bakar) adopted a modern written constitution. It was ceremony, precedent and custom that prevailed in constitutional matters. To say that traditionally the Malay States had unwritten, customary, constitutions,[17] is not to say that they had no rules or any distinction between politics and law; on the contrary Malay political culture emphasised an almost punctilious correctness of procedure, consultation and appointment. The constant disputes over royal succession in the Malay States, often exploited by the British for their own ends, tended to emphasise rather than undermine the importance of custom and precedent.[18]

In the case of Negri Sembilan, which based its federal, matrilineal and democratic constitution – it still does – on ancient Minangkabau custom known as *adat perpatih*, the constitution exhibited an almost arcane complexity and formality.[19] From the late eighteenth century it was a federation under the nominal sovereignty of the *Yamtuan* (a Sumatran Minangkabau prince) and had complex rules of succession. Its constitutional significance now is that the unique Malaysian system

---

[14] See, further, Mohamed Salleh Abas, 'Traditional elements of the Malaysian Constitution' in F Trindade and HP Lee (ed), *The Constitution of Malaysia: Further Perspectives and Developments: Essays in Honour of Tun Mohamed Suffian* (Singapore, Oxford University Press, 1986).

[15] A Harding, 'Nazrinian monarchy in Malaysia: The resilience and revival of a traditional institution' in A Harding and Dian AH Shah (eds), *Law and Society in Malaysia: Pluralism, Religion and Ethnicity* (Abingdon, Routledge, 2017).

[16] See eg J Rigby (ed) and R Wilkinson (trans), 'The Ninety-Nine Laws of Perak' in Hooker (n 12) 57–82.

[17] RJ Wilkinson, 'Constitutional and Adat Structure of Negeri Sembilan' in Hooker (n 12) 333–43; Winstedt (n 6) 81–90; M Hooker, *Adat Laws in Modern Malaysia* (Kuala Lumpur, Oxford University Press, 1972) chs 6–8.

[18] Adib Vincent Tung, *The Titles and Ceremonial Traditions of the Royalty and Nobility of the State of Perak, Malaysia* (Ipoh, Perak Academy, 2018) ch 2.

[19] Wilkinson (n 17).

of choosing the federal head of state (the *Yang di-Pertuan Agong*) by an election amongst the Rulers is taken from Negeri Sembilan's strange but fascinating constitution.

### III. THE COLONIAL CONSTITUTIONAL EXPERIENCE: THE RESIDENTIAL SYSTEM

'Seperti Raja dengan menteri'

(Like the King and his minister, i.e. in complete accord)

As Harper points out, the British did not come to Malaya to catch butterflies. Their intervention was precipitated by a number of commercial and strategic ambitions, and occurred in two stages, moving inexorably towards constitutional structures and eventually independence in 1957.[20]

First, in 1786, the Sultan of Kedah ceded to the East India Company Penang (then called Prince of Wales Island) and a strip of land known then as Province Wellesley on the Kedah mainland. Singapore was ceded to Britain by the Temenggong of Johor in 1819, and Malacca by an Anglo-Dutch treaty in 1824. These colonies were brought together in 1867 as the Straits Settlements colony, with their own Governor and a seat of government in Singapore. They were an attempt to establish profitable entrepot trade in a location, between China and India, in proximity to the Straits of Malacca. English law and legal institutions were introduced by a royal charter in 1826.[21] Although the British left in 1957, the common law, introduced by this charter, remained.

The second stage of intervention related to the Malay States, beginning in 1874 and ending in 1920. This stage involved the establishment of a series of protectorates in which the principle of indirect rule was observed. The traditional Ruler was obliged by treaty to accept the advice of a British Resident, but the local governance structure remained largely intact.[22] A contributory factor in this intervention was an unmanageable series of dynastic and law-and-order problems confronting the Malay States with progressively alarming results. Perak, for example, had more Chinese residents than Malays, and the constant battles between secret societies dragged law and order outside the government's control.

---

[20] Harper (n 1) 58.

[21] A Phang, *From Foundation to Legacy: The Second Charter of Justice* (Singapore, Singapore Academy of Law, 2006).

[22] R Emerson, *Malaysia: A Study in Direct and Indirect Rule* (Kuala Lumpur, University of Malaya Press, 1937: 1970).

The *Raja* requested British assistance and signed a treaty with the Crown (the Pangkor Engagement) at the island of Pangkor in 1874, under which Perak accepted a British Resident, setting a precedent for what became the 'residential system' throughout Malaya. The other Malay states eventually followed suit and by 1930 all were under the residential system. Johor, however, was recognised as an entirely independent state by a treaty of protection in 1885; the Sultan granted it a written Constitution in 1895, but it was finally brought under the residential system in 1914.

British policy was to encourage Chinese immigration in the expectation that Chinese labour and investment would galvanise Malaya into economic and social progress. This had also been the policy of the Malay Rulers in, for example, Johor, Selangor and Perak. The institution of the *Kapitan Cina*, or headman of the Chinese community, was recognised by the Malays before Malaya was taken over by the British: it is recorded that the most famous *Kapitan*, Yap Ah Loy, who is credited with the founding of Kuala Lumpur, was installed by the Sultan of Selangor in a formal ceremony in which Yap wore Malay costume.[23] The idea of the co-operation, yet functional separation, of the Malays and the Chinese was already an important aspect of government by the 1870s.

British constitutional policy lay in the avoidance of too much disturbance to Malay traditions and practice of government. However, the maintenance or enhancement of the authority of the Ruler over the chiefs would in turn enhance the power of the Resident. There was a good deal of reluctance to accept interference with time-honoured Malay constitutional assumptions.[24]

Nonetheless it is clear that although the British became more ambitious over time, great care had to be taken to observe constitutional niceties. Unfortunately, neither the Treaties nor the instructions given to the Residents contained any clear statement of the Resident's duties with regard to the Rulers and the existing system of government. Under the Treaties, the Ruler was in theory obliged to receive and act on the advice of the Resident, except in relation to matters pertaining to Islam and Malay custom. Interestingly enough, the Malay version of the Pangkor Engagement referred not to advice but to discussion (*berbicara*) between the Ruler and the Resident, which did not seem to suggest that the Ruler

---

[23] S Middlebrook and J Gullick, *Yap Ah Loy* (Kuala Lumpur, MBRAS Reprint No 9, 1983) 40.

[24] J Gullick, *Rulers and Residents: Influence and Power in the Malay States 1870–1920* (Singapore, Oxford University Press, 1992).

was always obliged to accept the advice proffered. It also seems likely that the significance of the exception concerning Malay custom and Islam was greater to the Malay mind than it was to the British. After all, before the British intervention, most government actually conducted by the Rulers could be said to pertain in some sense to Islam or Malay custom. On this view, the British would confine their advice to technical issues of policy and implementation such as railway construction or public health, rather than attempting to make wholesale changes to traditions.[25]

We can assess the nature of this constitutional system by looking at the earliest and precedent-forming example, that of Perak under Raja Idris and Resident Sir Hugh Low, one in which the *Raja* and his minister were indeed usually in accord, but only as a result of good sense on both sides. The Resident did not always refrain from giving advice on religious matters, technically within the purview of the Ruler, presumably on the basis that nothing in the 1874 Treaty prevented him from offering it. On the other hand the *Raja* sometimes ignored Low's advice even on matters within the Resident's purview. Low was able to achieve more by indirect means than others were able to achieve by direct means. In most instances the residential system was essentially rule by consensus, because neither the Resident nor the Ruler could afford the other to act against his will in matters of importance. In so far as the Ruler made the Resident aware of Malay sentiment on particular issues, it could be said that sometimes the Resident acted on the Ruler's advice rather than *vice versa*.[26]

In addition, there was a State Council in each State. Typically, for example in Perak, on which the other States based their State Councils, the State Council would consist of four Malay Chiefs, including the Ruler, two Chinese, and two European officials, including the Resident. The Resident nominated members who were appointed for life by their Ruler. The Ruler presided, but it was the Resident who took the initiatives. It was principally a consultative body, not a forum for opposition, though even this consultative function declined as the residential system became settled. Legislation was effected on the Resident's initiative by order of the Ruler-in-Council. There was no separation of powers: the State Council also exercised executive and judicial powers, acting as a final court of appeal, as the Ruler had done personally in previous times.

---

[25] E Sadka, *The Protected Malay States 1874–1895* (Kuala Lumpur, University of Malaya Press, 1968).

[26] CN Parkinson, *British Intervention in Malaya 1876–77* (Kuala Lumpur, University of Malaya Press, 1964) ch 10.

The residential system thus presaged the takeover by the British of the judicial system, which was then remodelled along the lines of the common law. Although the judicial system was not legally independent of the executive, the introduction of common-law principles tended to encourage the practice of judicial independence. As we will see in Chapter 8, judicial independence and the common-law traditions of the Bar were to become controversial issues.

Gradually, however, the powers of the State Council came to be restricted by the Colonial Office and the Governor of the Straits Settlements. The logic of consistency of action was hard to resist. From 1892 all draft legislation went to the Governor before the State Council. Crucial measures were sometimes not discussed in the State Council at all; the Malay leadership was able to delay, but hardly ever prevent their being passed.[27] A process of federalisation had begun.

Viewed as a preparation for democracy, the residential system and the State Councils cannot be said to have been effective. In fact the Malay political system prior to intervention was possibly more democratic; major decisions were often taken only after a mass meeting of 100 or more chiefs and many days of deliberation. In no way did the British attempt to build on the more democratic elements of Malay political tradition, except that the State Councils did at least provide an opportunity for Chinese representation, which was a constitutionally important innovation. The legacy of this system is that the Malay States as well as the Federation itself have a Cabinet system, constitutional monarchy and minority representation.

## IV. FEDERALISATION

'Kapal satu, nakhoda dua'

'A Malay proverb says that there cannot be two masters to one vessel; neither can there be four Rulers over one country' (Raja Idris of Perak, at the Rulers' Durbar, 1903)

The logic of centralisation, efficiency and development, encouraged by business and legal interests, soon led to attempts at federalisation, which ultimately deeply affected the nature of federalism as it is practised now. In 1895 Selangor, Negri Sembilan, Pahang and Perak were grouped together by treaty into the Federation of Malay States (FMS).

[27] Ibid ch 6.

The other States (Johor, Kedah, Perlis, Terengganu and Kelantan) came to be referred to as the Unfederated Malay States. This was not a federal constitution, although it was a forerunner of the present federal system introduced in 1948. There was no surrender of sovereignty and the Government was to be administered 'under the advice of the British Government'; the residential system remained, at least ostensibly; and there was division of 'state' and 'federal' powers. The Rulers agreed to accept the 'Resident-General' in Kuala Lumpur as the representative of the British Government under the direction of the Governor of the Straits Settlements, styled for this purpose as the High Commissioner of the Malay States. However, the Treaty entailed the end of the practice, if not the theory, of indirect rule, because the new arrangements resulted in the centralisation of executive power and marginalisation of the individuality of the various States.[28]

The State Councils, although in theory unaffected, had their powers drastically reduced in practice, becoming essentially rubber stamps for the legislative will of the federal authorities. Federal departmental chief officers were appointed, initially merely in an advisory capacity, but from 1902 they were given departments and exercised important and exclusive executive powers. By this innovation the beginnings of a cabinet system of government were introduced. This arrangement, in which the British Government imposed its will without any corresponding protection for the States, exposed the latter to encroachment on their powers. A centripetal federation was, one can see here, already in the making, and effectively only the Residents themselves stood in the way.

In 1904 even the judicial powers of the Resident and the appellate jurisdiction of the Ruler-in-Council, already eroded by the appointment in 1896 of a Judicial Commissioner for the FMS, were entirely removed and given to the Judicial Commissioner. This laid a foundation for the centralisation of the administration of justice and the introduction of the common law as the general law. '*Durbars*' or Conferences of Rulers, forerunners of the modern institution (see Chapter 5), were held in 1897 and 1903. Sultan Idris of Perak used the occasion of the 1903 Conference to express Malay unhappiness at the erosion of States' rights. A further step was taken in 1909 with the introduction, by means of a further treaty, of a Federal Council, headed by the High Commissioner, assisted by the Resident-General (from 1911 called Chief Secretary), and including the four Rulers, the four Residents and four unofficial members. The treaty provided that draft budgets for the States should

---

[28] J Sidhu, *Administration in the Federated Malay States* (Kuala Lumpur, Oxford University Press, 1980) ch 2 (the Appendices set out the relevant treaties).

be considered by the Federal Council, and blandly assumed that it, as well as the State Councils, would be empowered to enact laws. However, the treaty also reserved to the State Councils matters involving religion, traditional offices and the Rulers' prerogatives.[29]

By implication the treaty gave all other legislative powers to the Federal Council, and its Acts were to prevail over inconsistent State Enactments. This position was of doubtful constitutionality because legislative power could only be conferred on the FMS by express surrender of the sovereignty of the Rulers. Although the 1909 Treaty purported not to curtail any of the powers or authority of the Rulers, in fact it did so by centralising legislative power. However, it represented the first genuinely federal constitution in Malaya in that it constituted a federal legislature and divided legislative powers between the States and the Federation. Of course, this arrangement affected only four of the 13 States now forming Malaysia, but all the States have been profoundly affected by this 1909 Federal Constitution. The Rulers' influence was increasingly limited to customary and religious matters, and by convention they did not participate in Federal Council debates. Within the States, powers were vested more and more in the person of the Ruler, but exercised in fact by the British officials: 'By 1920 few could deny that the final vestiges of indirect rule had been trampled on and the Sultans were reduced to little more than glorified idols with feet of clay'.[30]

An Agreement of 1927, under which the Rulers could be represented on the Federal Council by the Resident, finally placed legislative powers under complete British control. From 1927 a reversal of policy resulted, however, in the pursuit *of decentralisation* in order to accommodate States' rights in the face of expanding federal control. Legislative powers were clearly divided between the States and the Federation, and some federal departments were devolved onto the State Governments. The first tentative steps had been taken towards the now familiar federal structure.

## V. THE MALAYAN UNION

'Seperti tulis di-atas ayer'

(Like writing on water)

During 1942–45 Malaya and Borneo were occupied by Japanese forces. The British cooperated with resistance elements, including communist

---

[29] *Agreement for the Constitution of a Federal Council, 1909*, cl 9.
[30] Sidhu (n 28) 126.

ones, to undermine Japanese rule. The reoccupation by allied forces in 1945 made moves towards independence unavoidable. It was now clear that colonial government had failed to fulfil its basic promise of protection, and the war had aroused greater consciousness of ethnic identity, and a new desire for self-determination, not least amongst those who had resisted the Japanese occupation.[31] Achieving independence, however, proved a complex matter. The territories now forming Malaysia then comprised a motley collection of Federated and Unfederated States together with Crown colonies. It had been a headache merely administering and defending them, and their constitutional differences were now an obstacle to independence. A British Cabinet Committee had decided during the war to create a unitary state in Malaya; Singapore and the Borneo States were left for later consideration. Malaya needed to be united to be defendable, a fact which was regarded as a precondition to independence.[32] There was, however, an obvious constitutional obstacle to unification. The British government had no authority to unify the Malay States, which were legally independent. The Malay Rulers were therefore bullied and threatened into signing the so-called MacMichael Treaties, which surrendered their authority to the Crown, and allowed the implementation of the Malayan Union Plan, which was introduced by the Malayan Union Order-in-Council on 1 April 1946.[33]

The details of this constitutional arrangement need not detain us, because nothing in it has had any lasting effect or influence, and by 1948 it had been replaced with a federal structure. Almost all of the main changes it made were controversial. The surrender of the Rulers' sovereignty in effect abolished the Malay States, whose history went back hundreds of years, and was regarded as an insult to Malay culture and tradition. As we have seen, the Treaties were also considered unconstitutional due to lack of consultation with the chiefs. The Union also gave citizenship equally to all residents, thus, in Malay thinking, demoting the Malays in their own land by making them equal to migrant people with only five years' residence, and exposing them to economic and political marginalisation. As if this were not bad enough the Union made no move

---

[31] W Roff, *The Origins of Malay Nationalism* (Kuala Lumpur, University of Malaya Press, 1967).

[32] Rais Yatim, 'The Road to *Merdeka*' in A Harding and HP Lee (ed), *Constitutional Landmarks in Malaysia: The First 50 Years, 1957–2007* (Kuala Lumpur, Malayan Law Journal/ LexisNexis, 2007).

[33] *Malayan Union Gazette Extraordinary*, 1 April 1946; J Allen, *The Malayan Union* (New Haven, Yale University Press, South East Asia Series No 16, 1967).

towards creating a democratic system of government, vesting practically dictatorial power in the Governor, who was able to control the exercise of all executive and legislative power, even to the extent of overriding any rejection of his proposed legislation by the mainly Governor-appointed 40-member legislature.

The reaction to this high-handed constitutional outrage was its total rejection by the Malays. The tumult was led by the Rulers and newly emerged political leaders from the Malay aristocratic class, notably Onn Jaffar and Tunku Abdul Rahman. They were joined by a thoroughly roused Malay populace and even former British officials. In March 1946, a new political party – the United Malays National Organisation (UMNO) – was formed by a congress of 42 Malay organisations with the express aim of defeating the Union. By June 1946 the arrival of a new Governor, Malcolm MacDonald, had prompted the abandonment of the Union and a decision to undertake plans for a federal structure to replace the Union.

## VI. THE FEDERATION OF MALAYA

'Bujur lalu, lintang patah'

(Lengthwise you get through, sideways you get broken)

Again the constitution-making process was orchestrated by the Government, four Rulers and two UMNO representatives being drafted onto a Committee comprising also six officials. The resulting constitutional arrangement also dealt with the Malay States and the former Straits Settlements of Penang and Malacca, but the Rulers and the States and State Councils were to be retained in a system of constitutional monarchy. The Government would be headed by a High Commissioner with powers over all matters except Malay custom and religion. The special status of the Malays would be recognised, and citizenship for non-Malays restricted to those with 15 years' residence. The Legislative Council would be chaired by the High Commissioner, and would comprise officials, the nine Presidents of the State Councils, and 50 appointed unofficial representatives of the various ethnicities. In this way the proposals, which became the Federation of Malaya Agreement 1948 (FMA), made important concessions to Malay sentiment but not to democratic participation. Indeed the powers of the High Commissioner hardly differed from those of the Governor under the Malayan Union.

The FMA was opposed by a number of interests which coalesced into the All-Malaya Council of Joint Action (AMCJA) in February 1947.[34] Alternative proposals, called 'the People's Constitutional Proposals', were advanced by the AMCJA in July 1947.

However, there was a limit to British willingness to consume a second helping of humble pie. A Consultative Committee was set up, but the FMA had already been negotiated. Furthermore, geopolitics intervened as the Communists advanced towards establishing a People's Republic in China and the Malayan Chinese, who formed the backbone of the Communist Party of Malaya (CPM), became ever bolder in confronting the colonial government. The CPM, having laid down its arms in 1945 after the allied victory over the Japanese, whom it resisted from the jungle, and having then joined the AMCJA, now moved towards armed rebellion. The AMCJA disbanded in June 1948 with the banning of many participating organisations and the outbreak of hostilities. In July 1947 Revised Constitutional Proposals had been published, but these hardly differed from the original FMA proposals. State Agreements were signed and the Constitution of the Federation of Malaya, based on the FMA, was passed into law by means of an Order-in-Council on 1 February 1948.[35] The Rulers had also agreed in the State Agreements to introduce written constitutions, where not already enacted, at the State level, by which they were to abide. The State Constitutions were promulgated (this time with the concurrence of the traditional chiefs), providing for a legislature (the Council of State), and also a cabinet executive (State Executive Council), whose advice the Ruler was required to follow. Thus Westminster-style government was finally implanted both at Federal and State levels.

The Constitution of the Federation followed the broad contours of the FMA. Its provisions were an important step towards the *Merdeka* Constitution only nine years later. The Federal Legislative Council, as it emerged from the FMA process, consisted of 49 members: the High Commissioner as Chairman, with 14 official and 34 unofficial members. It had wide legislative powers, but the High Commissioner had important reserve powers to refuse assent to a Bill passed by the Legislative Council, and to declare that a Bill before the Council should have effect

---

[34] Khong Khim Hoong, *Merdeka! British Rule and the Struggle for Independence in Malaya, 1945–57* (Petaling Jaya, INSAN, 1984) ch 3.

[35] *Federation of Malaya Order-in-Council 1948*, SI 108/1948 (UK). See also *Constitutional Proposals for Malaya: Report of the Working Committee, 24 April 1947* (Kuala Lumpur, Government Printer, 1947); *Federation of Malaya: Summary of Revised Proposals, 24 July 1947* (Kuala Lumpur, Government Printer, 1947).

even if not passed, if the High Commissioner considered this 'expedient in the interest of public order, public faith or good government'. A Federal Executive Council advised the High Commissioner, who was, however, empowered to act in opposition to their advice. It was later noted by the Reid Commission, which drafted the *Merdeka* Constitution, that, in spite of the potentially dictatorial powers vested in the High Commissioner, these were not actually exercised dictatorially: a convention emerged that no major policy changes would be made without the consent of all the State Governments. An informal Conference of Federation Executives, held before each meeting of the Federal Legislative Council, helped to ensure that a consensus emerged on major issues.[36]

It was also at this time that the various State Constitutions (Johor and Terengganu already had written constitutions) assumed something like their present form. Limited legislative power was exercised by the State Legislative Council, covering Islam and Malay custom and whatever was not covered by federal legislative powers. The Ruler, like the High Commissioner at the federal level, had reserve powers to perform actions which were contrary to the Council's advice. The State Government was headed by a *Menteri Besar* (Chief Minister). A system of federal grants to State Governments was operated. A Conference of Rulers was also set up, with powers to discuss and comment on Government matters, but with no powers to obstruct the advice tendered by the Government.

However, what was also important in terms of the shaping of the future constitution was the emergency, which began in 1948 and continued until 1960,[37] which resulted in the passing of a veritable armoury of repressive laws on sedition, publications and preventive detention, most of which became regular features of Malaysian law well into the twenty-first century. Moreover, the emergency tended to centralise government, limit States' rights, and of course facilitate the overriding of ordinary law and fundamental rights. The latter were not included in the Constitution, so that not even the judiciary could enforce them except in terms of statutory interpretation. The 1948 Constitution did not, however, in other respects, remain static; rather, it formed the basis for rapid constitutional and political development towards *Merdeka* and the 1957 Constitution.[38]

---

[36] Ibid.

[37] R Clutterbuck, *The Long, Long War: The Emergency in Malaya 1948–1960* (London, Cassell, 1966).

[38] Khong Khim Hoong (n 34) ch 4.

As always in decolonisation processes, the major issue was who would take over as the safe-pair-of-hands leadership, both negotiating early independence and forming the post-independence Government. In November 1950 the UMNO leader and principal candidate for Prime Minister, Dato' Onn Jaffar, an aristocrat from Johor, tried to make UMNO into a multi-racial party by proposing the admission of non-Malays into the party. UMNO was split over this issue, but Dato' Onn lost the debate, leaving UMNO in September 1951. Tunku Abdul Rahman ('the Tunku'), a prince of Kedah and a Cambridge-educated lawyer, opposed Dato' Onn's policy and became UMNO leader.

A multi-party system began to take shape with new parties created mainly along communal lines. In April 1951 a 'quasi-ministerial' or 'member' system was introduced, under which nine leading unofficial members of the Legislative Council were appointed by the High Commissioner as heads of ministries, forming a prototype of the modern Cabinet. Elections to Municipal Councils, the first elections to be held in Malaya, took place in December 1951. In the Kuala Lumpur Municipal Council elections of February 1952, UMNO, under the Tunku's leadership, allied itself with the Malayan Chinese Association (MCA) formed in 1949 by a prominent Malacca entrepreneur, Tan Cheng Lock. The surprising and historically important result was a landslide victory (12 seats out of 14) for the new 'Alliance'. What originated as a tactical local election pact became a winning formula repeated throughout Malaya in subsequent elections, and was later elevated, as we will see in Chapter 4, into a theory of government with long-term consequences for Malaysia. In all local elections during 1952–53 the Alliance won 94 out of 119 seats, although 30 of the increased number of 75 members of the Legislative Council were appointed from its main rival, Dato' Onn's multiracial Independence of Malaya Party.[39]

The Alliance, at a conference in August 1953, was able to agree on a firm independence platform of constitutional, responsible government; observance of basic liberties; constitutional monarchy; the reconciliation of the rights of communities; and the ending of the emergency. In December 1954 the Malayan Indian Congress (MIC), formed in 1946, also joined the Alliance, completing the unique inter-communal triptych which was to characterise post-*Merdeka* politics for several decades, and make an indelible mark on Malaysian constitutional development. A dominant-coalition party-system was already in place, which presumed

[39] R Milne and D Mauzy, *Politics and Government in Malaysia* (Singapore, Times Books, 1978) ch 4.

to represent all three of the main groups in Malaya. Its preferences would prove very hard to resist. The Government now agreed to Legislative Council demands for an election of 52 out of 98 members of the Council, to be held in 1955, and to a Malayan Chief Minister and Cabinet; the FMA was amended accordingly. The reconstituted Legislative Council was also to comprise (from 1956) a Speaker, who replaced the High Commissioner in that capacity; three officials; the nine State *Menteri-menteri Besar* (Chief Ministers); two 'Settlement' representatives for Penang and Malacca; 32 representatives of 'scheduled interests'; and seven members appointed in consultation with the majority party.

The Alliance proceeded to rout their opponents in the 1955 elections, winning 51 out of the 52 elected seats and 81 per cent of the vote. Elections were also held for all the State Legislative Councils and Settlement Councils by the end of 1955, with similar results. The Tunku became the first Chief Minister and formed a Cabinet, appointed by the High Commissioner in consultation with the Chief Minister, consisting of six Malay ministers, three Chinese ministers and one Indian minister, on whose advice the High Commissioner was on some matters now actually obliged to act, the British Government being responsible only for external defence and foreign affairs. It was also agreed that the British Residents would be withdrawn. The main planks of the *Merdeka* Constitution had, therefore, by 1955, been firmly laid.[40]

## VII. THE REID COMMISSION

'Jikalau kita beranak, ikut kata bidan'

(If a baby is being born, do what the midwife says)

A Constitutional Conference on the usual imperial pattern was held in London in January and February 1956 between representatives of the British Government, the Rulers, and the Government of Malaya. The Conference proposed independence for the Federation by August 1957 and the appointment of a Constitutional Commission. The proposals having been accepted by the Rulers and the British Government, the Commission was appointed and submitted its Report in February 1957. Following a period of public debate the Government of Malaya appointed a Working Party, consisting of four Alliance members, four Rulers, and two British officials, to consider the draft Constitution, which

[40] Khong Khim Hoong (n 34) ch 5.

was appended to the Commission's Report. Some changes were made to the draft, which was approved by the Federal and State Legislatures; the *Merdeka* Constitution was brought into effect on 31 August 1957. The event was celebrated by an impressive ceremony at the Padang, now known as *Dataran Merdeka* (Merdeka Square) in Kuala Lumpur, with the Tunku famously raising his fist with repeated cries of '*Merdeka!*'

Between early 1956 and mid-1957 the Constitution was settled through extensive debates, discussions and drafting exercises. Although there was a Constitution in place, it was in effect the constitution of a colony, not of a newly independent and democratic nation. Some things would not change, but new elements entered the constitutional mix.[41]

Prior to the London Conference, the three Alliance parties had over some months negotiated between them behind the scenes a common position on the future Constitution, and their Memorandum had been submitted to the Conference. The Memorandum's most important proposals involved a compromise: non-Malay citizenship should rise, but Malay special privileges should be retained. It also dealt with such issues as the national language and the monarchy. This position was destined to become in effect the cornerstone of the nation and the *Merdeka* Constitution, and is now often referred to as the social contract: a social contract not in Rousseau's sense of a notional contract between individuals and the state, but rather an actual, negotiated contract between ethnic communities – indigenous and migrant – planning to live in peace and harmony. This arrangement, which was to have very important long-term effects, is discussed in detail in Chapter 3.

The Reid Commission itself consisted of five persons under the chairmanship of Lord Reid, the prominent Scottish Judge. The other members were Sir Ivor Jennings, the Cambridge academic, whose experience of constitution-making in several countries was highly respected throughout the Commonwealth and who was also a personal friend of the Tunku; Sir William McKell, a former Judge and Governor-General of Australia; Justice B Malik, an Indian Judge; and Justice Abdul Hamid, a Pakistani Judge. None of the members was Malayan or (apart from Jennings) had any significant experience of Malaya. All were lawyers. Only Abdul Hamid was Muslim. However, all members except Lord Reid himself had experience of the operation of a federal constitution. It is clear that Jennings was the dominant intellectual force in the drafting process. Joseph Fernando draws attention to Jennings' unique

---

[41] This passage is based generally on J Fernando, *The Making of the Malayan Constitution* (Kuala Lumpur, MBRAS, 2002).

blend of academic brilliance, leadership, practical wisdom and sheer hard work during the second half of 1956; there can be no doubt that Malaysia owes a great deal to Jennings' efforts at that time,[42] not least the successful delineation of Federal, State and Concurrent powers in the Constitution's Ninth Schedule, which has stood the test of six decades, virtually without amendment.

This method of constitution-making by experts seems surprising, however, in view of the notable recent example of India, where there had been an elected Constituent Assembly. The constitution-making method adopted in Malaya, however, no doubt enabled independence to be reached rather sooner than might otherwise have proved possible. The most persuasive reason, however, for not having a Constituent Assembly, was that the main positions had already been negotiated amongst the key players, and there would be reluctance to countenance a departure from those positions that might lead to political disarray or even to the inter-ethnic rioting that was still fresh in memory from the immediate post-war period. The London Conference reflected these considerations by giving the Reid Commission terms of reference embodying the main positions of the Alliance Memorandum. Its task was perceived as the translation into legal and practical terms of that which was already politically settled. The job was therefore a technical drafting one, not a democratic process of nation-building. Nonetheless, even in this limited task the Commission had to employ sensitivity to the important issues that would be debated, by consulting widely and sympathetically. The resulting draft Constitution, set out in its Report,[43] although modified in certain respects, was accepted by all the relevant institutions in Malaya. Nonetheless, the *Merdeka* Constitution in its early days suffered from the fact that it was not drafted by the representatives of the people. It was often seen as a foreign document rather than an autochthonous one. While this argument has declined in cogency over time, a more democratically chosen body might well have come up with somewhat different recommendations.

The terms of reference agreed in London were to recommend a federal constitution with only a measure of autonomy for the states, a parliamentary democracy, constitutional monarchy, and a common

---

[42] J Fernando, 'Sir Ivor Jennings and the Malayan Constitution' (2006) 34(4) *Journal of Imperial and Commonwealth History* 577; H Kumarasingham, 'A foreign commission for domestic needs: The constitutional founding of Malaysia' in Kevin YL Tan and Bui Ngoc Son (eds), *Constitutional Foundings in Southeast Asia* (Oxford, Hart Publishing, 2019).

[43] *Federation of Malaya Constitutional Commission, 1956–7 Report* (Kuala Lumpur, Government Printer, 1957).

nationality that safeguarded the special position of the Malaya and the legitimate interests of other communities.[44] There was, however, no specific mention of fundamental rights or judicial independence.

During 1956, the Commission consulted widely all over Malaya, holding 118 meetings, including 31 at which evidence was presented, and considered 131 memoranda, notably those from the Rulers and the Alliance. The terms of reference bound the hands of the Commission in several respects, but on the other hand there was much latitude to be exercised in terms of addressing issues not specified. This involved critical choices. The modern Constitution was based on, and is still influenced by, the Commission's Report and the debates over it, and it is therefore important to set out the constitutional thinking of the time and the issues that were debated following the Report.

Some proposals proved controversial, and changes were made as a result of the recommendations of the Government's Working Party. The proposals were accepted by the Conference of Rulers in June 1957, and almost unanimously adopted by the Legislative Council in August. They were given effect by the Federation of Malaya Agreement 1957, the Federation of Malaya Independence Act 1957 (UK) and Orders-in-Council thereunder, the Federal Constitution Ordinance 1957, and State Enactments in the Malay States. This Constitution has remained continuously in effect since 31 August 1957.

## VIII. THE COMMISSION'S REPORT
## AND THE CONSTITUTIONAL DEBATES

'Sesal dahulu pendapatan, sesal kemudian apa guna-nya?'

(To be sorry in time is useful; but what is the use of being sorry afterwards?)

Most of the draft Constitution was either uncontroversial or had been agreed in advance. However, some issues not only resulted in intense debate, but have continued to prove problematical. These issues are the deeply connected ones, discussed in the later chapters of this book, of ethnicity, religion and fundamental rights.

An inevitable consequence of the terms of reference was the adoption of a Westminster-style executive based on the British model of constitutional monarchy.[45] The new office of constitutional head of the

---

[44] Ibid, para 3.

[45] The following section is based on the Commission's *Report* (n 44) and Fernando's study (n 42).

Federation (ultimately styled '*Yang di-Pertuan Agong*' and rendered in English in the Constitution as 'Supreme Head of the Federation'), was one whose powers resembled those of the British Crown. Given the nine existing monarchies of Malaya, the Commission naturally adopted the method of election which the Rulers themselves favoured, which was in essence a rotation of office amongst them on the basis of a five-year tenure. This system was in turn based on the system of precedence which had evolved among the Rulers themselves, and, more remotely, on the *adat* constitution of Negri Sembilan.[46] It is unique in constitutional law. The Rulers were to remain the Heads of Islam in the States. A Conference of Rulers (in existence already since 1948) was also recommended, which would have the principal function of electing or removing the *Yang di-Pertuan Agong*. However, its consent would also be required before certain laws could be passed, for example those concerning the privileges of the Rulers and the Conference itself. Notably, its consent would be required for legislation affecting the special position of the Malays and the legitimate interests of the other communities, but in relation to these matters each Ruler would be accompanied by his *Menteri Besar* (Chief Minister), and act on the advice of the State Executive Council. The Conference was also to have the right to be consulted about judicial appointments, as well as the power to discuss any national issues, each Ruler again being accompanied by his *Menteri Besar*.

Also in line with the terms of reference the Commission recommended a bicameral legislature comprising an elected 100-member *Dewan Rakyat* (House of Representatives) and a *Dewan Negara* (Senate), consisting of two members from each State, elected by the State Legislative Assemblies, augmented with 11 members appointed by the Federal Government as being persons of distinction or representative of racial minorities or indigenous people. The purposes of the upper house were to revise or delay ill-considered legislation and protect the constitutional rights of the States. For constitutional amendments, a two-thirds majority of those members present and voting in each House would be required, but for ordinary legislation the *Dewan Negara* would only have power to delay up to one year, with the *Dewan Rakyat* being able to override it by a resolution. The Commission envisaged that eventually the proportion of nominated Senators would decrease, that the number of members chosen by each State would be increased from two to three, and that they would be directly elected. The Government would have the power to proclaim an emergency and pass emergency laws inconsistent

[46] See above; and ch 4.

with the Constitution prior to Parliament sitting, when Parliament would assume this power.

Addressing the federal structure, the Commission separated federal and state powers in exhaustive detail, providing that neither the Federation nor the States would be able trespass on the powers of the other, although the federal legislature would have a strictly limited power to legislate for the States for the purpose of promoting uniformity. The Commission criticised the FMA for giving too much power to the States. Accordingly, the most important functions were to be allotted to the Federation. The theory adopted was that the States should not be financially overburdened, and thus become dependent on the Federal Government.

With regard to the judiciary, the Commission mandated the ordinary courts with responsibility for constitutional questions, so that the States' rights and fundamental rights would be guaranteed. The independence of the judiciary was not, however, well protected under the draft constitution. Judges were to be appointed by the Head of State on the advice of the Government in consultation with the Chief Justice. They were to retire at 65 but were to be removable in pursuance of an address passed by a two-thirds majority in each House.[47] The Commission considered that appeals to the Privy Council should be retained, as a valuable link between members of the Commonwealth, and also because the Privy Council's experience of other federal constitutions would be valuable. To the related issue of fundamental rights the Report devoted only two of its 194 paragraphs, arguing that these rights were firmly established, and finding there was no objection to recommending their inclusion, despite their view that apprehensions in some quarters about the future were 'vague and unfounded'.

What emanated from this approach was a limited scope and entrenchment of some rights based loosely on the contemporary examples such as India. The feebleness of the Commission's justification for entrenching fundamental rights is all too apparent from subsequent history, as we shall see. If the provision for judicial review of fundamental rights was merely to satisfy vague and unfounded apprehensions, it is hard to see why the Commission recommended the entrenchment of fundamental rights at all. The assertion that fundamental rights were already protected was optimistic in view of the emergency situation which prevailed. The failure to address obvious arguments in favour of

---

[47] In the final version of the Constitution, the judiciary was protected by a requirement to convene a special tribunal to consider a charge of misconduct: see ch 8.

entrenchment of fundamental rights seems bizarre in retrospect: it was indeed found objectionable even at the time. The arguments were as follows. First, Malaya was a diverse society with many races, religions and languages; a condition which required a more positive reassurance, especially to minority groups, that their rights would not be removed. Secondly, the principal need was for a strong central Government with institutional restraints to ensure against abuse of powers. Thirdly, the Constitution envisaged constitutional and democratic government and the separation of powers. Fourthly, certain rights were recognised by international instruments to be fundamental. The debate should really have been about how it would have been best to define and guarantee these rights, and what the role of the judiciary should be, not about whether guarantees were needed. As a result of this spineless approach, the Alliance Government was emboldened after 1957 to impose important and far-reaching restrictions on fundamental rights, especially after 1969, both in amending the draft Constitution, and by frequent, almost routine, legislative amendments in subsequent years that restricted those rights even further.

A further weakness in the Report in this area was that the five members were not unanimous on the question of judicial review. Justice Abdul Hamid, whose dissenting opinions on some other matters have proved to be rather more prophetic than his opinions on this matter, objected to judicial review on grounds of 'reasonableness' of the restrictions of the civil liberties of freedom of speech, assembly and association set out in Article 10. As we shall see, this was an important omission that has over time degraded the rights in Article 10.[48]

Despite objections being voiced to a restricted form of judicial review, the Tunku, a Cambridge law graduate and a barrister, supported by the Attorney-General, stood firm on the platform of a strong central Government, unimpeded by 'too much legal propriety', dealing effectively with the country's problems in a dangerous world. It was clear that the Government did not stand merely on current necessities, which could after all be dealt with under an emergency proclamation.

Thus far the Commission dealt with fairly standard constitutional questions, albeit with some local particularities to be considered. However, it also had to deal with the thorny questions of ethnicity and religion, and in particular the issue of special privileges. It was obvious to all that the diversity of Malaya presented several constitutional problems. Religion, which is now the most divisive issue in Malaysia, appeared

---

[48] See further, pp 163–164.

at that time to most of the actors a much more peripheral issue. Ethnicity appeared to be the real challenge, in response to which the Commission offered another equivocal response adverting to the incompatibility of equality and the granting special privileges to one group.

The problem was that the Malays as the majority, and, in their self-perception, indigenous[49] population, deserving of special recognition, were far behind other communities, especially the Chinese, economically. Colonial rule and the FMA itself had given the Malays some special privileges to avoid their being marginalised in their own country. For example, most positions in the police and the public service went to Malays. The issue was whether this should continue, and if so in what form and for how long. At issue was in effect the entire principle of the rule of law and a citizen's equality before it.

The Commission found that the special position of the Malays had been recognised and safeguarded with regard to land reservations, quotas for admission into the public service, business licences and scholarships. Since there was no opposition to the continuance of these privileges for the time being, the Commission recommended their continuance, subject to review by Parliament after 15 years. They clearly viewed the special privileges as 'sunset legislation', whose necessity would decline rapidly when the consequent laws and policies took effect, and as aspects of government which were essentially incompatible with the overriding principle of equality. There was a sharp difference here between the Commission and the Working Party as to the continuation of special privileges. While the Commission recommended that they should be reviewed after 15 years, the Working Party thought that the Government should review them from time to time, with no limitation. It was the Working Party view that prevailed, a view that was to have very far-reaching consequences.

The debates concerning religion in and around the Commission's Report are also important to understand in some detail.[50] The interpretation of the Constitution has become the weapon of choice in the struggle over the constitutional position of religion, as we shall see in Chapter 9. Given the penumbra of ambiguity of several provisions, the thinking of those involved in the drafting process becomes pre-eminently important. The Alliance wanted Islam to be the official religion of the Federation. The Rulers disagreed, reasoning that as Heads of Islam, being

---

[49] See, further, ch 6.

[50] D Shah, *Constitutions, Religion and Politics and in Asia: Indonesia, Malaysia and Sri Lanka* (Cambridge, Cambridge University Press, 2017) ch 2.

the religion of all the Malay States, they could not countenance religion being made in any sense a federal matter, which would undermine their position, since being Head of Islam was one of the few powers left in their hands. Moreover, at that time Muslims were actually in a minority, so there was no real case for making Islam the official religion based on it being the majority's religion. It was no doubt under Jennings' guidance that the Commission discerned a contradiction between the notion of a secular state and having an official religion.[51] Thus the majority of the Commission, Justice Abdul Hamid dissenting, recommended that the Federation should have a secular state, and that there should be no official religion. Abdul Hamid – changing his mind on this issue when the Commission reached the Rome hotel room where the originating version of the historic document was drafted – argued that it was harmless to accede to the Alliance position on religion, since many other constitutions had similar provisions. As Fernando points out, however, his argument was hardly to the point when in none of those cases was the society in question multi-religious.[52]

Predictably, the Alliance leaders were displeased with the outcome and demanded a provision on the official religion. Thus the stipulation in the current Article 3 of the Constitution that Islam is the religion of the Federation was inserted during the review process following the Commission's Report. UMNO stuck to its demand for an official-religion provision, and the other component parties of the Alliance were not disposed to unravel the carefully negotiated Alliance compromise. The Tunku himself was in favour of Article 3 on the grounds that the provision would not prevent the state from being secular in nature; was similar to provisions in constitutions of Muslim countries; was found in the Constitutions of some of the Malay States; and was agreed to unanimously by the Alliance, which also included non-Muslim parties. The non-Muslims' acceptance of Islam as the official religion was in essence a part of the social contract, from which they obviously derived other benefits. It was also clear in statements of the Alliance that the enshrinement of an official religion would not create a theocracy, nor would it affect the secular nature of the state, alter the rights of the Rulers as Heads of Islam, or abridge the religious rights of non-Muslims. The official Working Party in reviewing the draft Constitution also went along with the Alliance view. Even Malay opposition parties agreed with the Alliance view on religion, and non-Malay opposition parties did not

---

[51] Fernando (n 42).
[52] Ibid.

raise the issue, preferring to attempt to safeguard economic, language and education rights.

The Constitution, properly contextualised, actually only entrenched the position which had applied in practice under British rule in the Malay States, namely, that within the federal political system provision for Islam was essentially a state matter and dealt with by the Ruler in consultation with the Religious Council. In brief, it had only a ceremonial or symbolic role to play in the Constitution at the federal level, and this was the only new element. An Islamic theocracy was not contemplated and the issue of making Islam the official religion was in essence a symbolic recognition of Malay-Muslim identity and the special position of that community. Malaysia was in other words considered an Islamic state only in the sense that Islam was established and enjoyed a special position, but this had no impact on religious freedom or on the structure and operation of the state. There was in fact no proposal that the matter of religion be taken any further than Article 3.[53]

Despite the apparent failure to address fully the religious predisposition of the Malays, the 1957 Constitution was approved by the Federal and State Legislatures and all major interests. It was Malay nationalism defined in relation to the Chinese and Indian communities, rather than Islam defined in relation to Christianity, Buddhism and Hinduism, which characterised the politics of this period.

The Reid Commission can be applauded on several fronts but also criticised on several fronts. That they were right about the basic structure of government in the new Federation is established by the test of time. Their recognition of the importance of the social contract was also wise. At the same time, it is surprising that they set so little store by fundamental rights, judicial review, and the importance of religion, and enjoyed so much confidence in parliamentary democracy, Alliance rule and emergency powers. In all these respects, however their responses were not untypical of thinking in the 1950s Commonwealth world of decolonisation. One could also argue that they had little choice in these matters given the situation of Malaya at the time. We will see, however, that these very issues will return in several contexts for further discussion.

There were winners and losers in all this, no doubt. The Chinese and Indian communities gained some access to the political system through the extension of citizenship and their participation in the Alliance victory in the constitutional debates. Their property and businesses

---

[53] J Fernando, 'The Position of Islam in the Constitution of Malaysia' (2006) 37(2) *Journal of Southeast Asian Studies* 249.

were protected; their cultures and languages recognised and tolerated. But they would not necessarily be equal citizens. The Malays saw their language, status and religion firmly established, and they were guaranteed an increasing share of the economy. These were, moreover, positions largely placed above any real political debate. But they were achieved at a cost. The *Merdeka* Constitution had placed the Alliance effectively in charge of the Constitution as well as the Government, given their electoral dominance and the requirement of only a two-thirds parliamentary majority for most constitutional amendments, and had thus created the possibility of an accrual of extremely wide powers with little accountability for their exercise.

## IX. THE CREATION OF MALAYSIA

'Bagai semut menghimpunkan lemukut – melukut'

(As ants collect a quantity of husk, bit by bit)

The constitutional developments of 1946–57 failed to address the issues with a regional perspective, and there was therefore unfinished constitutional business – Singapore, Sarawak, North Borneo (Sabah) and Brunei. Singapore became a separate Crown colony in 1946. Sarawak had recently become a Crown colony, ceded by Rajah Charles Vyner Brooke in 1945 after a century of rule by the White Rajahs. North Borneo was already a Crown colony, while Brunei was a British protectorate.[54] There were reasons for caution. Further federation involving Borneo was opposed by Indonesia and the Philippines; Indonesia wanted to see a federation of North Kalimantan comprising North Borneo, Sarawak and Brunei, while the Philippines claimed possession of North Borneo. The addition of Singapore would increase the proportion of Chinese citizens in Malaysia, placing the Malays in a possibly permanent minority. The Prime Ministers of both Malaya and Singapore envisaged the creation of Malaysia, embracing the Federation of Malaya, Singapore, Sarawak and North Borneo.[55] Brunei was not interested in sharing its increasing oil wealth, but elections and a UN Commission in the Borneo States, as well as a referendum in Singapore, supported the new Federation.

Accordingly, the Malaysia plan proceeded, despite the persistence of objections, especially from Indonesian President Sukarno, who

---

[54] An 1888 treaty had made Sarawak, North Borneo and Brunei protected States.
[55] Tan Poh-Ling, 'From Malaya to Malaysia' in Harding and Lee (n 32).

denounced it as a British neo-colonial plot. The Federation of Malaya, the United Kingdom, North Borneo, Sarawak and Singapore Governments entered into the Malaysia Agreement 1963. The Malaysia Act 1963 was passed by the Federation's Parliament to give effect to the Agreement in Malaya and to amend the Constitution, and new constitutions for the three new States of Malaysia were provided by a UK Order-in-Council. The chief effect of all this was simply that three new States joined the Federation. There was no suggestion that an entirely new Constitution was required. Still, the negotiation of terms for the admission of these three new States entailed special constitutional provision being made for them, and an elevation of their status above that of the States of the existing Federation in terms of their legislative powers, guarantees of their continued autonomy, and (in the cases of North Borneo, now renamed Sabah, and Sarawak) disproportionately high representation in Parliament.

These changes introduced a new complexity into Malaysia's ethnic and political diversity. Singapore left the Federation in 1965 when disagreements between the Singapore and Kuala Lumpur Governments became too problematical.[56] Sabah and Sarawak, however, remained within the Federation, but with somewhat different laws and legal institutions from those of Malaysia, as well as different powers from the other States. Thus the Malaysian Federation took a slightly different form from that of Malaya in that it is a two-tier Federation with three subjects, one of which is itself a Federation of eleven subjects. These changes affected the manner in which the political system functioned more than they affected the actual constitutional structure. However, they necessitated in the Borneo States a separate High Court and separate legal professions, as well as state powers over immigration and changes with respect to citizenship, language and ethnic status. As we shall see in Chapter 6, these arrangements have proved controversial in Sabah and Sarawak, where it is commonly felt that the terms and understandings of the 1963 Agreement have not been adhered to.

One other matter requires mention here. In a fascinating case brought literally a few hours before Malaysia's inauguration, the constitutionality of the entire enterprise was thrown into doubt by the State of Kelantan, which sought an interim injunction effectively preventing the new country from being formed on the ground that Kelantan had not been consulted about the changed federal structure, and that it was

---

[56] Kevin YL Tan, 'Singapore: In and Out of the Federation' in Harding and Lee (n 32).

accordingly not bound by the relevant constitutional amendments.[57] In a judgment with heavy implications for the nature of Malaysian federalism, the Chief Justice held[58] that the amendments to the Constitution creating Malaysia did not require Kelantan's consent, as there was no implied constitutional requirement to that effect. The amendments had been effected according to the express terms of the Constitution itself, having been appended to the Federation of Malaya Agreement 1957, to which Kelantan was a party. Moreover, anticipating future arguments over the extent of the power to amend the Constitution, he said that in doing these things he could not see that 'Parliament went in any way beyond its powers or that it did anything so fundamentally revolutionary as to require the fulfilment of a condition which the Constitution itself does not prescribe'. This left open the idea that a constitutional amendment could be so fundamentally revolutionary as to require fulfilment of such a condition.[59]

Thus the new Federation was born amidst legal and international controversy as Indonesia mustered power to attempt to strangle the newborn in its cradle. Malaysia was nonetheless formed on 21 September 1963.[60] Sukarno and the Indonesian *konfrontasi* were faced down in what has been called Malaysia's finest hour.[61] With Singapore becoming an independent republic on 9 August 1965 and Sukarno cast aside by the Indonesian military in September 1965, *konfrontasi*, which had seen guerrilla warfare in Borneo, paratroop landings in Malaya, and bombings in Singapore, came to an end. This was also the last chance of the communist party, in league with Sukarno, to take over Malaysia. The CPM insurgency limped on in the Northern Malayan jungle near the Thai border until 1989, by which time there were few of the CPM left to surrender to the Malaysian Government. There were many struggles to come, but the infant had survived and the constitutional structure for the whole region had been settled.

---

[57] See, further, Johan Shamsuddin Sabaruddin, 'The Kelantan Challenge' in Harding and Lee (n 32), 47.

[58] *Government of Kelantan v Government of the Federation of Malaya and Tunku Abdul Rahamn Putra Al-Haj* (1963) MLJ 355.

[59] For discussion of the 'basic structure doctrine', see p 199.

[60] Malaysia's National Day is 31 August, which is *Merdeka* Day for the Federation of Malaya only; 50 years of independence were celebrated in 2007, although the Borneo States had been independent only since 1963. For the problematical issue of whose birthday, which is a source of displeasure in East Malaysia, see J Chin, 'Federal – East Malaysia relations: Primus inter pares?' in A Harding and J Chin (eds), *50 Years of Malaysia: Federalism Revisited* (Singapore, Marshall Cavendish, 2014) 152.

[61] Tan Poh-Ling (n 55) 32; J Mackie, *Konfrontasi: The Indonesia-Malaysia Dispute 1993–1966* (Kuala Lumpur, Oxford University Press, 1974).

## X. CONCLUSION

Naturally, Malaysian constitutional history did not cease in 1963, and there have been many other changes. These changes will be dealt with in later chapters. The purpose of this chapter has been to indicate the main features of the history that led to the emergence of the Malaysian polity in 1963. Changes since then have been important but have not affected the design fundamentally. This polity has elements that are traditional, colonial and nationalist. It represented a delicate balance that was seriously disturbed and then redrawn in 1969–71, as we will see in Chapter 3. A major theme underlying every chapter in this book is the way in which the state has had to respond to the fact of ethnic and religious diversity: a process that is still very much ongoing.

## FURTHER READING[62]

Sri Murugan Alagan, *The Federal Constitution: A Commentary* (Subang Jaya, Thomson Reuters, 2019).

B Andaya and L Andaya, *A History of Malaysia* (London, Macmillan, 1982).

Abdul Aziz Bari and Farid Sofyan Shoaib, *Constitution of Malaysia: Text and Commentary* (2nd edn, Petaling Jaya, Prentice Hall, 2006).

J Fernando, *The Making of the Malayan Constitution* (Kuala Lumpur, MBRAS, 2002).

A Harding, *Law, Government and the Constitution in Malaysia* (The Hague, Kluwer, and Kuala Lumpur, Malayan Law Journal, 1996).

A Harding and HP Lee (eds), *Constitutional Landmarks in Malaysia: The First 50 Years, 1957–2007* (Kuala Lumpur, Malayan Law Journal/LexisNexis, 2007).

Lim Wei Jiet, *Halsbury's Law of Malaysia: Constitutional Law* (Kuala Lumpur, LexisNexis, 2019).

Kevin YL Tan and Li-ann Thio, *Constitutional Law in Malaysia and Singapore* (3rd edn, Singapore, LexisNexis, 2010).

---

[62] This list includes general Malaysian constitutional law publications in addition to items specific to the subject matter of this chapter.

# 2

# Executive Power and the Configuration of the State

Structure of the Executive Power – Appointment of Governments – The Cabinet – The Public Service – Privatisation – Public and Private Interface – GLCs and the Liability of Ministers

## I. INTRODUCTION

'Kemana nak pergi layang-layang? Tali ada di-tangan kita'
(Where can the kite go? Its strings are in our hands)

WITH THE OBJECT of facilitating development, the intention of the constitution-making process of 1957 was to create a strong central government with limited autonomy for the States. Typically of constitutional drafting of the 1950s, the *Merdeka* Constitution gave no concrete indication of the type of state[1] ideology that was envisaged, nor did it set out any directive principles or priorities of government.[2] The fundamental policies and principles of operation of the state were therefore left to the leadership of the new nation to develop, and democratic institutions to mould over time. As a result, the fundamental nature of the Malaysian state and citizenship in a plural society, whether considered juridically or politically, has been a matter for continued argument over most of the time since 1957.[3]

This chapter looks at the constitutional structure of the Federal executive branch (that of the States being left to Chapter 6) and the

---

[1] In this book 'state' (as noun or adjective) refers to the federal executive power, or where the context demands the Malaysian state generally, including the legislative and judicial branches; and 'State(s)' (as noun or adjective) refers to the 13 subjects of the Federation or any of them.

[2] The *Rukunegara* was a concerted attempt to supply the omission: see below, at p 61 ff.

[3] The arguments over the notion of an Islamic state are discussed in ch 9.

limits on its powers. Consistently with the objective of picturing the lived experience of constitutional government, the chapter will examine how the state has been transformed over time and upon what principles it has operated. The overwhelming power of the state will be seen as an important historical factor in every chapter of this book, affecting profoundly the nature and operation of all aspects of the constitutional system. We have seen in Chapter 1 how the events of 1969 led to fundamental changes in the state's definition, direction and design. The Malaysian state, geared to development and a social contract renegotiated with the *Rukunegara* amendments in 1969–71, and propelled by the New Economic Policy (NEP),[4] proved remarkably stable for a long time. Five decades on from 1971, however, it cries out for renovation, although there seems to be no real agreement as to the type or extent of renovation that is needed. The Pakatan Harapan (PH) Government of 2018–20 promised but failed to deliver fundamental reform, and was replaced by the Perikatan Nasional (PN) Government (2020 to date), which comprised parties and factions that did not offer to further the reform process.[5] The stated objective of the Malaysian Government under Mahathir's *Wawasan 2020* (Vision 2020), which dates from 1991, was to achieve the status of a fully developed country, not only in terms of economic progress but also in terms of national unity in a tolerant, democratic and caring society, by 2020. This project was far from fulfilment by 2020. Given the fragmented politics post-2018, no clear state agenda has since emerged or seems likely to do so.[6]

First, we will look at the executive power as formally and legally defined in and structured by the Constitution, embodying a constitutional monarchy, a Westminster-style parliamentary executive, and a prime-ministerial system of government. This will involve looking at the operation of cabinet government. We then move to examine the administrative structure of the state at the Federal level, in terms of the public

---

[4] The NEP technically ended in 1990, but was replaced by the 'National Development Policy' and then in 2000 by the 'National Vision Policy'. It has become conventional, however, to refer to the policy of *bumiputera* preference, which is at the core of the social contract, as the 'NEP'. Since 1966 there have also been five-year 'Malaysia Plans' implementing development policies in detail.

[5] See, further, pp 85 ff.

[6] A Harding, 'Constitutional trajectory in Malaysia: Constitutionalism without Consensus?' in MW Dowdle and MA Wilkinson (eds), *Constitutionalism Beyond Liberalism* (Cambridge, Cambridge University Press, 2017); A Harding, 'Law and development in Malaysia: A vision beyond 2020?' in Salim Ali Farrar and P Subramaniam (eds), *Law and Justice in Malaysia: 2020 and Beyond* (Kuala Lumpur, Thomson Reuters, 2021).

service, statutory agencies, regulation and privatisation, engaging here with the public-private interface. Detailed consideration of these topics, some of which are at first sight hardly relevant to the Constitution, serves to set out the 'toolbox' of the executive power, which is by far the largest of the three powers of government that are separated under the Constitution. A critical issue here is the legal accountability of the Prime Minister and other ministers in respect of the discharge of their functions (political accountability being dealt with in Chapter 4). By examining accountability under public, private and criminal law we can, first, define the state and the public/private interface, with special reference to Government-linked Companies (GLCs); and, secondly, we can examine constraints on the exercise of power that have become of prime importance since the emergence of the 1MDB scandal and its revelation of extensive kleptocracy in Malaysian government.

The chapter concludes with a discussion of the social contract as a basic principle for the actual functioning of the state, clearly recognised – enshrined even – in the Constitution at Article 153. The social contract is infrequently understood and debated, partly because criticism of the policies constituting it is prohibited in terms of the social contract itself, and partly because, dealing with the fundamental issue of ethnic preference, it is a deeply sensitive topic.

## II. CONSTITUTIONAL STRUCTURE OF THE EXECUTIVE POWER

'Air di tulang bumbungan, turunnya di cucur atap'

(The water on the roof falls to the eaves – in other words power naturally flows from top to bottom)

### A. Constitutional Monarchy

The institution of a constitutional monarchy and a Westminster-model executive[7] was a given factor in the constitution-making process of 1957.

---

[7] See YAM Raja Azlan Shah, 'The Role of Constitutional Rulers in Malaysia' in FA Trindade and HP Lee (eds), *The Constitution of Malaysia: Further Developments and Perspectives* (Singapore, Oxford University Press, 1986); V Sinnadurai (ed), *Constitutional Monarchy, Rule of Law and Good Governance: Selected Essays and Speeches of HRH Sultan Azlan Shah* (Petaling Jaya, Sweet and Maxwell Asia, 2004).

This model was also imposed on the States, whose Constitutions were obliged under the Federal Constitution to conform to Westminster principles.[8] As a result the constitutional conventions associated with this model, relating to the head of state, the head of government, the legislature, and the relations between them, are codified in the Federal and State Constitutions, and have been definitive in Malaysian constitutional practice. These conventions have also been the subject of controversies that have usually arisen in the operation of the State Constitutions, but became problematical at the Federal level during 2020.[9] Discussion of constitutional conventions will also be found in Chapters 4, 5 and 6.

The problem is, in essence, that of interpreting conventions which developed in Britain as unwritten customs dependent on precedent and political practice,[10] but which now find themselves as written law in Malaysia.[11] For example, the convention that the head of state must act on government advice is enshrined in the constitutional text at Article 40(1) and (1A); and the principle of collective ministerial responsibility to Parliament is set out in Article 43(3). Westminster-style conventions, although clearly evident in Malaysian constitutional law, may, however, not operate in precisely the same way in Malaysia as they do in Britain and other Commonwealth States, because Malaysia has a different history of democratic politics.[12] It has in fact to some extent developed its own constitutional conventions or interpretations of them and, unlike in Britain, the courts have played an important part in interpreting and enforcing these conventions.[13] Some aspects of these conventions in relation to the executive are discussed below.

The starting point for looking at the Federal executive is that the executive authority of the Federation is vested in the *Yang di-Pertuan Agong*, but this power is exercisable by the *Yang di-Pertuan Agong* or the Cabinet or any Minister authorised by the Cabinet, and where

---

[8] See Federal Constitution, Sch 8: Provisions to be Inserted in State Constitution.

[9] See below.

[10] G Marshall, *Constitutional Conventions: The Rules and Forms of Political Accountability* (Oxford, Clarendon Press, 1986).

[11] See further, A Harding, 'Conventions and practical interpretation in Westminster-type constitutional systems' (ICONN, forthcoming).

[12] A Harding, 'Acting (or not acting) on (law or unlawful) advice in Malaysia: From Windsor to Kuantan and back again', *ICONNECT Blog*, 20 November 2020.

[13] See below for these cases.

the *Yang di-Pertuan Agong* acts he does so on the advice of the Government.[14] Indeed Article 40(1A) (introduced in 1994) states this principle explicitly:

> In the exercise of his functions under this Constitution or federal law, where the *Yang di-Pertuan Agong* is to act in accordance with advice, on advice, or after considering advice, the *Yang di-Pertuan Agong* shall accept and act in accordance with such advice.

In certain cases, however, such as the appointment of the Prime Minister, the *Yang di-Pertuan Agong* has discretion to exercise,[15] but this exercise of discretion is bounded by precedent and the constitutional responsibilities that this discretion entails. This discretion is discussed below.

The position thus established ensures that, although the *Yang di-Pertuan Agong* is the nominal Head of the Executive, the Prime Minister and the Cabinet are the real executive power. The convention that the head of state must act on the advice of the government has, with one exception (the refusal of an emergency proclamation in October 2020, discussed below) always been followed in Malaysia in much the same way as it has in Britain, at least at the Federal level. This does not necessarily mean that the *Yang di-Pertuan Agong* is unable to voice any opinions, but rather that in the last analysis he must act on government advice, whatever his personal views might be. The Proclamation of Constitutional Principles,[16] introduced in 1992 during a controversy over the powers of the Rulers, rehearses Bagehot's classic statement of the limited rights of the monarch: 'to be consulted, to encourage and to warn'.[17] Since this document represents both government and royal opinion on the constitutional role of the monarchy, although not binding in law, this statement can be taken to represent constitutional practice as understood in Malaysia. It should, however, be qualified by two considerations: first, that the *Yang di-Pertuan Agong* is one of nine Rulers who are members of the Conference of Rulers and he will normally reflect the views of the Rulers collectively, or at least not stray too far from their views; and secondly, that a more expansive view of royal powers is taken

---

[14] Arts 39–40; RH Hickling, 'The *Yang di-Pertuan Agong* as the head of the executive' [1991] *Supreme Court Journal* 43.

[15] Art 43; see also Art 40(2).

[16] Kobkua Suwannathat-Pian, *Palace, Political Party and Power: A Story of the Socio-Political Development of Malay Kingship* (Singapore, NUS Press, 2011) App 1.

[17] W Bagehot, *The English Constitution* (Glasgow, Fontana, 1867: 1963) 111.

in Malaysia compared to more strictly 'Westminster' systems. This latter consideration is discussed in more detail below.

The most important function of the *Yang di-Pertuan Agong* is to act as a symbol of unity for a diverse population. This role is therefore largely ceremonial, but in addition to the prerogative powers defined in the Constitution the *Yang di-Pertuan Agong* is the Head of Islam in the Federal Territories.[18]

## B. The Prime Minister

The power in Article 43(2) to appoint the Prime Minister is as follows:

> the *Yang di-Pertuan Agong* shall first appoint as *Perdana Mentri* (Prime Minister) to preside over the Cabinet a member of the House of Representatives who in his judgment is likely to command the confidence of the majority of the members of that House.

There have been 14 Federal general elections (styled here 'GE14' and so on) since *Merdeka*; on each occasion up to GE14 in 2018 the Alliance / Barisan Nasional obtained a clear majority in Parliament, and its Chairman, consistently also the President of UMNO, was automatically appointed Prime Minister. UMNO therefore provided Malaysia's political leadership for 61 years after independence. GE14 provided the first occasion when there had been a change of government since 1957 and marked a significant juncture in Malaysian political history.

With regard to constitutional conventions, the appointment of Tun Dr Mahathir Mohamad as Prime Minister on 10 May 2018 was not entirely without controversy or difficulty. It was clear on that day that the Pakatan Harapan (PH) coalition had won the election, but there was delay in issuing the official results, giving rise to fears that some unconstitutional action might deprive the PH and the electorate of their just deserts. It was also not entirely certain, in the eyes of some at least, that Tun Mahathir should be appointed, as he was the leader of a small party (Parti Pribumi Bersatu Malaysia, PPBM) that had won

---

[18] The federal territories comprise the City of Kuala Lumpur; Putrajaya, named after the Tunku (Abdul Rahman Putra Al-Haj), and constructed to the south of Kuala Lumpur in the 1990s, the administrative capital of Malaysia; and Labuan, an island offshore of Sarawak (in both geographical and financial senses), which is federal territory due to its economic significance as a kind of special economic zone.

only 13 seats. Nonetheless he had been endorsed by all the PH parties during the campaign as their candidate for Prime Minister. Following initial uncertainty the *Yang di-Pertuan Agong* met with the various party leaders and received a letter signed by all of the PH's newly elected members; he was also visited by the heads of the police, the army and the civil service, who stressed the need to appoint the Prime Minister immediately to avoid public disorder. He then concluded that Tun Mahathir was likely to command the support of a majority of Members of Parliament (MPs), and late on 10 May he was finally sworn in as Prime Minister.[19]

The appointment process was also in question during the political crisis in the days leading up to 1 March 2020, when the Federal government changed hands for the second time, this time without an election but due to defections from the PH, causing the government to collapse. Tensions over succession issues within the Parti Keadilan Rakyat (PKR), the largest of the PH parties, led to a realignment of PH parties and factions with a view to the construction of a new government involving opposition parties. This prompted Tun Mahathir to resign as Prime Minister on the basis that he no longer had the confidence of a majority of MPs. The *Yang di-Pertuan Agong* accepted his resignation and then appointed him as 'Interim Prime Minister', although this position does not in fact appear in the Constitution. There followed a period of confusion in which Tun Mahathir tried unsuccessfully to construct a new government whose composition would bypass party affiliations, but the remnants of the PH regrouped in support of his continuing as Prime Minister. The *Yang di-Pertuan Agong* interviewed all MPs to gauge their support, without being able to reach any conclusion. He also met with party leaders, and called a meeting of the Conference of Rulers. Meanwhile Tun Mahathir insisted that he had the support, via statutory declarations, of 114 MPs: a small majority in a House of 222. Nonetheless, His Majesty on 1 March 2020 appointed as Prime Minister Tan Sri Muhyiddin Yassin, the President of PPBM, who also claimed majority support. Although it

---

[19] For the whole story of this change in government, see the papers in the online symposium edited by Jaclyn Neo, Dian AH Shah and Andrew Harding, entitled 'Malaysia Boleh! Constitutional implications of the Malaysian tsunami', available at http://www.iconnectblog.com/2018/06/introduction-to-i-connect-symposium-malaysia-boleh-constitutional-implications-of-the-malaysian-tsunami; and see A Harding and others, *ICONnect-Clough Centre Global Review of Constitutional Law 2018*, available at https://papers.ssrn.com/sol3/papers.cfm?abstract_id=3471638; ET Gomez and Mohamed Nawab Mohamed Osman (eds), *Malaysia's 14th General Election and UMNO's Fall: Intra-Elite Feuding in the Pursuit of Power* (Abingdon, Routledge, 2020).

can be strongly argued that the issue of support should have been tested on the floor of the *Dewan Rakyat*, the House was not summoned until some seven weeks after the appointment.[20]

Difficulty can also occur around the issue of dismissal of a Prime Minister. It remains unclear whether the *Yang di-Pertuan Agong* has a reserve power actually to dismiss the Prime Minister. Article 43(4) merely says, consistently with Westminster-type practice:

> If the Prime Minister ceases to command the confidence of the majority of the members of the House of Representatives, then, unless at his request the *Yang di-Pertuan Agong* dissolves Parliament, the Prime Minister shall tender the resignation of the Cabinet.

The latest guidance from the Federal Court in a 2010 case[21] involving the *Menteri Besar* of the State of Perak appears to indicate that, despite any provision giving the Head of State a power of dismissal, he could nonetheless declare the office of Prime Minister vacant if, in his view, the latter has lost the confidence of a majority of MPs; moreover, in doing so he could take into account evidence of matters occurring other than in the legislature. This decision, apparently resolving doubt as to whether there was an implied power for the Head of State to dismiss a Chief Minister, is, however, questioned by a large body of constitutional opinion.[22] We can also note here that when UMNO was declared by the High Court to be an unlawful society in February 1988, the Opposition demanded Prime Minister Tun Mahathir's resignation on the ground that he was no longer the leader of any (lawful) political party.[23] However, the test of a Prime Minister's tenure, as in both the 2018 and 2020 instances, is clearly the confidence of a majority of MPs, not the leadership of any party or coalition, and there was no indication that Mahathir had lost the confidence of the majority of MPs on that occasion: indeed BN leaders expressed confidence in him, and Government Bills continued to be passed in the *Dewan Rakyat*.

Each of the first six Prime Ministers of Malaya / Malaysia held office for at least five years, although Tun Mahathir's second tenure

---

[20] For a full account and critique of this process, including the so-called 'Sheraton move', from a constitutional perspective, see A Harding and Dian AH Shah, 'Constitutional quantum mechanics and a change of government in Malaysia', ICONNECT Blog, April 2020, available at www.iconnectblog.com/2020/04/constitutional-quantum-mechanics-and-a-change-of-government-in-malaysia.

[21] *Datuk Nizar Jamaluddin v Datuk Seri Zambry Abdul Kadir* [2010] 2 MLJ 285.

[22] See ch 5. The State Constitutions are identical to the Federal Constitution in this respect.

[23] See ch 8.

was less than two years. Tun Mahathir (Prime Minister 1981–2003 and 2018–20) defined the nature and trajectory of the developmental state during the 22 years of his first premiership, imposing his personal and controversial stamp on the polity as no other Prime Minister has done. He survived many crises, taking Malaysia much further towards authoritarian government than any of his predecessors or successors. However, during his second tenure he appeared as a champion of reform in the face of the infamous corruption scandal relating to the sovereign wealth fund company 1Malaysia Development Berhad (1MDB), which led to the downfall of the BN Government in GE14. The fact that Malaysia has had only nine Prime Ministers since 1957 is an index of relatively stable government during this period – at least up until 2018, after which political power seems to have fragmented to some extent.

All of Malaysia's Prime Ministers this far have been male, Malay-Muslim, UMNO or former UMNO politicians. The power accruing to these Prime Ministers has usually been great. Not only did they control UMNO and the BN coalition, and thereby the Federal Government (up to 2018), but they also indirectly controlled most State Governments for most of the time via their control over the BN. They were rarely even challenged from within UMNO or the BN. Until GE12 in 2008 they also commanded more than a two-thirds majority in Parliament as well as controlling the Senate, thereby enabling them to propose successful amendments to the Constitution: a power which they exercised with some frequency.[24]

Mahathir's first premiership expanded the power of the Prime Minister considerably. Unlike all of his predecessors he was not a lawyer but a medical practitioner by training and proved more impatient of constitutional checks and balances than other Prime Ministers. However, in his second term, in a remarkable change of ideology, and commencing this term at the age of 93, he appeared as a reformer and champion of multi-party democracy. During his first term he challenged the power of the judiciary in 1988 (see Chapter 8), the Rulers in 1983 and 1993 (see Chapter 5), and dissent within UMNO in 1987 and 1998,

---

[24] HP Lee, 'The Process of Constitutional Change in Malaysia' in Tun Mohamed Suffian, HP Lee and FA Trindade (eds), *The Constitution of Malaysia: Its Development 1957–1977* (Kuala Lumpur, Oxford University Press, 1978); A Harding and HP Lee, 'Constitutional Landmarks and Constitutional Signposts: Some Reflections on the First Fifty Years' in A Harding and HP Lee (eds), *Constitutional Landmarks in Malaysia: The First Fifty Years, 1957–2007* (Kuala Lumpur, Malayan Law Journal/LexisNexis, 2007).

and got his way in all of these instances. He also held important ministerial portfolios during his premiership, taking over Finance, Home Affairs, and Defence during the period from 1998 to 2003. In 2018, on the other hand, he was prevailed upon not to assume the education portfolio in addition to the premiership. Najib Razak, however, held the finance portfolio in addition to the premiership, which enabled him to control government-linked companies through the Minister of Finance Incorporated.[25]

Mahathir not only had virtually unlimited power but exercised it extensively and personally, playing a significant role even in planning and executing major projects such as the Multimedia Super Corridor, Kuala Lumpur International Airport, the Petronas Twin Towers, and the new administrative capital, Putrajaya. He also orchestrated Malaysia's successful response to the financial crisis of 1997–78, resisting international criticism and demands.[26] During his period in office it became increasingly apparent that it was political rather than legal constraints on the Prime Minister's power that counted. These constraints existed mainly within UMNO and the Cabinet.

Given the importance of the Prime Minister in the Malaysian system of government, we will now look more closely at the sources and extent of the power of this office.

First, the Prime Minister is head of the executive in a parliamentary system, exercising power as the office-holder on whom the very constitutional existence and continuance of the government depend, as the minister presiding over the Cabinet, and through his power to offer advice to the *Yang di-Pertuan Agong* in appointing ministers and other members of the government, as well as officials, and heads and members of statutory agencies, where the Prime Minister is usually required to consult specified persons.[27] The Prime Minister's Office (PMO) has responsibility for government oversight and the organisational aspects of government, including the civil service, policy coordination and law enforcement, and special responsibility with regard to justice, religion and the economy and development. Independent agencies also, in

---

[25] For the dangers inherent in the Prime Minister holding multiple portfolios, see ET Gomez, *Minister of Finance Incorporated: Ownership and Control of Corporate Malaysia* (IDEAS, 2018) 219ff.

[26] RS Milne and DK Mauzy, *Malaysian Politics under Mahathir* (London, Routledge, 1999) 67–68, 75–76, 175–78.

[27] Eg see Constitution, Art 122B (the judiciary).

practice, report to the PMO in fulfilment of the statutory duty of reporting to the Government.[28] None of these functions involves the Prime
Minister exercising statutory powers directly, except with regard to official appointments. In short, the Prime Minister exercises considerable
political influence on the policy and operation of government, but almost
all governmental statutory functions are vested in ministers or statutory
agencies. The PMO became increasingly large and important during
Mahathir's premiership, and has usually housed a number of ministers
in addition to the Prime Minister. Currently the PMO has five ministers
and five deputy ministers in addition to the Prime Minister, exercising
extensive functions related to law, Parliament, religion, economic affairs,
and Sabah and Sarawak affairs.[29]

## C. The Cabinet

The *Jemaah Mentri* (Cabinet) is an institution expressly envisaged by
the Constitution, in that Article 43 requires a Cabinet to be appointed
to advise the *Yang di-Pertuan Agong* in the exercise of his functions.[30]
The other Ministers are to be appointed by the *Yang di-Pertuan Agong*
on the advice of the Prime Minister, but these must be members of
either of the Houses of Parliament, to which the Cabinet is collectively
responsible. It is the resignation of the Cabinet which must be tendered
in the event that the Prime Minister loses the confidence of Parliament.[31]
Cabinet government is a particularly important feature of the Malaysian
'consociational' political system[32] in which there is a need to consolidate
Government policy across several political parties that represent various
ethnic communities and disparate interests.

The internal operation of the Cabinet is described in gratifying detail
in Rais Yatim's *Cabinet Governing in Malaysia*.[33] From this revealing

---

[28] See eg the Malaysian Anti-Corruption Commission Act 2009 (Act 694), s 14(5).

[29] For the PMO, see www.pmo.gov.my.

[30] For discussion of the Cabinet, see further Abdul Aziz Bari, *Cabinet Principles in Malaysia: The Law and Practice*(2nd edn, Petaling Jaya, The Other Press, 2002); and Rais Yatim, *Cabinet Governing in Malaysia* (Kuala Lumpur, DBN Enterprises, 2006).

[31] Art 43(4). And see *Datu Amir Kahar bin Tun Datu Haji Mustapha v Tun Mohamed Said bin Keruak, Yang di-Pertua Negeri Sabah and Ors* [1995] 1 MLJ 169; A Harding, 'When is a resignation not a resignation? A crisis of confidence in Sabah' (1995) 84 *The Round Table* 353.

[32] Milne and Mauzy (n 26) 16–19.

[33] Rais Yatim (n 30).

account by an experienced former Cabinet member, who is also a lawyer and a scholar, it becomes clear that, although the power of the Prime Minister is acknowledged to be very great, the Cabinet is nonetheless also of considerable importance.

The structure of the Cabinet is dictated more by political than by administrative or governmental considerations. It is necessary for the Prime Minister to exercise great caution in its composition. Not only is the Prime Minster under the usual constraints of having to reflect opinion and assuage factions within his party and reward political associates, it is also necessary for the Prime Minister to include members of the component parties of the coalition he heads, members of the various ethnic communities, and representatives of the various States, especially Sabah and Sarawak. In recent years there has also been a small number of women in the Cabinet. The Cabinet is and has to be reflective of Malaysia's pluralism. The appointment of Ministers to the Cabinet is thus a balancing act in which the Prime Minister takes into account the candidates' experience, expertise, party, State, race, religion and gender. Which offices are to be represented in the Cabinet is also a matter for the Prime Minister to decide, but it has been conventional that all Ministers, in the sense of political heads of all Federal Government Departments, excluding deputy ministers and parliamentary secretaries, are Cabinet members. Thus the Cabinet is in effect the entire Government. Under Prime Minister Najib Razak, the Cabinet consisted of 30 ministers who between them held all the Government's ministerial portfolios. The number has generally increased since the original 10 in 1955, the largest being the present astonishing number of 70 under Prime Ministers Muhyiddin Yasin and Ismail Sabri, which means that a large majority of Government MPs are also Cabinet members. Naturally, a Cabinet of such enormous size is unlikely to be more than a rubber stamp for Government decisions already made.

Due to its size and nature the Cabinet tends on the whole not to be a forum for the making of fundamental policy decisions, but rather for the settling of administrative matters. Accommodation between coalition parties, which one might assume to take place in Cabinet, tends in fact to take place outside the Cabinet. The Cabinet normally meets for four hours once a week around an oval table at the Cabinet Office in Putrajaya. Cabinet papers are voluminous. Proceedings are conducted in a mixture of Malay and English, according to the speaker's preference, and the atmosphere is informal. The Prime Minister leads the meeting and invariably has his way: 'Ministers do not forget', comments Rais Yatim, 'that under the Malaysian political system the PM calls

the shots'.[34] This does not mean there is no debate, and some ministers are reported to have been outspoken in Cabinet.[35] Ministers can
introduce their own items for discussion and contribute to discussion
of matters not under their portfolios. Budgetary matters are very much
under the control of the Prime Minister and the Finance Ministry;
nonetheless under recent Prime Ministers there has been more participation in budgetary decisions, and rarely does a minister encounter
total rejection of the Ministry's proposed programme. Cabinet papers
are of course secret, and collective responsibility has normally been
strictly observed (less so under the recent PH and PN governments),
with any ministers making public statements which deviate from the
Government line being brought into line by the Prime Minister either in
Cabinet or by means of an 'amicable phone call' followed by a ministerial clarification.

As we have seen, ministers are collectively responsible to Parliament.[36]
Individual ministerial responsibility is not explicitly referred to in the
Constitution, but clearly does exist: ministers' question-time, for example, has been a standard aspect of parliamentary proceedings. In 2018
Tun Mahathir reversed a change introduced by the previous government,
restoring 'Prime Minister's Question-time'. However, it has proved difficult for Parliament, where the BN had a majority until 2018, to be more
than a forum for the Opposition to criticise ministers. An incident in
2005 regarding approved permits for importing vehicles indicates the
true nature of ministerial responsibility. The then Minister of Trade and
Industry, Datin Seri Rafidah Aziz, an experienced and forceful Cabinet
Minister, was criticised by Government MPs via the media for lack of
transparency in the way her ministry had granted import permits. A spat
followed between Rafidah and Mahathir, her former boss, with claims
and counter-claims over the facts. In the event, although she was criticised
in Parliament, the General Assembly of UMNO rather than the floor
of Parliament was the main forum in which displeasure over Rafidah's
conduct was voiced, encompassing irregularities in permit approvals but
also her failure to meet with Mahathir to discuss their disagreement,
regarded as discourteous according to Malaysian cultural norms. As a
result of the criticism Rafidah, known as 'Rapid-fire' and the 'iron lady'
of Malaysian politics, resigned in a flood of tears. This was, however,
a rare rather than a typical incident.

---

[34] Ibid 11.
[35] Milne and Mauzy (n 26) 168–69.
[36] Art 43(3).

In 1982 Prime Minister Mahathir laid down a list of ethical require-ments for his ministers which has been a touchstone for the Cabinet ever since; it includes, for example, a requirement to declare assets once every two years and avoid using any Government facilities for personal benefit.[37] There are frequent demands for increased regulation of minis-terial and civil-service ethics.

### D. Administrative Agencies and the Public Service

Any consideration of the state needs to take account of the very large bureaucracies beyond the Cabinet and Government Departments. There are numerous Government agencies embracing an array of functions, locations, degrees of autonomy, and legal bases. In addition, there are many GLCs, and of course in addition most of this is repeated in each of the 13 States.

Pursuing the theme of development, it can be noted that large numbers of these agencies are described as having an explicitly development-related function. To take the example of information and communica-tions technology, which is regarded as a critical aspect of Malaysia's development,[38] no fewer than 15 agencies have relevant functions. They range from the Ministry of Information and Communications to the Malaysian Communications and Multimedia Commission, the Malaysian Technology Development Corporation, the Multimedia Development Corporation (MDec), and the Multimedia Super Corridor (MSC), which falls under MDec's remit. They involve a federal ministry and statutory agencies as well as a GLC.

One obvious feature of all of these agencies is their lack of independ-ence. All are under the control of the Federal Government via lines of responsibility leading to a minister and the Cabinet, and in most cases they are appointed by the Government. This is true even of GLCs.[39] Leadership of GLCs has been a controversial issue. The PH Government of 2018–20 attempted to reverse a policy of political appointments to

---

[37] Rais Yatim (n 30) 64.

[38] Abu Bakar Munir, 'Privatisation in Malaysia: A Case Study of the Telecommunications Department' in W Neilson and E Quah (ed), *Law and Economic Development: Cases and Materials from South East Asia* (Singapore, Longman, 1993) 169; M Wigdor, *No Miracle: What Asia can Teach all Countries about Growth* (Farnham, Ashgate, 2013) 194 ff.

[39] M Likosky, *The Silicon Empire: Law, Culture and Commerce* (Aldershot, Ashgate, 2005) 169.

GLC chief executive positions; the PN Government indicated its intention to place backbench MPs in such offices.[40] In practice the operation of ministerial responsibility insulates administrative agencies from parliamentary criticism. Even agencies that are formally independent of the Government are often nonetheless treated as if the minister has to answer for them in Parliament.[41] Given the great overarching power of the Government over GLCs and the multiplicity of government and quasi-governmental agencies, and the lack of political accountability, the case law discussed earlier relating to legal accountability of ministers, especially in relation to their control over these companies and agencies, becomes of prime importance.

Naturally the civil service (known in Malaysian law as the 'public service') is a crucial component of the state. The public service includes general Federal and State service as well as the military and the police. It is responsible for the effective delivery of policy, and for the rational, pragmatic and continuous formulation and development of policy, irrespective of which group of politicians is in power. In Malaysia the Constitution in Part X deals at some length with the public service, providing for independent service commissions to control matters of appointment, advancement, transfer, discipline and dismissal. By this means the Constitution ensures that appointments are made on merit; that human resources are used effectively; and that public servants are not dismissed unfairly, or for political or other extraneous reasons.[42] The Constitution lays down in some detail the composition and powers of the service commissions: the Armed Forces Council, the Judicial and Legal Service Commission, the Public Services Commission, the Police Force Commission, and the Education Service Commission. To ensure the independence of the public service, no member of any legislature may be a member of a commission, or a member of the public service, or an officer or employee of a local or statutory authority. Additionally, a Chairman or Deputy Chairman of a Commission may not be a member of any board of directors or management of a commercial or industrial undertaking.

---

[40] 'Decision to appoint MPs as GLC heads may see history repeat in Malaysia', *Business Today*, 15 April 2020, available at https://www.businesstoday.com.my/2020/04/15/decision-to-appoint-mps-as-glc-heads-may-see-history-repeat-in-malaysia.

[41] See, further, M Puthucheary, 'Ministerial Responsibility in Malaysia' in Tun Suffian, HP Lee and FA Trindade (eds), *The Constitution of Malaysia: Its Development 1957–1977* (Kuala Lumpur, Oxford University Press, 1978).

[42] For a full explanation, see *Government of Malaysia v Mahan Singh* [1975] 1 MLJ 3.

Members of Commissions are usually to be appointed by the Government for terms of five years, with eligibility for reappointment, and have security from dismissal.[43] In practice, the Government's power to appoint commissions means that they are not really independent. Senior positions equivalent to head or deputy head of a department are, however, filled not by the relevant Commission, but by the *Yang di-Pertuan Agong* on the recommendation of the Commission, and after considering the advice of the Prime Minister; the *Yang di-Pertuan Agong* may refer the recommendation back to the Commission for reconsideration. A similar position obtains for independent agencies not mandated by the Constitution, such as the Malaysian Anti-Corruption Commission and the Judicial Appointments Commission. In July 2018 the PH Government announced a policy whereby in future independent agencies would report, not to the PMO but to Parliament; by the time it relinquished office in 2020, however, no action had been taken to implement this far-sighted policy.

The Government is generally able to secure its desired candidates as senior public servants, agency heads and GLC heads, and there is little doubt that public servants, rather than being strictly neutral, are expected to support Government policies. In 2018 Prime Minister Mahathir roundly criticised senior members of the public service for campaigning openly for the BN in GE14, and for not being loyal to the Government of the day.[44] Clearly after 61 years of BN control, the public service as a whole had difficulty in fulfilling this basic requirement, and the failure of the PH reforms is in part attributed to resistance from the public service.[45] On the other hand, the professional reputation of the public service was given a boost during the Covid-19 pandemic in 2020, when the Director-General of the Health Ministry, rather than the minister, became the leading public figure both in formulating and publicly explaining Government policy; Malaysia had had no Government and no Health Minister for a critical period of 11 days at the beginning of the outbreak.[46]

---

[43] Arts 137–40.

[44] 'Mahathir to civil servants: Reject orders that break the law', *Straits Times*, 16 August 2018, available at www.straitstimes.com/asia/mahathir-to-civil-servants-reject-orders-that-break-law.

[45] N Chan, 'Unpacking the idea of Malaysia's "deep state"', *New Mandala*, 20 February 2020, available at https://www.newmandala.org/unpacking-the-idea-of-malaysias-deep-state.

[46] 'Dr Noor Hisham a top professional in covid-19 fight', *The Star*, 16 April 2020, available at www.thestar.com.my/news/nation/2020/04/16/dr-noor-hisham-a-top-professional-in-covid-19-fight.

Members of the public service hold office at the pleasure of the *Yang di-Pertuan Agong*, which means that they do not have a title to their posts, as judges and members of service commissions do, and can therefore be dismissed without cause, or without any charge having to be established against them. However, this does not mean that public servants may be summarily dismissed or demoted: there are some procedural restrictions, including the right to be heard.[47]

Given the relative security of tenure enjoyed by most public servants, the main problem has been that of ensuring quality of service delivery and linkage of the public service to overall development goals. Ever since the Montgomery and Esman Report in 1966,[48] the Government has sought various ways of doing this, notably via the privatisation and 'new public management' programme.[49] Since 2010 a Government Transformation Programme has attempted to improve public access to Government services, increase the accountability of the public service, and by adopting 'National Key Result Areas' link these efforts very explicitly to specific development goals such as improving standards of living, urban transport and rural infrastructure, and reducing corruption.

### III. PRIVATISATION AND THE PUBLIC–PRIVATE INTERFACE

'Seperti gergaji dua mata, tarek makan, soring makan'

(Like a double-edged saw, it bites when you pull it, and it bites when you push it)

It has long been recognised that development is not simply a result of government policies, but that it requires cooperation between government and private interests, both domestic and international. The distinction between public and private power, even though not explicit in the text of the Constitution, is therefore of great importance in understanding the

---

[47] Art 135.

[48] JD Montgomery and MJ Esman, *Development Administration in Malaysia* (Kuala Lumpur, Government Printer, 1966); MJ Esman, *Administration and Development in Malaysia: Institution Building and Reforms in a Plural Society* (Ithaca, Cornell University Press, 1972).

[49] Ahmad Sarji bin Abdul Hamid, *The Civil Service of Malaysia: Towards Vision 2020* (Kuala Lumpur, Government of Malaysia, 1994); Norma Mansor and Raja Noriza Raja Ariffin, 'Public administration in Malaysia: Origins, influence and assessment' in M Weiss (ed), *The Routledge Handbook of Contemporary Malaysia* (Abingdon, Routledge, 2014).

modern state and its constitutional parameters. In Malaysia the relationship between the public and private sectors has always been a porous one, and in some situations, such as with the 1MDB scandal, appears to have dissolved completely. In the circumstances prevailing in 2021, amid the consequences of that scandal, the public–private distinction has assumed particular constitutional significance in terms of accountability of the executive branch. In this section we examine the public–private interface in the context of privatised entities and GLCs; and in the process, our emphasis being on contextual constitutional analysis, we look at accountability, both legal and political, for the exercise of powers in relation thereto by members of the executive branch.

## A. Privatisation and Development

Privatisation is a loose concept implying a bundle of laws and other instruments ranging from stock market flotation of Government assets and Government contracting, to legislation and administrative regulation. In the Malaysian context it has involved transfers of assets to the private sector; charging citizens market prices for consumption of particular services; contracting out performance of public functions; and undertaking large public–private projects. While privatisation has been an almost universal phenomenon, especially since the 1980s, there were particular incentives for the Malaysian state to move in this direction.[50] The divesting of state assets to *bumiputera* citizens would accelerate the meeting of NEP targets of wealth distribution. The implementation of new public management in public administration, exposing the state to elements of competition and market-driven management would improve the rather obviously poor efficiency in service delivery in state enterprises. The large public debt – a major priority for foreign lenders – would be reduced. Foreign and domestic investment would be attracted to the large projects that would result from public–private partnerships. It was seen as essential, however, that privatisation should not compromise major development objectives. It would have to be regulated in such a way that assets would not simply fall into foreign hands, and would have always to serve the uniquely Malaysian priorities set out in the NEP.[51]

---

[50] KS Jomo, *Privatising Malaysia* (Boulder, Westview Press, 1995).
[51] G Felker, 'Malaysia's development strategies: Governing distribution-through-growth' in Weiss (n 49).

Malaysia was in fact one of the first developing countries to implement a policy of privatisation, which commenced under Prime Minister Tun Mahathir's Japan-fixated 'Look East Policy' in 1983. It was later encapsulated in the Privatisation Master Plan 1991.[52] The intention was partly, as elsewhere, to dismantle or slim down the muscle-bound power of the state, surrendering government functions to private enterprise, releasing energy and creating incentives. In the Malaysian context it was, however, pre-eminently a means of garnering resources for infrastructural or technological projects in the interests of national development. The 'public and private sectors … [are] a team that work together to develop the country', as Mahathir himself expressed it.[53] Japan's development was offered as an explicit model under the Look East Policy; but a team of British accountants and lawyers advised on the implementation of privatisation, as the UK had just gone through an extensive privatisation process,[54] and a number of legal instruments were required to give effect to privatisation, where the British common-law system and Westminster constitution offered common elements with Malaysia. The adoption of an Asian development model was, however, a clear statement that 'Malaysia Incorporated', as it came to be called, would become in some respects a typical Asian developmental state. This implies governance under which democratic principles may in practice be limited in scope and development policies predominate; broad administrative discretion, favouring of a narrow range of preferred business interests and setting priorities; limits on judicial review and civil liberties; and the use of emergency or police powers if necessary to inculcate social and industrial discipline and minimise dissent.[55] The Asian developmental state envisages the state having a critical role in laying down industrial policy, directing sectoral development, and creating the necessary infrastructure for growth. There was also more than a suggestion in Malaysia that

---

[52] *Privatisation Master Plan* (Prime Minister's Department, Kuala Lumpur, Government Printers, 1991); see also *Malaysia's Privatisation Policy: The Rationale, Policy and Process* (Prime Minister's Department, Kuala Lumpur, Government Printers, 1992).

[53] Quoted in Likosky (n 39) 147.

[54] KS Jomo, 'Privatisation in Malaysia: For what and for whom?' in T Clark and C Pitelis (eds), *The Political Economy of Privatisation* (London, Routledge, 1993) 438.

[55] For examples of all of these features, see Likosky's discussion of the initial problems over the MSC in light of the spat between Mahathir and US presidential candidate Al Gore, the Anwar Ibrahim affair, and the resignation of Alvin Toffler from the Advisory Board of the MSC: M Likosky, 'Cultural Imperialism in the Context of Transnational Commercial Collaboration' in M Likosky (ed), *Transnational Legal Processes: Globalisation and Power Disparities* (London, Butterworths/ LexisNexis, 2002).

it was 'Asian values' that would guide the process.[56] Although it might seem paradoxical that a developmental state ambitious to acquire and fully utilise public power would indulge in privatisation, the manner in which this was done in Malaysia did not imply that the state was letting go of any kite strings.

An early instance of privatisation Malaysia-style that had implications for public procurement was the controversial North-South Highway Project, the largest infrastructural project ever undertaken in the country, and also its largest BOT (build-operate-transfer) project. The contract for this project was awarded to a young entrepreneur who owned a company, United Engineers Malaysia (UEM), that had no track record of such projects; but he had good connections to the PMO, and UEM was owned by a company linked to UMNO, the ruling party. Moreover, the project for which the tender was submitted was one suggested by the entrepreneur himself, and two other companies submitted lower bids. An apparently open international tendering process was undertaken, but UEM got the contract largely because it was able to offer a convincing array of sub-contractors who were in turn impressed with the political connections of UEM.[57] The contract created a political storm, with the Opposition DAP Leader, Lim Kit Siang, pursuing extensive litigation, ultimately unsuccessful, seeking to have the contract cancelled.[58] It also led to alterations in tendering procedures.

Another striking example is telecommunications,[59] which were privatised in two stages in the 1980s and 1990s. First, in 1984, the functions of the Government's Telecommunications Department were transferred to Telekom Malaysia (TM), a government-owned company; but the Department retained regulatory power. TM was then partially privatised in 1990. However, the Government retained most of the shares, and although no formal monopoly over telecommunications has been created, the PMO has the power of licensing. As a result, TM, although a commercial success (hardly surprising given its de facto monopoly and its political connections and status), is in essence an arm of the developmental state rather than a private entity. It is a crucial part of the MSC, discussed below, and also operates a university producing knowledge workers.[60]

[56] A J Langlois, *The Politics of Justice and Human Rights: Southeast Asia and Universalist Theory* (Cambridge, Cambridge University Press, 2001) 13–16, 32–38.

[57] Likosky (n 39) 153–55.

[58] *Government of Malaysia v Lim Kit Siang* (1988) 2 *Malayan Law Journal* 12.

[59] Abu Bakar Munir (n 38).

[60] Likosky (n 39).

During the 1990s Mahathir personally developed an ambitious plan, the Multimedia Super Corridor (now called 'MSC Malaysia'), which is designed, by attracting foreign companies to invest in it, to create Asia's 'Silicon Valley' and was to propel Malaysia towards a knowledge economy as envisaged by the National Development Plan and 'Vision 2020', in order to create a fully developed economy by 2020. The Corridor, about 40km long, close to Kuala Lumpur and its International Airport, and boasting a fibre-optic backbone, benefits from special laws and facilities. A Bill of Guarantees ensures that investors have confidence in their investment and are not subject to *bumiputera* preference policies (discussed below). An impressive International Advisory Panel comprising the likes of Alvin Toffler and Kenichi Ohmae was established to oversee the development of the project. The instruments used were many. MDec was set up in the form of a GLC, whose Chairman and board members were to be appointed by the Government – indeed a third of the board must be members of the Government. MDeC is also funded by the Government, in its own terms 'combining the entrepreneurial efficiency and effectiveness of a private company with the decision-making authority of a high-powered government agency'. It is designed to act as a one-stop agency for investors that is also free of civil service red tape. As with TM, MDeC is a Government project, owned and operated in effect by the Government. It too is an arm of the developmental state.[61]

Despite the extensive privatisation programme the Federal Government has refused to let go of its assets, finding in privatisation a means of avoiding (largely speaking) parliamentary and judicial scrutiny while reducing the financial burdens on, but not compromising the objectives of, the developmental state. The privatisation programme came to an end with the currency crisis in 1997. The MSC continues and its liberalisation of the regulatory process for foreign investment has been extended to more economic sectors and also zones such as the Iskandar Development Region in Johor.[62] Indeed, free zones, export-orientated zones, corridors and growth areas have been a major theme of economic development involving the public and private sectors. One case, the Port

[61] Ibid ch 6; B Ramaswamy, A Chakrabarty and M Cheah, 'Malaysia's leap into the Future: An evaluation of the Multimedia Super Corridor' (2004) 24(11) *Technovation* 871–83.

[62] Tey Tsun Hang, 'Iskandar Malaysia and Malaysia's Dualistic Political Economy' in C Carter and A Harding (ed), *Special Economic Zones in Asian Market Economies* (London, Routledge, 2011).

Klang Free Zone, became mired in allegations of large-scale corruption engulfing leading Chinese BN politicians.[63] Since 2018 little has changed. Tun Mahathir in his second term as Prime Minister continued with the policies outlined here, which he himself iterated, reviving some of his pet projects. However, the 1MDB scandal had starved the treasury of funds and measures were taken to scale down the intensity of Malaysia's engagement with what could be called 'hyper development'.

It is difficult at the present time to assess the overall impact of the 1MDB affair on executive accountability and the structure of the state. Prosecutions are still ongoing and there is a large question mark over the future of mooted reforms, commenced by the PH government, designed to prevent kleptocracy from reoccurring. However, the constitutional status of GLCs has been clarified in a number of cases, discussed below. This is an area that will have to be thoroughly considered in any reform process, as the abuses of public power and public funds have been very extensive and extremely damaging to public trust in government.

## B.  Government-linked Companies, the State and the Public–Private Interface

With regard to GLCs generally, as a matter of law these operate in general terms under the aegis of company law rather than public law, so that the only difference between GLCs and ordinary public companies is the identity of the shareholder(s). Malaysia has been innovative, not just in privatisation of services and projects, as discussed above, but in creating many GLCs designed principally to further national developmental priorities via large-scale investment, without being shackled by public-service rules, policies, and procedures, and with the flexibility to act as creatures of private rather than public law. The Minister of Finance Incorporated has a majority shareholding in 68 companies (sovereign wealth fund Khazanah and development company 1MDB being prominent amongst them) as well as holding ordinary shares in many more. Nonetheless, there has sometimes appeared to be ambiguity around the precise orientation of GLCs, in the sense that it has been unclear whether their objects and performance have served the public interest. As a result, a GLC Transformation Programme was commenced in

---

[63] 'PKFZ: The scandal with no culprits', *Malay Mail*, 17 March 2017, available at www.malaymail.com/news/malaysia/2017/03/17/pkfz-the-scandal-with-no-culprits/1336987.

2004 under the Putrajaya Committee on GLC High Performance. Under the PH Government the performance of GLCs became a major political issue, largely as a result of the 1MDB episode, and a number of CEOs of GLCs were replaced. Thus the Minister of Finance is responsible for the performance of GLCs via both the principle of ministerial responsibility and his statutory ownership of all or a majority of shares in the GLC.[64]

The question then arises whether the Prime Minister and other relevant ministers at Federal and State level are subject to principles of public law relating to exercise of administrative powers when they act in relation to GLCs, or are only subject to company law. This is a critical issue in the context of Malaysian government practices, and has given rise to some important case law that in effect defines not just the extent of legal accountability of ministers but the dimensions of the state itself and its legal capacities.

Malaysian law recognises the distinction – now familiar in administrative law in common law countries – between public and private law, and this distinction is highly relevant to the extent of judicial review of GLCs.[65] In *Pengurusan Danaharta Nasional Bhd v Tang Kwor Ham and Ors*[66] the question arose whether a GLC, Danaharta, could be subject to judicial review of its actions. To be amenable to judicial review Danaharta had to be a 'public authority'.[67] The Court of Appeal by a majority held that Danaharta was a public authority. Gopal Sri Ram JCA for the majority held that Danaharta, although registered as a company under the Companies Act 1965, was wholly financed by public funds; and its affairs were directly or indirectly under the control of the Minister of Finance, representing the Federal Government. Moreover, the powers of Danaharta were, apart from its Memorandum of Association, conferred upon it by statute. He explained the legal position of GLCs on the basis of three types of company:

1.  Limited companies (public or private) incorporated under the Companies Act having a purely private character, some of which may have Federal or State Government as a substantial shareholder.

---

[64] Minister of Finance (Incorporation Act) 1957 (Act 375).
[65] *Wong Koon Seng v Rahman Hydraulic Tin Bhd and Ors* [2003] 1 MLJ 98; *Pengurusan Danaharta Nasional Bhd v Tang Kwor Ham and Ors* [2006] 5 MLJ 60.
[66] Ibid.
[67] Rules of the High Court, Order 53 rule 2, and the Courts of Judicature Act 1964, sch 1, para 1.

(Malaysian Airlines was offered as an example.) These are not subject to judicial review.

2.  Hybrid companies, which have multiple shareholders including Government, and are similar to other limited companies except that they perform public functions regulated by statute, and are given statutory powers. These are amenable to judicial review depending on whether the act or omission complained of is within the confines of its private character, or is ultra vires the powers conferred on it by statute. Only in the latter case is the matter subject to judicial review. (Telekom Malaysia was offered as an example.)

3.  Companies of which the Government is the sole shareholder, which are funded from public money and have either statutory powers or duties conferred on them. 'In form these entities are companies. But in truth and substance they are each an instrument of government'. These companies are subject to judicial review.[68]

Other GLC cases concern the criminal and tortious liability of ministers. The Federal Court clarified the criminal liability of ministers as public servants in *Mohd Khir bin Toyo v Public Prosecutor*.[69] The former *Menteri Besar* of Selangor had been found guilty of an offence of accepting a valuable thing with inadequate consideration under section 165 of the Penal Code, which relates to 'public servants'. The charge related to transactions relating to the Selangor State Development Corporation, of which he was *ex officio* Chairman. The Federal Court held that he was a public servant by virtue of his position as chairman of PKNS, and in the light of the definition of 'public servant' in section 21 of the Penal Code. It was held that his official work as chairman of PKNS was an integral part of his work as *Menteri Besar*.

Tortious liability was discussed in two cases, brought separately by a DAP MP and Tun Mahathir against Prime Minister Najib Razak, that arose directly out of the 1MDB affair. In *Tony Pua Kiam Wee v Government of Malaysia*,[70] the plaintiff sued the Federal Government and Najib Razak for the tort of misfeasance in public office, inter alia, by abusing his public office as Prime Minister, Minister of Finance and

---

[68] See also *Tenaga Nasional Bhd v Tekali Prospecting Sdn Bhd* [2002] 2 MLJ 707, Court of Appeal.

[69] *Mohd Khir bin Toyo v Public Prosecutor* [2015] 5 MLJ 529, Federal Court.

[70] *Tony Pua Kiam Wee v Government of Malaysia & Anor* [2019] 12 MLJ 1; see also *Tun Dr Mahathir Mohamad and Ors v Datuk Seri Mohd Najib bin Tun Abdul Razak* [2018] 3 MLJ 466.

Chairman of 1MDB's Board of Advisors, to unlawfully enrich himself, his family members and close associates with funds belonging to 1MDB; by influencing the way 1MDB was managed such that it led to the dissipation / misappropriation of its funds and assets; and giving evasive or wrong answers in Parliament when queried about the true facts concerning 1MDB, its transactions and its financial status. The relevant issue of law on appeal was whether these acts were committed as a 'public officer' in terms of the tort of misfeasance. The Federal Court, overruling the Court of Appeal, held that the Prime Minister, as a member of the administration, was a 'public officer' for these purposes. Two Court of Appeal decisions were overruled in this case, and it was held:

> The doctrines of the rule of law and the separation of powers underpin and comprise the 'internal architecture' of our Constitution … So, to conclude that the definition of public officer in Malaysia excludes members of the administration such as a Prime Minister, so that members of the administration like the defendant/respondent in the instant appeals, may allegedly act with impunity, so as to knowingly and/or recklessly dissipate public funds and remain immune to civil action under this tort, is anathema to the doctrine of the rule of law and the fundamental basis of the Federal Constitution.[71]

Most notable of all, however, is the criminal case against former Prime Minister Najib Razak, arising out of misappropriation of funds amounting to RM42 million intended for another GLC, SRC International Sdn Bhd. The defendant was charged with seven counts of criminal breach of trust, money-laundering, and abuse of position for gratification, under the Penal code, the Anti-Money-Laundering Act, and the Malaysian Anti-Corruption Commission Act, respectively. He was convicted in the High Court in July 2020 on all seven charges, and received concurrent sentences amounting to 12 years' imprisonment of corruption and money-laundering, for which he received a sentence of 12 years, plus a fine of RM210 million. Mohamed Nazlan J in pronouncing sentence stated as follows:

> What the Court seeks to affirm is the sanctity of the rule of law and the supremacy of the Constitution. No one, not even one who was the most powerful political figure and the leader of this country, enjoys a cloak of invincibility from the force of law … The ascension of the accused to the pinnacle of leadership of the nation and his grip of political power reposed on him by the citizens of this country the position of trust in our system

---

[71] *Tony Pua Kiam Wee* (n 70) 41 (per Nallini Pathmanathan FCJ).

of constitutional democracy. His conviction of all seven charges concerning abuse of position, criminal breach of trust and money laundering constitutes nothing less than an absolute betrayal of that trust.[72]

Taken together, these striking developments in case law not only help to define the state as against the private sector, and the powers of the Prime Minister and other ministers especially in relation to GLCs, but also enhance considerably their legal liability in public, private and criminal law in that and other matters. The rule of law has indeed been upheld in this case, which is on appeal to the Court of Appeal, with a stay of execution, at the time of writing. It should be noted, however, that the former Prime Minister and other former ministers face many more charges and so it will take some years for these cases, including appeals, to be determined.

We have seen in this section how the Malaysian state, within the confines of Westminster-model government, has been configured in ways that serve the requirements of a developmental state. Power has been highly centralised in the office of Prime Minister. Accountability for the various branches of the all-enveloping executive power has been gradually increased over time.

## IV. CONCLUSION

'Hujan mas perak negeri orang: hujan keris lembing negeri kita'

(Though it rains gold and silver there, it is still a foreign land: though it rains swords and daggers here, it is still our land)

In this chapter we have seen how the state, structured along the lines of the Westminster constitution as a constitutional monarchy, emerged from the independence process. Its basic organisational principles had been determined, but not its subsequent power or direction. We have seen how the executive leadership, in the office of the Prime Minister and the Cabinet, has been determinative of policy and direction through only eight top executives since 1957, and how a variety of instruments has been employed, including privatisation, to address the ethnic problems and lofty ambitions of a developmental state.

---

[72] *Pendakwa Raya v Dato' Seri Mohd Najib bin Hj Abd Razak* [2020] MLJU 1254 at 3011.

However, a deep-seated fault line threatening the new, democratic, state was its failure to address basic socio-economic justice despite the social contract of the mid-1950s. The 'May 13 incident' (discussed in Chapter 3) was an axial moment that blew apart the Tunku's consensus around the existing social contract and demanded a restructuring of the state, the adoption of more specific objectives and targets than previously, and coercive methods to limit freedom of speech. The social contract is explained in the next chapter.

Central to all of these changes is Malaysia's often problematical attempt to secure its own vision of development as a stabilising factor for its fraught and fractious pluralism. A new Malaysian state appears slowly to be emerging – with considerable difficulty – from the womb of the old. Whether its shape would be recognisable to those two Cambridge lawyers and Westminster-model advocates, Sir Ivor Jennings and the Tunku, is for the time being a matter of speculation.

FURTHER READING

AJ Harding and Dian AH Shah (eds), *Law and Society in Malaysia: Pluralism, Religion, and Ethnicity* (Abingdon, Routledge, 2017).

HP Lee, *Constitutional Conflicts in Contemporary Malaysia* (2nd edn, Oxford, Oxford University Press, 2017).

HRH Sultan Nazrin Shah, *Striving for Inclusive Development: From Pangkor to a Modern Malaysian State* (Oxford, Oxford University Press, 2019).

J Neo, Dian AH Shah and A Harding (eds), 'Malaysia Boleh! Constitutional Implications of the Malaysian Tsunami', ICONNECT Online Symposium, June 2018, available at http://www.iconnectblog.com/2018/06/introduction-to-i-connect-symposium-malaysia-boleh-constitutional-implications-of-the-malaysian-tsunami.

# 3

# *The Social Contract*

Origins and Rationale of the Social Contract – May 13 Incident – *Rukunegara* Amendments – Affirmative Action – Implementation – Critiques

## I. EXPLANATION OF THE CONCEPT AND ITS ORIGINS

'Aur bergantung ke tebing, tebing bergantung ke aur'
(The river bank depends on the bamboo, the bamboo depends on the river bank)

THIS CHAPTER OFFERS an analysis of the defining concept of the Malaysian state, in which the twin goals of managing ethnic relations and national development have been brought together in the social contract. The social contract was formed in the manner described in Chapter 1 and then redefined in 1971, following the events of 13 May 1969 (the 'May 13 incident'), a process that is addressed in the next section. The chapter explains how the social contract has been implemented in practice and the critiques it has attracted. As we shall see, it has constitutional dimensions of fundamental significance.

Since 1970 the implementation of Malaysia's social contract via the New Economic Policy (NEP) and its successors has been a major function of state-orchestrated development, involving the creation of prosperity, the reduction of poverty, and the provision of opportunity to the *bumiputera* majority.[1] However, the social contract is also vague. We saw in Chapter 1 the history of, and the general rationale for, its creation. But what exactly are its terms? Who are its parties? How is it implemented? Most importantly now, can it be changed and, if so, how? Confusion surrounds these issues, and the lack of any real freedom to address them has proved not so much a necessity in a plural society as a

[1] E Gomez and KS Jomo (eds), *The State of Malaysia: Ethnicity, Equity and Reform* (London, RoutledgeCurzon, 2004).

dysfunctional form of political process. The social contract is an abstraction, not contained in any particular document, and has to be construed mainly from the provisions of the Constitution itself, the circumstances surrounding their adoption, and the changing discourse on interethnic relations.[2]

The original 'terms' of the social contract, crystallised in the *Merdeka* Constitution in 1957, were reasonably clear. The contract was concluded between leaders representing the three communities in their capacity as leaders of the three main parties in the Alliance (UMNO, MCA and MIC). They could fairly claim to negotiate on behalf of their respective ethnic communities because they had demonstrated that, collectively, they had the overwhelming support of the electorate. This was an electorate to which the idea of being represented communally but in a manner which embraced accommodation and compromise proved perennially appealing.[3] The essence of the agreement was that the special privileges of the Malays would remain, while citizenship would be extended liberally to non-Malays.[4]

Such a social contract, even guaranteed by the adoption of a moderate, consociational form of politics under the Tunku, might seem unsatisfactory in terms of what it clearly allowed; in terms also of what it (less than clearly) did not allow; and in relation to those whose needs it failed to address, such as the *orang asli* and non-*bumiputera* poor and other disadvantaged minorities. Nonetheless, apart from the fact that it was very fulsomely supported by the electorate, the social contract has to be understood as a response to the deep fears of all communities that existed in the early decades of Malaysia's existence, and which still persist in many ways today. In 1957 the Malays owned about 1 per cent of an economy that was 66 per cent in foreign ownership, and their poverty rate was 70 per cent; by 1970 those figures had changed to just 2.5 per cent of the economy and a 64 per cent poverty rate, figures that compared very unfavourably with those for other ethnic groups.[5]

---

[2] Norani Othman, MC Puthucheary and C Kessler (eds), *Sharing the Nation: Faith, Difference, Power and the State 50 Years After Merdeka* (Petaling Jaya, SIRDC, 2008).

[3] Wilson TV Tay, 'Dimensions of *Ketuanan Melayu* in the Malaysian constitutional framework' in A Harding and Dian AH Shah (eds), *Law and Society in Malaysia: Pluralism, Religion, and Ethnicity* (Abingdon, Routledge, 2017).

[4] K von Vorys, *Democracy without Consensus: Communalism and Political Stability in Malaysia* (Princeton, New Jersey, Princeton University Press, 1975).

[5] KS Jomo and Chang Yii Tan, 'The Political Economy of Post-Colonial Transformation' in KS Jomo and Wong Sau Ngan (eds), *Law, Institutions and Malaysian Economic Development* (Singapore, NUS Press, 2008) 27; Lee Hwok-Aun, 'Affirmative action: Hefty measures, mixed outcomes, muddled thinking' in M Weiss (ed), The Routledge Handbook of Contemporary Malaysia (Abingdon, Routledge, 2014) 174.

Thus in 1957, and even, one might argue, in 1969, at the time of the May 13 incident, the Malays were in danger of losing not just political status but even their aspirations for development. The non-Malays stood to lose their tenuous status as migrants and their own hard-won economic position and opportunities. Worse, they could lose their cultural and language rights, as had happened with the Indonesian Chinese. The memory of post-war ethnic reprisals was also still fresh. The social contract was not seen as a dangerously discriminatory new order but rather as the best compromise that could be expected in fraught circumstances. Whatever the objections, it was thought better for those disadvantaged to live within its constraints than risk losing all. To some advocates of Malay rights this all means that the state embodies a fundamental and continuing notion of '*ketuanan Melayu*' (Malay dominance).[6] As we will see, however, the social contract is a compromise which *balances* the rights and interests of different communities, and the Constitution, while preserving some traditional elements and special privileges, does not embody Malay dominance as such but rather a pluralist democracy.[7]

The concessions embodied in the social contract were significant. For Malays the impossibility of ever being in a minority in their own country was traded for acknowledgment that their position was special; from the perspective of many Malays the Chinese were suspected of allegiance to communist China rather than Malaya. Non-Malays lost the opportunity for equal citizenship, but for many this was traded for the chance to enjoy citizenship at all, which had not been available to them before. In other words, even as liberal, pluralist democracy and constitutionalism were being adopted, this group accepted the status of second-class citizens. Beyond that, it was clear from the retention of the States and their Malay monarchies in a federal structure, the designation of *Bahasa Melayu* (the Malay language) as the national language, and the establishment of Islam as the official religion, that the state was in essence a pluralist artefact underpinned by a substratum of Malay culture.[8]

The social contract was reflected principally in Article 153 of the Constitution, which permitted the Government to act in a manner contrary to the principle of equal protection of the law, which is

---

[6] Wilson Tay (n 3).

[7] J Fernando, *The Making of the Malayan Constitution* (Kuala Lumpur, MBRAS, 2003) ch 6.

[8] Von Vorys (n 4). See also Tun Mohamed Salleh Abas, 'Traditional Elements in the Malaysia Constitution' in of FA Trindade and HP Lee (eds), *The Constitution of Malaysia: Further Developments and Perspectives* (Singapore, Oxford University Press, 1986).

guaranteed by Article 8, in protecting the 'special position' of the Malays and the 'legitimate interests' of other communities, thereby authorising a quota system in various areas of activity. Article 153 was derived from the Federation of Malaya Agreement 1948, which simply required the High Commissioner 'to safeguard the special position of the Malays and the legitimate interests of the other communities'.[9] The practice of reservation to Malays of positions in the public service, and certain scholarships and licences, as well as reservation of land, had commenced during the immediate post-war period under colonial government. Article 153 clarified and extended these practices and gave them constitutional legitimacy.

## II. THE MAY 13 INCIDENT
## AND THE *'RUKUNEGARA'* AMENDMENTS

'Gajah sama gajah bergaduh, pelanduk mati di tengah-tengah'

(When elephants fight, the mouse deer that gets between them is killed)

The May 13 incident[10] in 1969 remains the most traumatic episode in Malaysia's history; one which threatened to eclipse the Constitution and democratic, parliamentary government. In the event, it radically affected their nature and trajectory. The state was dramatically redefined, with changes to the social contract, the emergence of new redistributive policies, the instigation of emergency rule, and limits to free expression.

The general elections of May 1969 were especially racially charged. On 10 May results for Peninsular Malaysia were announced, and it became apparent that the opposition parties had achieved an excellent result, depriving the Alliance Government of its two-thirds majority;[11] winning the States of Penang, Perak and Kelantan, and reducing considerably the Alliance share of the vote, especially among the non-Malays. The opposition parties staged provocative victory processions on 12 May, and on 13 May a large pro-Government procession of Malays

---

[9] *Federation of Malaya Agreement 1948* (Kuala Lumpur, Government Printer, 1948) cl 19(i)(d).

[10] C Das, 'The May 13th Riots and Emergency Rule' in A Harding and HP Lee (ed), *Constitutional Landmarks in Malaysia: The First Fifty Years, 1957–2007* (Kuala Lumpur, Malayan Law Journal/LexisNexis, 2007); Goh Cheng Teik, *The May 13th Incident and Democracy in Malaysia* (Kuala Lumpur, University of Malaya Press, 1971); L Comber, *13 May 1969: A Historical Survey of Sino-Malay Relations* (Kuala Lumpur, Heinemann, 1983).

[11] This is the special majority required to amend the Constitution: see Art 158.

made its way to the Selangor *Menteri Besar*'s house. Tensions were at tinder-box level, and an incident involving Malay and Chinese youths immediately sparked serious and unprecedented rioting in many parts of Kuala Lumpur. In the next few hours many people died or suffered serious injuries in an orgy of violence, and there was also much looting and damage to property. The precise course of events and its causes remain a matter of dispute.[12] What really matters in terms of understanding Malaysia's history over the last five decades is what was said or believed to have happened and how that was used to restructure the state and justify authoritarian rule. Undoubtedly, unscrupulous politicians used racial issues for their own advancement, and it was true that the social contract had essentially failed to deliver much in the way of redistribution at that point.

The situation which was created by the May 13 incident was such that extraordinary measures had to be taken. Ever present, of course, was the threat that the disturbances would spiral even further out of control. Therefore on 15 May an emergency was proclaimed under Article 150 of the Constitution extending to the entire Federation, on grounds of a threat to national security. Since the emergency was proclaimed at a time when Parliament had already been dissolved, and the elections had not been completed in Sabah and Sarawak, there was no Parliament to meet. In fact, although obliged under Article 150 to summon Parliament as soon as was practicable, the Government simply suspended the elections, which were not in fact completed until February 1971; only then, some 22 months after the Proclamation, was Parliament summoned. For all of this period Malaysia was under emergency rule. This period of executive dictatorship had lasting effects on the Constitution and the legal system.

Of interest here is the unorthodox ad hoc structure of government which was developed by the Government to deal with the emergency. It immediately enacted the Emergency (Essential Powers) Ordinance No 1/1969, which gave the Government extremely wide powers, to 'make any regulations whatsoever ... which [the *Yang di-Pertuan Agong*] considers desirable or expedient for securing the public safety, the defence of Malaysia, the maintenance of public order and of supplies and services essential to the life of the community'. The entire executive and legislative power of the Federation was vested in a Director of Operations (Tun Abdul Razak, Deputy Prime Minister and later Prime Minister, 1971–74).

---

[12] Kua Kia Soong, *May 13: Declassified Documents on the Malaysian Riots of 1969* (Petaling Jaya, Suaram, 2007).

For our present purposes what is significant is the immediate politi-cal aftermath in which a raft of amendments to the Constitution, passed in 1971, and going far beyond any amendments before or since, fundamentally altered the nature of state and government.[13] The important objective was clearly to return the country to normal parlia-mentary government and democracy, albeit in a different form from that prevailing before the elections. To this end a National Consultative Council (NCC) was set up to consider ways of restoring racial harmony. It became clear, however, that Parliament would not be summoned unless the Government was sure that the constitutional amendments that it had proposed would be passed, whether with or without oppo-sition support. The creation of the Barisan Nasional (BN) to replace the Alliance, with wider political support, gave the Government the likelihood of the two-thirds majority it sought, so the elections were completed, Parliament summoned, and the amendments passed. The administrative structure of emergency rule was dismantled, but the Proclamation and emergency powers still remained. Ordinance No 1 remained in force, which meant that the Government still exercised the legislative power granted to it by that Ordinance, and Tun Razak was by that time the Prime Minister, allowing for a smooth (and the first) constitutional transition of power.

The return to normality was not a return to the pre-1969 Constitution, but to a radically altered version of constitutionalism. The constitutional amendments, termed in this book the '*Rukunegara* amendments', after the national ideology[14] which they were supposed to implement in the Constitution, were far-reaching, and took Malaysia a significant step away from several tenets of the *Merdeka* Constitution.[15] Principally, the amendments redefined the social contract so as to give more special privileges to the Malays, extend their scope to natives of Sabah and Sarawak, and entrench those privileges even further than was already the case. They also expressed the social contract as a list of 'sensitive issues' that could not be discussed, except as to policy implementation, in any forum, including even the floors of the Federal and State legislatures.

As for the causes, the official position was that the special privileges had failed to deliver real social change, and the NEP was the remedy. One immediate effect of all this was to change the leadership in 1970 from the Tunku, moderate, tolerant and regarded by some factions as rather too

---

[13] Das (n 10).
[14] See below.
[15] A Harding, 'The *Rukunegara* Amendments of 1971' in Harding and Lee (n 10).

conciliatory, to Tun Razak, who was seen as more of a technocrat, less charismatic, but a firmer supporter of Malay rights.

At a stroke the *Rukunegara* amendments had redefined ethnic relations and the political economy of Malaysia, the roles of executive and legislative powers, and the limits of freedom of expression. They had in effect converted a liberal democracy observing basic rights into an authoritarian semi-democratic police state with large exceptions to basic rights.

The *Rukunegara* amendments also added a new aspect to the social contract. The *Rukunegara* itself,[16] promulgated on national day 1970 by the *Yang di-Pertuan Agong*, was negotiated between political leaders representing different communities as a concerted attempt at nation-building by forming an agreed national ideology transcending Malaysia's diverse and deeply polarised society. It took Indonesia's *Pancasila* as a model, establishing parameters of debate and bases for national reconciliation; in particular, for present purposes, it involves respect for the Constitution and the rule of law. The ideology established is progressive, inclusive and liberal-democratic. By the 1971 amendments, policy on the sensitive issues (Article 153 privileges and legitimate interests, citizenship, the national language, and the monarchy) was placed beyond public debate, and even parliamentary privilege, it was provided, would not protect freedom of expression with regard to these issues. It was permissible, however, to debate the implementation of such policy. This was all enforced by means of the law of sedition, under which relatively small fines were usual, prison sentences much less so.[17]

There is a dark side to the social contract. Its remodelling took place under the cloud of emergency rule, with parliamentary democracy suspended, elections uncompleted, and citizens preventively detained without trial under the Internal Security Act. Agreements reached behind the closed doors of inter-party meetings were placed beyond public debate. The foundations were laid for an authoritarian style of government which contradicted many of the basic tenets or assumptions of the *Merdeka* Constitution. The amendments provided the basis for the construction of a state that denied basic civil liberties and entrenched

---

[16] Harding (ibid) 115. The text of the *Rukunegara* is appended to that chapter at 130–32. The word is made up of '*rukun*' (principles) and '*negara*' (nation). It can be argued that it is a milk-and-water document that few could object to. However, its principles are often breached and are worth regular reiteration: see C Lopez, 'Inter-faith relations in Malaysia: Moving beyond Muslims versus "others"' in Weiss (n 5) 333.

[17] For judicial responses to sedition prosecutions and the limits to free speech, see Harding (n 15).

the Alliance (expanded and renamed the BN) in power for more than six decades.

The settlement of 1971 also demanded a few changes to the terms of the social contract which were in effect a complete revision of the contract. The main changes were the expansion of its scope to include in the *bumiputera* category natives of Sabah and Sarawak; the adding of admission to tertiary education as an area for the operation of quotas; and the entrenchment of the social contract – placing it, as a list of 'sensitive issues', beyond political debate, except as to its implementation.[18] These changes in effect subordinated all elements of the state to development and restricting criticism of policy, but also adapted the developmental state to the particular problems of Malaysia's multi-cultural society.

### III. THE SOCIAL CONTRACT: IMPLEMENTATION AND CRITIQUES

'Bahawa kita memiliki telaga, Mengapa masih memegang talinya, Sedang orang mencapai timba?' (Usman Awang)

(We possess the wells; So why are we holding the ropes, While others are grabbing at the pails?)

It is important to understand that Article 153 is not a licence to ignore the Constitution or the rights of citizens, or to indulge generally in official or institutionalised discrimination. It obliges the *Yang di-Pertuan Agong*, acting on advice (in other words the Government), to exercise his functions under the Constitution and Federal law in such manner as may be necessary to safeguard the special position of *bumiputera* and, by giving binding directions to the relevant authorities, to ensure the reservation for *bumiputera* of a reasonable proportion of positions in the Federal public service; scholarships and other similar educational or training privileges; and permits or licences for the operation of any trade or business, where required by Federal law. Specific authority to impose quotas for admission to institutions of higher education was added in the form of Article 153(8A) in 1971.

Thus Article 153 represents a significant but balanced exception to equality before the law, allowing quotas in specified areas of public decision-making affecting individual opportunities. However, there are some express limitations. It does not allow unequal treatment of federal employees of different races once they are employed (as opposed to

---

[18] Art 10(4).

unequal access to public service positions); or deprivation of a public office or scholarship already held by any person. Similarly, it does not allow deprivation of a licence already held, or refusal to renew or allow transfer of a licence when such renewal or transfer might reasonably be expected in the ordinary course of events (here the Constitution gives effect to the familiar administrative law notion of a legitimate expectation). Also, Parliament may not restrict business or trade solely for the purpose of reservation of quotas.

With the application of Article 153 to 'natives of Sabah and Sarawak', these communities too were made parties to the social contract. The communities protected by Article 153 are routinely referred to in Malaysia, and also in this book (although not in Article 153 itself) as '*bumiputera*'.[19] Although the meaning of this term fluctuates somewhat in common usage, from an official perspective it includes: Malays, who are in turn defined by the Constitution as Muslims habitually using the Malay language and Malay customs and domiciled in Malaysia, and anyone with one Malay parent; natives of Sarawak, belonging to a scheduled list of indigenous groups, or having a parent belonging thereto; and similarly natives of Sabah. The indigenous '*orang asli*' (or 'aborigines' as they are called by the Constitution) comprise a number of indigenous groups who are confined mainly to the mountainous jungle areas of central Malaya (see Chapter 7). The Constitution provides for the validity of 'any provision for the protection, wellbeing or advancement of the aboriginal peoples of the Malay Peninsula (including the reservation of land) or the reservation to aborigines of a reasonable proportion of suitable positions in the public service'. However, they are not designated as *bumiputera*, even though, as we have seen, the indigenous 'natives' of Sabah and Sarawak, such as the Iban and Kadazan, are so designated. Essentially, it is for the department in question to decide if a given person is a *bumiputera* or not. Given the nature of Malaysia's diverse society, this issue is clearly an official headache embodying little in the way of social or economic logic. But the essential point is that by broadening the group of 'Indigenous people' this group was able to construct a clear majority within Malaysia. The creation of Malaysia in 1963 followed by the departure of Singapore (with its 75 per cent Chinese population) in 1965 made this majority possible, and it was partly the prospect of such a majority that had driven the plan to form Malaysia in the first place.

---

[19] Meaning, literally, 'princes of the soil', or in English usage 'sons of the soil', but the term as used is gender neutral.

Oddly enough, the courts have never had to pronounce on the scope and meaning of Article 153 or the concepts of 'special position' or 'legitimate interests'. The lack of any litigation on these issues is probably attributable to their designation as sensitive issues; a fact of which lawyers would be acutely aware in providing advice. The likelihood is that litigating rights under Article 153 would also risk inflaming public feelings, inviting the possibility of prosecution under the Sedition Act. Nonetheless, although some litigation (see the *Merdeka University* case below, and cases on religion discussed in Chapter 9) has indeed concerned socially sensitive issues, Article 153 itself has somehow not featured in such cases. It is of course also a good argument that the use of litigation to test the proper extent of constitutional power could function as a much safer means than other, more overtly political, means of raising issues with ethnic or religious implications. Sensitive cases involving religion, as we will see in Chapter 9, have in fact been dealt with in the courts in the face of great tensions among the public. Attempts have been made by Malay/Muslim groups in a suit against Chinese and Tamil schools organisations to have vernacular schools ruled unconstitutional, invoking Article 152 of the Constitution which governs use of the national language.[20]

One other instance of litigation, relating to the national language, comes the closest that any litigation has come to a conflict over the social contract. The controversial case of *Merdeka University Bhd v Government of Malaysia*[21] examined the right of a private university to use a language other than the national language as the main medium of instruction. The promoting company, supported by a large number of Chinese interests, applied to the Government under the Universities and University Colleges Act 1971 for permission to set up a private university, in which Chinese would be the main medium of instruction. Permission was refused on the grounds that the proposed university would conflict with the national education policy. The refusal was challenged in judicial review proceedings, partly on the grounds of contravention of Article 152

---

[20] *Mohamed Khairul Azam bin Abdul Aziz v Menteri Pendidikan Malaysia & Anor* [2020] 1 MLJ 398, Fed Ct; Lim Wei Jiet, 'The case for the constitutionality of vernacular schools', *Malaysiakini*, 23 December 2019, available at www.malaysiakini.com/news/504604.

[21] *Merdeka University Bhd v Government of Malaysia* [1982] 2 MLJ 243; see also V Sinnadurai, 'Rights in respect of education under the Malaysian Constitution' in Trindade and Lee (n 8); and for discussion of judicial review in relation to privatisation, Gan Ching Chuan, 'Administrative law and judicialised governance in Malaysia: The Indian connection' in T Ginsburg and Albert HY Chan (eds), *Administrative Law and Governance in Asia* (London, Routledge, 2009).

of the Constitution, under which the use of languages other than the national language is permitted, but not for 'official purposes', which are defined as 'any purpose of the Government, whether Federal or State, including any purpose of a public authority'. The definition of 'public authority' includes 'a statutory authority exercising powers vested in it by federal or state law'. A majority of the Federal Court held that the proposed university would be a statutory authority within this definition, so that it could not use Chinese as the main medium of instruction; the Government's decision was therefore held constitutionally valid. The reasoning was that even a private university established under statutory provisions was subject to some degree of public control in its affairs and involved a number of public appointments to office in its framework; acted in the public interest; and was eligible for grants-in-aid from public funds.

This decision seems incorrect in that it confuses a public authority exercising statutory powers with a private body exercising private rights but subject to statutory regulation, even though statutory bodies are also providing the same service. The case is an example, coming at a time when the national language was being promoted in all forms of education as a basis for national unification, of how the policy demands of the developmental state have been all-pervasive in Malaysia. It was highly controversial and appeared to cut against the notion of a pluralist and inclusive state.

Since then, however, changes have been made to education policy that now allow private tertiary institutions to use English, as the medium of globalisation, information technology and science; and Arabic, as the medium of Islam. National primary and secondary schools, on the other hand, have always been able to use Chinese and Tamil, and even to admit pupils other than those who have these languages as their mother tongue.[22]

As we saw in Chapter 1, there was no agreement amongst the Alliance parties in 1956–57 on the question of the duration of the special privileges under the provision which became Article 153. The Reid Commission said that after 15 years Parliament would have to reconsider the special privileges, but the outcome was that no duration was fixed. Given that the 15 years would have expired in 1972, it is probably fortunate that this benchmark was not adopted, as history in fact decreed the exact opposite – the special privileges were at that time

---

[22] Peter KW Tan, 'The medium-of-instruction debate in Malaysia: English as a Malaysian language?' (2005) 29(1) *Language Problems and Language Planning* 47–66.

not abolished but actually increased in scope and deeply entrenched in the Constitution. This issue was dealt with in the 1971 settlement not by settling a particular duration (although the NEP itself set targets, especially 30 per cent *bumiputera* economic ownership, to be achieved by 1990), but by protecting all the changes made by the *Rukunegara* amendments with not just the usual two-thirds majority required for constitutional amendments, but also a requirement for the consent of the Conference of Rulers.[23]

Another area of lack of clarity in the social contract is the concept of 'legitimate interests of other communities', which are also protected by Article 153. No definition has been given of this term in any judicial or statutory interpretation. However, we can probably understand it in this light: assuming the city of Johor Bahru decided to allot 1000 new taxi licences, it would be constitutionally valid to decide to allot a quota of say 70 per cent to *bumiputera* taxi drivers; on the other hand it would be constitutionally invalid to take away the licences of 500 current non-*bumiputera* licence-holders and allot all or even a percentage of these to *bumiputera*.[24] At any rate, the notion of legitimate interests was understood in general terms as indicating that non-Malays would not be restricted in conducting business or having their property rights restricted; but no particular programme was implied, as opposed to some limited and obvious restrictions on the special privileges themselves. The NEP and the social contract embodied in the amended Article 153 have thus been implemented principally by the quota system which is designed to provide opportunities for *bumiputera* citizens. Other instruments, however, have been adopted to implement the overall policies of wealth creation and distribution. Statutory boards were set up, designed to provide special programmes or assistance for *bumiputera* – principally Malay peasants. A notable example is the Federal Land Development Authority (FELDA), which is the world's largest plantation operator and has settled rural poor on smallholdings with loans to grow mainly oil palm. FELDA started operations in 1956, but its size and remit were greatly expanded during the 1960s and 1970s. It has settled as many as one million rural poor on its estates as oil-palm producers. The Majlis Amanah Rakyat (MARA, the People's Council of Trust) has carried out economic and social development in rural areas since 1966, with the objective of encouraging *bumiputera* entrepreneurship. MARA also set

---

[23] Art 159(5).
[24] Art 153(4), (7), (8).

up the Institut Teknologi MARA (ITM, now UiTM following its establishment as a university in 1999) in 1966 to provide training courses for young *bumiputera*.[25]

Non-statutory rules and policies are designed to ensure that investors enter joint ventures with *bumiputera* partners to the extent of 30 per cent *bumiputera* ownership.[26] The Industrial Coordination Act 1975 required both foreign and domestic investors to comply with employment policies benefitting *bumiputera*. Only 30 per cent *bumiputera*-owned companies were allowed to be listed on the Kuala Lumpur Stock Exchange. Tax concessions and Government procurement have been used to effect employment and share allocation quotas in the private sector. Special *bumiputera* discounts of at least 7 per cent were imposed on developers for the purchase of new housing, given effect by conditions placed on planning permissions. In relation to the public service, there was already a formal 4:1 *bumiputera* quota for Division 1 officers. This was continued and applied to the unified Administrative and Diplomatic Service and the police, while a 3:1 quota applied to the Judicial and Legal Service and the Customs Department. However, the pattern of actual recruitment to Division 1 posts was varied so that almost all new recruits were *bumiputera*.[27]

It is in relation to education, especially tertiary education, however, that Article 153 has had most effect. One important facet of Malay unrest in 1969 was the fact that Malays lagged behind other races in respect of university places. The universities admitted students on merit alone, which resulted in an ethnic imbalance in admissions. A Government Committee recommended that universities should ensure as far as possible that the ethnic composition of the student population within the university and within each faculty should reflect the composition of Malaysian society. This was given effect with the Government giving binding directions to tertiary institutions under Article 153 to reserve admission quotas, resulting in a dramatic increase in scholarships and

---

[25] Mohd Nazim Ganti Shaari, 'Whither the *bumiputera* identity of Universiti Teknologi MARA (UiTM)' (2011) 29(2) *Kajian Malaysia* 67, critiquing the identity of UiTM.

[26] For conditions for doing business and the 30 per cent *bumiputera* ownership policy, see Wong Partners, 'Doing Business in Malaysia', available at www.bakermckenzie.com/-/media/files/insight/publications/2017/10/belt-road/doing_business_in_malaysia_2016.pdf?la=en.

[27] M Dass and K Abbott, 'Modelling new public management in an Asian Context: Public sector reform in Malaysia' (2008) 30(1) *Asia Pacific Journal of Public Administration* 59; AJ Harding, *Law, Government and the Constitution in Malaysia* (The Hague, Kluwer, and Kuala Lumpur, Malayan Law Journal, 1996) 231–39.

places for *bumiputera* students.[28] *Bumiputera* university admissions rose from 40 per cent in 1970 to 63 per cent (roughly, demographically, a par figure) in 1985.[29]

All these efforts have inevitably raised the issue of whether the targets have been met and what the implications of success or failure might be.[30] The Malaysian state has indeed achieved economic development. Since 1970, and especially after Mahathir became Prime Minister in 1981, economic growth rates have been high, albeit not consistently so, at least up until the Covid-19 pandemic struck in 2020. Recessions in 1985/6 and 2008/9, in addition to the Asian currency crisis of 1997/8, have held back economic development, but the overall trajectory represents notable achievement. Malaysia no longer appears on most lists of 'developing countries', and poverty has been very substantially reduced.

At the same time the consequences of the NEP have by no means received universal applause. It is criticised for creating a comfortable urban Malay middle class and large numbers of state-dependent citizens, while ignoring real poverty amongst all communities. The so-called 'ali-baba' phenomenon involves *bumiputera* borrowers acting as frontmen for non-*bumiputera* entrepreneurs; this has created much resentment and defeats the object of redistribution and increased opportunity. Often the government itself has stressed that the need and the intention is to encourage thrusting new entrepreneurs pushing the economy forward, not to provide handouts which do not produce proportionate common benefits. Corruption and cronyism in government are other phenomena that have spurred criticism.[31] One overall assessment states that Malaysia has 'achieved various numerical outcomes but floundered in the ultimate goal of cultivating capability, confidence and self-reliance, towards genuinely and effectively redressing *bumiputera* socio- economic disadvantage'.[32]

In addition, the factual issues regarding success of the NEP and its successor policies, the National Development Policy and the (current) National Vision Policy, are fraught with controversy. The main objective of the NEP was to increase *bumiputera* equity ownership from 1.5 per cent in 1969 to 30 per cent by 1990. The other main aspect of the NEP was

---

[28] Tun Mohamed Suffian, *An Introduction to the Constitution of Malaysia* (2nd edn, Kuala Lumpur, Government Printer, 1976) 312–19.

[29] Lee Hwok-Aun (n 5) 169.

[30] Zainal Aznam Yusof, 'Affirmative action in Malaysia: An overview of progress and limitations' in G Brown, F Stewart and A Langer (eds), *Affirmative Action in Plural Societies: International Experiences* (Basingstoke, Palgrave Macmillan, 2012).

[31] Gomez and Jomo (n 1).

[32] Lee Hwok-Aun (n 5) 172.

to reduce poverty (seen largely as a rural Malay issue, in practice) from 49 per cent in 1970 to 16 per cent in 1990. Officially, the poverty rate is now below 3 per cent.[33] The NEP has without doubt succeeded in many respects, although there are still issues of uneven development. Accounts of success or failure in this objective render the issue murky, as there are no agreed criteria for assessing ownership, and official statement indicate that there is still some way to go. Some critiques doubt the 30 per cent target in principle, while others claim that increasing equity ownership does not lead to the intended social changes. However, since there is no agreed method for benchmarking success precisely, the true position is difficult to ascertain and objective debate has been difficult to conduct while the issue has continued to be regarded as 'sensitive'. When an NGO research unit issued a report in 2006 contradicting the Government's figures, and alleging that the true percentage for *bumiputera* equity ownership might be as high as 45 per cent, the Director of the unit, a prominent academic, was forced to resign amid serious recriminations and invective from Government ministers.[34] Debate about the meeting of targets, moreover, has had to substitute for debate about the principles of the NEP, because it is still an offence under the Sedition Act to question the policy, albeit that such questioning has become more frequent in recent years. The closer official statements have come to saying that the 30 per cent target is being achieved, the more difficult it has been to close off debate about what comes next, whatever limitations the law imposes on freedom of speech.

Indeed, since the early 2000s signs that the NEP's star is waning have appeared. The Government itself has been cautiously and by degrees addressing dysfunctional aspects of the *bumiputera* preference policy, no doubt aware of its need to satisfy non-*bumiputera* voters given the splintering of the Malay vote since 1999 between UMNO and the emergence of newer opposition parties. The '30 per cent' rule in foreign investment approvals was rescinded in 2009, and earlier, for all investments, in the MSC and other special economic zones (see Chapter 2). Quotas for university admission were abolished in 2004, and in 2008 the scholarship quota was adjusted from 90–10 per cent to 55–45 per cent in favour of *bumiputera*.[35]

---

[33] See https://worldpoverty.io/map.

[34] 'ASLI Director quits over controversial findings', *The Star*, 11 October 2006, available at www.thestar.com.my/news/nation/2006/10/11/asli-director-quits-over-controversial-findings.

[35] Lee Hwok-Aun, 'Malaysia's *bumiputera* preferential regime and transformation agenda: Modified programmes, unchanged system' (2017) 17(2) *Trends in Southeast Asia.*

There is clearly widespread belief that the social contract is outdated and changes are required. Placing an extra constitutional obstacle in the path of change (ie the consent of the Conference of Rulers, by amendment to Article 159) might prove to have been unwise. An alternative solution is offered by the fact that Article 153 allows the Government a discretion as to when and how to exercise the powers it grants, as with the adjustment in scholarship quotas. If the Government were of the view that the special position of *bumiputera* citizens is no longer in need of protection it could simply decline to use the powers involved and rescind the relevant regulations. This would be perfectly legal but, of course, would also have the disadvantage of leaving the system in place for possible future use.

Any process to dismantle or replace the social contract will have to be handled carefully. There is attachment to its principle as a matter of group rights, as well as to the benefits that it has bestowed on a large proportion of the population. Many would regard their removal with dismay, and might argue with some force that the social contract and the NEP have been a success. Given the continued existence of ethnic and religious tensions, which were apparent in opposition to the PH government of 2018/20, the social contract will no doubt continue to be a matter of sensitivity and controversy.

FURTHER READING

ET Gomez and J Saravanamuttu (eds), *The New Economic Policy in Malaysia: Affirmative Action, Ethnic Inequalities, and Social Justice* (Singapore, NUS Press, 2013).

A Harding, 'Constitutional trajectory in Malaysia: Constitutionalism without Consensus?' in MW Dowdle and MA Wilkinson (eds), *Constitutionalism Beyond Liberalism* (Cambridge, Cambridge University Press, 2017).

Lee Hwok-Aun, *Affirmative Action in Malaysia and South Africa: Preference for Parity* (London and New York, Routledge, 2021).

Norani Othman, MC Puthucheary and C Kessler (eds), *Sharing the Nation: Faith, Difference, Power and the State 50 Years After Merdeka* (Petaling Jaya, SIRDC, 2008).

# 4

# *Parliamentary Democracy in a Plural Society*

Role and Definition of Parliament – Elections and the Composition of the Dewan Rakyat – Political Parties and the Political Process – Parliamentary Process – Parliamentary Accountability – The Dewan Negara – Emergency Powers

## I. INTRODUCTION

'Nyamok berkepak, dunia nak chondong-kah?'
(If a mosquito flaps its wings, will the world keel over?)

AN EARLY DEMOCRATIC experiment in the form of municipal elections took place in the Straits Settlement of Penang in 1911; yet it was not until 1951 and in the same State that elections on a universal franchise were first held. These were quickly followed by similar developments in Kuala Lumpur, Johor and Terengganu. The first federal elections were those for the Federal Legislative Council which were held in 1955, but Parliament in its present form did not sit until 1959 after GE1. Since then, both State and Federal elections have been held on a regular basis (14 of them altogether), every four or five years, except for the emergency period of 1969–71, during which elections were suspended.[1] The *Merdeka* Constitution, like the constitutions of many other newly constituted states of the period that had previously been governed by Britain, envisaged a parliamentary democracy on the model of the Westminster constitution. Of course, the overall constitutional configuration differed from the Westminster model in some important

---

[1] For details of the conduct of elections, see Azhar Azizan Harun, 'The electoral process' in Mohamad Ariff Yusoff, Roosme Hamzah and Shad Saleem Faruqi (eds), *Law, Principles and Practice in the Dewan Rakyat (House of Representatives) of Malaysia* (Subang Jaya, Thomson Reuters, 2020).

respects: supremacy, for example, lay with the Constitution rather than the will of Parliament;[2] a Bill of Rights was included along the pattern of the Constitution of India; and a federal structure also entailed some differences from the British system of government.

The electoral system was decided by the Reid Commission without any serious debate or even consideration of alternative systems. It was formed along Westminster lines with a single-member, simple-plurality system (usually known as the 'first-past-the-post' or FPTP system), which still applies today to both the lower house, the *Dewan Rakyat*, and the State Legislative Assemblies. Proportional representation was, however, considered before *Merdeka* by a committee of the Federal Legislative Council, but rejected on the ground that the electorate would have difficulty in understanding it. However, although the electoral system is constantly debated in public fora,[3] and Parliament now has a Special Select Committee on Elections, no legislative attempt has been made to revisit this reasoning in light of changed circumstances, such as increased literacy and a greater plurality of parties. In Malaysia, where communally defined parties have been the norm but ethnicity is not evenly spread across constituencies, the FPTP system in effect requires parties to seek alliances across communal lines, giving rise to a number of coalitions of parties. The existing system is highly advantageous for the coalition that is able to secure a majority of the vote, as this usually delivers an even higher proportion of seats.[4] For small and medium-sized parties the present system is disadvantageous. At GE14, for example, PAS obtained around 17 per cent of the vote and around 8 per cent of the seats in Parliament, while the MCA obtained more than 5 per cent of the vote but only one seat or less than 0.5 per cent of the seats.[5]

In addition, the Constitution incorporates many of the Westminster conventions, notably those governing the relationships between the Government, the monarchy, and Parliament.[6] These conventions – in fact codified rules in the Malaysian Constitution – have been much in use

---

[2] Art 4.

[3] See eg Wong Chin Huat, 'Malaysia's first-past-the-post (FPTP) electoral system: Malpractices and mismatch' in ML Weiss and Faisal H Haziz (eds), *Towards a New Malaysia? The 2018 Election and Its Aftermath* (Singapore, NUS Press, 2020).

[4] Francis Loh Kok Wah, 'Centralised federalism in Malaysia: Is change in the offing?' in ML Weiss (ed), *The Routledge Handbook of Contemporary Malaysia* (Abingdon, Routledge, 2014).

[5] See https://election.thestar.com.my.

[6] AJ Harding, 'The Westminster model constitution overseas: Transplantation, adaptation and development in Commonwealth states' (2004) 4(2) *Oxford University Commonwealth Law Journal* 143.

and the subject of much doubt as to their interpretation in recent years; examples are discussed in Chapters 2 and 5, as well as later in this chapter. The most important of these is that the appointment and survival of the Government depend on it having a parliamentary majority (the operation of this convention is discussed in Chapter 2). Since, therefore, the Government, by definition, must command a parliamentary majority, Parliament has invariably endorsed the will of the Government. It is recorded that about 80 per cent of bills have been passed with no amendment at all,[7] although a number of bills have been withdrawn.

However, after GE14 in 2018 the PH Government, despite having a majority in the *Dewan Rakyat*, had no majority in the upper house (the *Dewan Negara*), a majority of whose members had been appointed during the previous BN Government's period in office (the *Dewan Negara* is not dissolved when Parliament is dissolved). As a result, the PH Government was able to pass very few bills and was discouraged even from tabling bills. In 2019, for the first time, a bill was rejected by the *Dewan Negara*; this was a bill to repeal the Anti-Fake News Act 2018. For the first time in Malaysian history a Bill for Amending the Constitution also failed to obtain the required two-thirds majority,[8] although another such Bill, lowering the voting age to 18, was passed, but has not been implemented.[9] Since Senators hold office for a period of three years, an incoming government in future may well find the *Dewan Negara* an obstacle to legislation, as the PH Government did following GE14; reform of that house has been under consideration and may well come about.[10] This is discussed below.

In essence, parliamentary process has normally been something of a formality. As one noted scholar has expressed it: 'Parliament legitimates; it does not legislate.'[11] It is, rather, criticism of bills or demands for reform made *outside*, rather than on the floor of, Parliament that has acted as a check on legislative power. For example, in the case of the Bersih 2.0 rally calling for free and fair elections in 2011, the Government agreed to set up a parliamentary committee to look into the electoral system.[12] At the same time, Parliament has often been a major forum for political

---

[7] Mohamad Ariff and Shad Saleem Faruqi, 'The constitutional position of Parliament' in Mohamad Ariff Yusoff and others (n 1) 36.

[8] Bill DR 7/2019.

[9] Constitution (Amendment) Act 2019, amending Art 47. This amendment is supposed to be implemented along with automatic voter registration in 2021.

[10] Azhar Azizan Harun (n 1) 114–16.

[11] Shad Saleem Faruqi, *Our Constitution* (Subang Jaya, Thomson Reuters, 2019) 234.

[12] Azhar Azizan Harun (n 1) 115.

debate and calling the Government to account. However, its weakness was exposed during the 1MDB scandal, when foreign media proved more adept at exposing corruption than the Malaysian Parliament, which was manipulated by the Prime Minister so as to avoid parliamentary accountability almost entirely.[13]

Parliament is defined as consisting of the *Yang di-Pertuan Agong*, the *Dewan Negara* and the *Dewan Rakyat*, and is therefore bicameral.[14] The consent of all three is required to pass legislation; but in the case of the *Yang di-Pertuan Agong* a Bill becomes law automatically if he fails to assent to it within 30 days of it being presented to him.[15] The *Dewan Rakyat* is the more important, functional part of Parliament. The *Yang di-Pertuan Agong* has the power to summon, prorogue and dissolve the *Dewan Rakyat*, acting on government advice. In addition to being the institution that exercises the Federal legislative power, Parliament fulfils the functions of executive oversight, and redressing of grievances, and controls Federal government spending. The Prime Minister and Cabinet ministers must normally be members of one of the two houses, as one would expect in a Westminster-type structure, but only the Prime Minister has to be a MP.[16] In March 2020 Prime Minister Muhyiddin took an unusual step by appointing a senator, Tengku Zafrul Aziz, a technocrat banker, as Minister of Finance. As we saw in Chapter 2, the Prime Minister himself has very often held the post of Finance Minister.

These basic determinants having been outlined, this chapter proceeds to examine in constitutional terms the nature and functioning of the parliamentary system. It will become apparent that parliamentary democracy has over the years been limited in its traction within the political system both as a concept and as a matter of practice. Tight election results in GE12, GE13 and GE14 have, however, somewhat revitalised Parliament as an institution, and concerns about the electoral system have also renewed interest in the nature of democratic representation at the Federal and State levels. The chapter will therefore also examine the political process and the electoral system, within the system of parliamentary democracy as it has operated in Malaysia since *Merdeka*.

---

[13] DS Jones, '1MDB corruption scandal in Malaysia: A study of failings in control and accountability' (2020) 23(1) *Public Administration and Policy* 59.

[14] Art 44. In this chapter 'Parliament' refers to the constitutional definition set out in the text; but 'MP' will refer to Members of the House of Representatives (rendered here in accordance with Malaysian convention as the '*Dewan Rakyat*'), and Members of the Senate (*Dewan Negara*) being normally referred to in English as 'Senators'.

[15] Art 66(4A).

[16] As was indicated in ch 2, Senators as well as MPs are found in the Cabinet.

The State Assemblies are also of some importance, but are dealt with separately in Chapters 5 and 6. The chapter concludes with discussions of the *Dewan Negara* and of emergency powers, which impinge on the legislative and oversight role of Parliament.

## II. ELECTIONS AND THE COMPOSITION OF THE *DEWAN RAKYAT*

'Gajah berhati, kuman pun berhati juga'

(The elephant has a heart, but so has the mite)

The composition of the *Dewan Rakyat* is governed by Article 46 of the Constitution, which requires a constitutional amendment to change the number of seats; before a constitutional amendment of 1983, Parliament could alter this number simply by passing a law. At present the *Dewan Rakyat* consists of 222 members, but Article 46(2) specifies the number of members elected from each State and from the Federal Territories. The House has grown in number from the 98 members of the Federal Legislative Council (of whom only 52 were in fact elected) which replaced a wholly appointed Federal Council following the first legislature election in 1955. The increase in numbers naturally reflects a large growth in population (from around 6.3 million in 1957 to around 32.8 million), but also the increase in the number of States from 11 to 14 with the formation of Malaysia in 1963 (reducing to 13 with Singapore's departure from the Federation in 1965). Another effect of the advent of Malaysia was the granting temporarily of over-representation in the *Dewan Rakyat*, in terms of the proportion of seats to population, to Sabah and Sarawak, which was one of the guarantees given to those States under the Malaysia Agreement 1963.[17] Currently, however, a dramatic increase in population in Sabah has resulted in disproportionate representation: Sarawak (population 2.6 million) with 31 seats has a proportion of one seat per 84,000 population (well below the national average of 148,000), while Sabah (population 3.5 million) has 25 seats and a proportion of one seat per 144,000 population.[18] The dispensation of seats is not only unfair as between these two States: significant outliers are highly urbanised areas such as Selangor (population of 5.8 million and 22 seats; ie one seat

---

[17] See ch 6. It is a further grievance that when Singapore left the Federation, its parliamentary seats were in effect redistributed to Peninsular Malaysia but not to Sabah or Sarawak.

[18] These numbers denote residents rather than voters; Sabah has had a large influx of foreign workers in recent years.

per 264,000 population).[19] Thus there is no clear or consistent relation between the number of seats apportioned and the size of a State's population or electorate. The apportionment of parliamentary seats between the States is also set out in Article 46 of the Constitution, but is required to be reviewed by the Election Commission of Malaysia (ECM) at least once every eight years.

This situation is indeed odd for a Federal system, in which one would expect reasonably equal treatment of the various States. While a balance somewhat in favour of rural areas with their attendant difficulties is not unusual in electoral systems generally, the very considerable disproportion between the metropolitan conurbation, with its concentration of opposition support, and the rest of Malaysia seems lacking in any objective justification. Not all rural areas are even necessarily favoured under this system: urban Penang, for example, has 13 seats with a proportion of one seat per 113,000 population, while rural Terengganu with eight seats has a proportion of one seat per 131,000 population. There are also enormous disparities between individual seats. In GE14, for example, 120,000 votes were cast in Damansara, while only 12,000 were cast in Putrajaya, an astonishing ten-fold difference that raises serious constitutional difficulties. Apart from such disparities, which are incompatible with a modern democracy, it is also alleged that the present 'first-past-the-post' system reinforces ethnic divisions. The electoral system seems in many respects in need of a thorough review and overhaul.[20]

The functions of the ECM, set out in Article 113 of the Constitution, are mainly the conduct of Federal and State elections; preparing and revising the electoral rolls; reviewing Federal and State constituency boundaries once every eight years, with the review taking no longer than two years; reviewing Federal or State constituency boundaries in the area affected, consequent on an increase in the number of elected members of the *Dewan Rakyat* or of a State Legislative Assembly, with the review again taking no longer than two years; and making rules for the purposes of these functions.[21] Although in appointing members of the ECM regard is to be had 'to the importance of securing an Election Commission which enjoys public confidence',[22] and the Commissioners

---

[19] Population figures are approximate and as of 2020.

[20] Wong Chin Huat, 'A new electoral system for a new Malaysia', *New Mandala*, 4 November 2018, www.newmandala.org/a-new-electoral-system-for-a-new-malaysia.

[21] Art 113.

[22] Events surrounding the *Bersih* 2.0 rally, 11 July 2011 (see below), indicated a considerable lack of public confidence at that time in the ECM.

enjoy security of tenure similar to that of judges, it was not a truly independent body until after GE14 when, following criticism of the ECM for being biased towards the BN, its members resigned and were replaced.[23] Its performance in GE14 in 2018 was widely regarded as utterly abysmal, restricting voter participation in several respects, imposing unreasonable requirements on opposition parties, and being late in returning official results when the outcome was already well known, almost precipitating a law-and-order crisis.[24]

The seven Commissioners are appointed by the *Yang di-Pertuan Agong* after consultation with the Conference of Rulers; since the former acts on the advice of the Government, it is effectively the Government that appoints the ECM. The Commission reports directly to the Prime Minister with regard to the delimitation of both Federal and State constituency boundaries, but the Prime Minister is required to submit the report to the *Dewan Rakyat* with a draft order, which may amend the recommendations but has to be approved by the House before it can take effect. The last delimitation exercise took place in 2018, prior to GE14. The State Legislative Assemblies and Governments actually play no special role in all this, even though the delimitation of State constituencies is potentially a highly sensitive issue of great interest to them. In effect therefore the Government can control even State constituency boundaries, a factor of some importance when several States are under opposition control. It is highly questionable whether the Prime Minister should play such a decisive role in this matter.

The review procedure adopted by the ECM is laid out in Schedule 13 of the Constitution, and includes an opportunity for objections to be made against its recommendations. State Governments can and do object to such recommendations, and this triggers a requirement to hold a public enquiry. Elections themselves may only be challenged by means of an election petition in the High Court under Article 118. Each election spawns many such petitions. There is no appeal from the High Court's decision, nor can there be judicial review of an election court, as it is not an inferior court.[25]

---

[23] 'EC members quit to frustrate tribunal probe, says AG', *The Star*, 31 January 2019, available at www.thestar.com.my/news/nation/2019/01/31/ec-members-had-quit-to-frustrate-tribunal-probe-says-ag.

[24] See the articles on the 2018 election in the ICON Symposium reported at www.iconnectblog.com/2018/06/introduction-to-i-connect-symposium-malaysia-boleh-constitutional-implications-of-the-malaysian-tsunami.

[25] *Ignatius Stephen Malanjun v Election Judge, Sabah* [1989] 2 MLJ 433.

The delimitation of constituencies must be carried out 'as far as possible' in the light of four principles, set out in Schedule 13 to the Constitution.[26] These are:

1. The *congruency principle*: constituency boundaries should not cross State boundaries, and State constituency boundaries should not cross Federal constituency boundaries. In practice this means that Federal constituencies are each divided into a number of State constituencies.
2. The *administrative principle*: regard must be had to the administrative facilities available for registration and polling.
3. The *rural-weightage principle*: the number of electors within each constituency 'ought to be approximately equal except that, having regard to the greater difficulty of reaching electors in the country districts and the other disadvantages facing rural constituencies, a measure of weightage for area ought to be given to such constituencies'. This principle does not specify how far it can be taken without breaching the principle of equality between constituencies (and therefore between voters). Originally the permissible margin of difference in numbers of voters between constituencies was 15 per cent, which seems an acceptable margin.[27]
4. The *status-quo principle*: regard must be had to the inconvenience attendant on alterations of constituencies, and to the maintenance of local ties.[28]

These principles do not say that citizens should be treated equally with regard to the value of their votes – indeed they indicate quite the reverse. Nor do they provide any hierarchy of principles, as opposed to just a list, leaving the ECM to decide which principles have precedence and to what extent. In practice the rural-weightage principle has proved the most significant. By legitimising large discrepancies between urban and rural constituencies, this principle has overall allowed proportionally more Malay than non-Malay representation in Parliament, since Malays have largely been more concentrated in the rural areas than in the urban areas. Up to 1973 the provision (Schedule 13, section 2(c)) referred to rural constituencies 'in some cases' containing 'as little as one half of the electors of any urban constituency'. With the repeal

---

[26] The designation of these principles, adopted for clarity of exposition, is based on AJ Harding, *Law, Government and the Constitution in Malaysia* (The Hague, Kluwer and Kuala Lumpur, Malayan Law Journal, 1996) 100–01.

[27] Article 116(4) as it stood before amendment in 1960.

[28] The names given to these principles are the author's own.

of these words the ECM was given carte blanche to create an even more alarming gulf between these two kinds of constituency. Given the timing of this change in the law, coming as it did hard on the heels of the *Rukunegara* settlement, the NEP and increasing authoritarianism (discussed in Chapter 1), it seems lacking in any real justification. In fact, it led to the enormous disparities in representation that were set out above. In one extreme case highlighted before the Parliamentary Select Committee on Electoral Reform in 2011, the BN-held constituency of Putrajaya had 6,008 voters while PR-held Kapar had 112,224 voters, more than 17 times Putrajaya's numbers.[29] As we have seen, a similar situation obtained in GE14.

Even if this law was justified in 1973 it is hard to see how it can be justified almost half a century later, given that poverty has been dramatically reduced and greater opportunity, mobility and vastly improved communications are the norm. It is apparent that a great deal of gerrymandering has occurred, with rural weightage being 'extreme in some carefully selected constituencies'.[30] Before 1960 allowance was to be made in delimitation for 'the distribution of different communities in the constituencies', which was interpreted to mean that ethnic differences were not to be taken into account in drawing boundaries.[31] In any event it is surely appropriate to address the problems of rural areas, and also deprived urban areas – whatever their ethnic mix – and poverty generally, with programmes targeted to their actual needs as opposed to distorting the electoral system and creating inequality in the electoral sphere where, above all, citizens should be equal. Indeed, given the lack of real effectiveness of Parliament as a means of critiquing policy, this form of electoral discrimination does not even effectively address the problem of rural disadvantage. The present author has commented on this issue as follows:

> The Malaysian Constitution has not gone so far as to resuscitate the rotten borough of 18th-century England in the form of the rotten *kampong* [Malay village], but there is a real danger of lack of legitimacy if the electoral system diverges too sharply from the principle of 'one-man-one-vote-one-value'.[32]

That danger is mitigated only by the fact that, in spite of these defects, which were alleged to work very much against them, the opposition PH

---

[29] 'A retiree exposes gerrymandering in Sabah', *Malaysiakini*, 27 November 2011.
[30] D Mauzy, 'Resilient hybrid regimes' (2006) 2(2) *Taiwan Journal of Democracy* 47, 64.
[31] Azhar Azizan Harun (n 1) 112.
[32] A Harding, *Law, Government and the Constitution in Malaysia* (Kuala Lumpur, MLJ/LexisNexis, 1996) 101.

coalition was able to win GE14, creating an erroneous impression of an electoral system that is essentially fair.

Many other defects have been noted in the electoral system. These include phantom voters, vote-buying, on-the-spot ministerial offers of development funding, and threats of economic sanctions for areas returning opposition candidates.[33] On top of these problems is the long-standing issue of party-hopping, which has occurred regularly and involves large sums of money changing hands.[34]

Another concerning aspect is the actual numbers of electors. Currently there are fewer than 15 million registered voters: less than half the population. This is attributable partly due to a very young population with a large proportion of citizens under 21 years of age, a large non-citizen population, and the fact that many Malaysians live far from their home towns and have not registered to vote. By 2023 it is estimated by the former chair of the ECM that about 7.3 million more voters will be on the electoral roll, due to lowering the voting age to 18 and to provision for automatic registration.[35]

On four occasions (2007, 2011, 2012 and 2015) a mass rally was organised by Bersih,[36] a coalition of non-governmental organisations (NGOs) and political parties, demanding 'free and fair elections'. Consistently with its name, Bersih demanded reforms in several areas, including the cleaning up of voter registration, reforming overseas and postal voting, instituting longer campaign periods, taking stern action against electoral corruption, and lowering the voting age to 18. Bersih also claimed that as many as 3.5 million voters were in effect disenfranchised. Several of these issues have now been addressed by the ECM. However, official sympathy for a free and fair electoral system was not apparent before GE14 and few reforms occurred after it. The demand for a lowering of the voting age to 18 was, however, acceded to in 2019, when the Constitution was amended accordingly.[37] In 2018 the PH Government set up an Electoral Reform Committee, whose initial report in late 2019 recommended looking at adopting a system of proportional representation, in addition to

---

[33] Mauzy (n 30) 18.

[34] Politicians changing party are popularly known as '*katak*' (frogs). On a number of occasions such party-hopping has resulted in a change of government at the State level (see ch 6), and even, as we saw in ch 2, at the Federal level. See, further, Jaclyn Neo, 'Constitutionalizing clear rules for political transition: Entrenching the Malaysian tsunami' (*I-CONnect*, 16 May 2018), available at www.iconnectblog.com/2018/05/constitutionalizing-clear-rules-for-political-transition-entrenching-the-malaysian-tsunami-i-connect-column.

[35] Azhar Azizan Harun (n 1) 107.

[36] 'Bersih' means 'clean' in the Malay language.

[37] Constitution (Amendment) Act 2019.

other reforms.[38] At the time of writing its full report had not yet been presented to the Government, and reforms may be impossible to achieve before the next election.

The ECM itself, as we have seen, is not fully independent of the Government. Its powers are limited and have not even been exercised as broadly as they might be. The ECM has no role to play in enforcing electoral law except to provide evidence of irregularities, which are often widespread, to the prosecuting authorities. A former Chair of the ECM has levelled many trenchant criticisms of the electoral system, in particular the lack of accountability and rationality in the delimitation process.[39] Since GE14, however, although the relevant laws, inadequate as they are, remain the same, 10 by-elections have been held without any criticism of the ECM's performance. This lends support to the idea that 'independent agencies' can operate well and independently, depending on the appointment system and the actual appointees. A proposal in 2018 that such agencies should report directly to Parliament, rather than to the Prime Minister, appears to be a desirable reform, but has not been acted upon.[40]

It seems clear that major reforms are still required at every level if Malaysia is to achieve a free and fair electoral system consistent with a twenty-first-century democracy, and it is to be hoped that this will be recognised across the political spectrum.

### III. POLITICAL PARTIES AND THE POLITICAL PROCESS

'Banyak orang, banyak ragam-nya'

(Many people, many whims)

The political aspects of state formation and government formation in Malaysia have been discussed in Chapters 1 and 2, where reasons were offered for the emergence and dominant position of UMNO and the BN over six decades. One of the many paradoxes in the Malaysian political system, however, is that, despite increasingly authoritarian

---

[38] 'Electoral Reform Committee proposes proportionate representation system for parliamentary seats', *Malay Mail*, 2 October 2019, available at www.malaymail.com/news/malaysia/2019/10/02/electoral-reform-committee-proposes-proportionate-representation-system-for/1796495.

[39] Azhar Azizan Harun (n 1).

[40] Nine agencies to begin reporting to new Parliament, *The Star*, 2 October 2019, available at www.thestar.com.my/news/nation/2018/07/15/nine-agencies-to-begin-reporting-to-new-parliament.

government from 1970 up until 2008, especially during Dr Mahathir's earlier premiership, political parties have flourished, at least numerically. Currently 31 parties are registered with the Registrar of Societies; 17 of these parties are represented in Parliament, with no party holding more than 42 out of 222 seats. Coalitions naturally flourish, and there are four of these in Parliament,[41] with the PN coalition commanding an overall majority of about six seats, as far as can be ascertained in Malaysia's currently highly fluid politics.

Fluidity has also been a feature of Malaysian political parties themselves. Although several parties date from the 1940s or 1950s, new parties have appeared often, 22 of the current 31 having been registered since 2007. While some have lasted for a short time, others have attained instant success; PKR, led by former Deputy PM Anwar Ibrahim, for example, was registered in 2003, obtained seats in the legislatures in GE11 (2004), led four State Governments after that election, was in government 2018–20, and is now one of the two main Federal opposition parties. Parti Pribumi Bersatu Malaysia (Bersatu) was established by Mahathir in 2016 and by 2018 he headed the PH coalition, Bersatu holding several Cabinet seats; splintering of the party followed with Mahathir and other MPs expelled and Muhyiddin, by then Bersatu President, taking over as Prime Minister, as narrated in Chapter 2. Currently Bersatu has 26 seats in Parliament, having won 12 in GE14, and Mahathir has established yet another new party, Pejuang, a splinter group of Bersatu, while a new reform party, MUDA, comprising mainly younger politicians from different groups, has also been established, although neither is yet registered by the Registrar of Societies, giving rise to litigation in both instances.

Although floor-crossing or party-hopping statutes, designed to prevent members changing parties, are a feature of some State Legislative Assemblies,[42] there is no restriction of this kind in the Federal legislature, where the only relevant rule is that a Member who resigns their seat is disqualified for five years.[43] This rule was effected by a constitutional amendment passed in 1990 to prevent opposition parties using staged resignations as a means of testing the Government in by-elections. Currently there is much discussion as to the merits of enacting a Federal 'anti-hopping' law. One major obstacle to such development is that the courts have held such law to be contrary to the right of freedom

---

[41] PH, PN, BN and Sarawak's GPS.
[42] See ch 5.
[43] Art 48(6).

of association,[44] so that such law would require to be enacted in the Constitution by amendment thereto, or else to be authorised by such amendment, which would of course require to be passed by two-thirds majorities in each house.

All parties, and indeed all societies, are required to be registered under the Societies Act 1966.[45] This Act, with 70 sections, presents many obstacles, including a good deal of red tape and several mechanisms whereby the Government can control parties and civil society organisations. The Act recognises a distinction between political parties and other societies, defining a political party as a society that seeks to participate in elections at any level.[46] A society is defined as including 'any club, company, partnership or association of seven or more persons whatever its nature or object, whether temporary or permanent'. It is an offence, until a society is registered, to organise or take part in any activity of or on behalf of it without the written permission of the Registrar of Societies. The minister can declare unlawful any society which in his opinion is, or is being used for purposes which are, prejudicial to security, public order or morality. The Registrar and the minister have wide powers to refuse or cancel registration on a number of grounds connected with security, peace, welfare, public order or morality, affiliation or connection outside the Federation, and unlawful purposes. Decisions under the Act may be appealed from the Registrar to the Minister, whose decision is final. Controversial amendments to the Act were passed in 1987 following a crisis over the illegality of the ruling party (see Chapter 8). In practice political parties, as opposed to some religious groups (see Chapter 9), have not been declared illegal under the Act, but there are delays and frustrations in registering and in observing requirements. Beyond that, civil society flourishes despite close statutory regulation.[47] All societies are required to observe the Constitution, and the Societies Act threatens societies with de-registration if any of their activities or affairs in any manner violate or show disregard for: the system of democratic government headed by constitutional monarchy; the position of Islam as the religion of Malaysia; the use of the national language for official purposes; the position of the Malays and of the natives of Sabah and Sarawak; or the legitimate interests of the other communities.[48] In this

---

[44] *Noordin Salleh v Dewan Undangan Negeri Kelantan* [1992] 1 MLJ 343.

[45] Societies Act 1966, Act 355, amended in 1972 (Act A102), and 1981 (Act A515).

[46] Societies Act 1966, s 2.

[47] M Weiss, *Protest and Possibilities: Civil Society and Coalitions for Political Change in Malaysia* (Stanford, Stanford University Press, 2005).

[48] Societies Act 1966, s 2A.

way political parties are, consistently with the Sedition Act and Article 10 of the Constitution (for which see the discussion of the social contract in Chapter 3), strictly confined in the manner in which they address the 'sensitive issues'.

The political system was described, until 2008 at least, as a dominant-coalition system, very similar to a dominant-party system but incorporating the element of inter-ethnic accommodation. The BN, at its height comprising 16 parties, but now only four, took to a logical conclusion the system inaugurated by the Tunku in the 1950s, in that many of the parties that have formed it, beyond the original three ethnic parties of the Alliance, have also represented other ethnic groups, especially native communities of Sabah and Sarawak. However, there is no doubt that within the BN coalition UMNO was and is dominant. The Chairman of the BN was always until 2018 the PM. Although the component parties of the BN held Cabinet seats, they had little influence on policy despite their claim, which was often doubted, to obtain the best deal for their ethnic group. It is indeed hard to find a single example of a major policy explicitly prevented, abandoned or modified in the face of intra-BN opposition. A pattern was set by the 1959 crisis over Chinese education, which has always been a thorny issue in Malaysian politics: UMNO on that occasion resisted attempts by the MCA to block changes in education policy that affected Chinese education. MCA supported the Tunku at the expense of splitting the party.[49] At the same time UMNO policy-making kept in mind the need to secure the votes of supporters of other BN parties, not just its own. Maintaining a close connection with Malay political leaders has been a priority for Chinese business interests. In this respect it can be noted that support for the MCA and the MIC (the two original coalition partners of UMNO) has eroded seriously over recent years, especially in GE14. However, the logic of inter-ethnic accommodation remains compelling, especially as the Malay vote has become increasingly split between (now) four of the main parties (Bersatu, UMNO, PKR and PAS).

Currently the intra-party and inter-party relations of Malaysian political parties are in a state of radical indeterminacy and rapid shifts in alignment. This represents in many respects an improvement on the BN dominant-coalition system of 1957–2008, opening the opportunities for much-needed change, especially in Parliament. For now, the shape of the party system remains extremely fluid.

---

[49] RS Milne and DK Mauzy, *Malaysian Politics under Mahathir* (London, Routledge, 1999) 91–96.

## IV. PARLIAMENTARY PROCESS

'Sudah tahu bertanya pula'
(You have been told already, but here you come asking questions)

Proceedings in both Houses are within the powers of the House to decide, subject to the relevant constitutional provisions, and both Houses have power to make Standing Orders governing their procedure.[50] Moreover, the independence of Parliament is protected under Article 63(1): '[t]he validity of any proceedings in either House of Parliament or any committee thereof shall not be questioned in any court'.[51] The principles of separation of powers and parliamentary independence were upheld in the Federal Court in a decision relating to the Select Committee on Competence, Accountability and Transparency in the Selangor State Legislative Assembly, in which some assemblymen questioned the legality of the Committee's establishment.[52] Although it is usual in Westminster-type parliaments for the Speaker to be appointed from amongst sitting members, which was indeed the case in Malaysia until 1964. Since then, Speaker has been appointed from outside Parliament, and is not allowed to vote. Opposition members often criticise the Speaker or his decisions, and sometimes question the Speaker's impartiality. Nonetheless, occasionally the Speaker has played an important role in securing proper and thorough parliamentary process; in 1971, for example, the personal intervention of the Speaker secured a seven-day extension to the debate on the Constitution (Amendment) Bill introducing the *Rukunegara* amendments.[53]

In 2020–21 the Speaker's absurd repeated refusal, going against Westminster principles, to allow the debating of several parliamentary no-confidence motions allowed the PN government to remain in power despite the fact that its majority had never been demonstrated. By most accounts the government had at various times lost its majority or had a razor-thin majority of one or two.[54] Together with the de facto

---

[50] Art 62(1).

[51] *Teng Chang Khim and 5 Ors v Dato' Raja Ideris bin Raja Ahmad and 2 Ors* [2014] 4 MLJ 12.

[52] Ibid.

[53] A Harding, 'The *Rukunegara* Amendments of 1971' in AJ Harding and HP Lee, *Constitutional Landmarks in Malaysia: The First Fifty Years, 1957–2007* (Kuala Lumpur, LexisNexis, 2007) 94.

[54] Standing Orders allow the Government to decide the order of business, but this, it is submitted, is overridden by the requirements of the Constitution. Government business is only Government business if the Government has a majority and that, if disputed, can only be tested by a motion of confidence.

suspension of Parliament for eight months (January to August 2021) during the proclamation of a Covid-19 related emergency, this situation presented parliamentary democracy's lowest ebb since 1969–71.

The role of Leader of the Opposition is also crucial for effective accountability in Parliament. Since 1971 the Leader of the Opposition is a position recognised by Malaysian law and carries with it a salary. Parliament has undoubtedly been enhanced as an institution by the fact that from 1969 to 1999 and then again from 2004 to 2008 the former DAP leader Lim Kit Siang, a lawyer and a prolific author and blogger, was an effective and indefatigable Leader of the Opposition, and remains an MP at age 80. He was one of the longest serving opposition leaders in the world and ensured that parliamentary proceedings never became a pure formality, even if his criticisms had little overt effect on legislation or Government policy. Lim pursued his political aim to bring the Government to account not only via parliamentary debates and question time, but also in numerous court cases, and was also, despite being Leader of the Opposition, detained without trial under the Internal Security Act for periods of 18 and 17 months respectively during the 1969 and 1987 crackdowns.[55]

Parliamentary procedure in Malaysia will be very familiar to those acquainted with procedure in Westminster-type parliaments. This applies even to fine details of ceremony; for example, the mace, in the charge of a Sergeant-at-Arms, precedes the Speaker into the *Dewan Rakyat* and is placed below the table when the House resolves itself into committee, an indication that the more informal procedure appropriate to the committee-stage then applies. The mace contains sealed in its base pieces of rubber, tin and grains of rice padi, the main produce of Malaysia.

Once elected, Parliament continues for a period of five years from the date of its first meeting, unless it is dissolved. This rule has been followed with the exception of the period of emergency rule from 1969–71. Dissolution takes place on the advice of the Prime Minister, and there is no legal principle of a fixed-term Parliament, so that the decision to call an election is that of the Prime Minister. On dissolution a general election follows within 60 days. Standing Orders of the *Dewan Rakyat*[56] lay down the procedure and are made by the House itself. A session, of which each Parliament usually has four or five, and which usually lasts for about one year, begins, by convention, with the 'speech from the throne', in which the Government outlines its legislative

---

[55] See, further, Harding and Lee (n 53) 301.
[56] Mohamad Ariff Yusoff and others (n 1) App 5.

programme for the session, and ends with prorogation, which must not last more than six months. Since 1984, prorogation does not discontinue Bills that are before Parliament or pending royal assent.[57] Sessions normally consist of five or six meetings, which can last a few days or a few weeks, depending on business. Parliament has usually sat only for about 80 days in the year. The quorum is 26 and before the opposition obtained a large number of seats in GE12 (2008) there were occasions when Government MPs deserted the chamber, making opposition and even sometimes Government business impossible to transact.

Almost all Bills are in practice Government Bills. Legislative procedure in Parliament itself tends to be rather attenuated, and there is also little public debate beforehand on the principles of the legislation. The Cabinet approves the legislative policy, and after internal consultation within the Government it also gives final approval for the drafting of a Bill. Even MPs are often given very little notice of a Bill being introduced, and white papers are virtually unheard of. Indeed bills are normally embargoed until they receive a first reading in Parliament, which severely limits public debate. An extreme case was the Constitution and Malaysia (Singapore Amendment) Bill 1965, by which Singapore was expelled from the Federation. This momentous Bill, seen by MPs only the same day it was passed, took three hours to pass all stages through both Houses – one of the fastest divorces in history. MPs from Sabah and Sarawak, and even the Governments of those States, were not consulted in spite of their particular interest in the matter, and even the Cabinet did not discuss it. This was admittedly a special case, but on 27 August 1967 no fewer than 24 Bills were passed in the *Dewan Rakyat*; and in 1993 a highly controversial constitutional amendment affecting royal immunity from suit (see Chapter 5) was passed in both Houses in less than three days. This once routine 'bouncing' of Parliament has not, however, been repeated to the same extent in recent decades. But the lack of transparency and debate around legislation remains a problem. Some have advocated reform in this area, even to the extent of establishment of an independent law reform commission to consider legal reforms and draft relevant bills, as exists in some other Westminster-type systems. This reform was announced by the PH Government in February 2020, just before it lost power.

Bills may be introduced in either House, and receive three readings, as well as going through a committee stage, in each House, and receive the royal assent before becoming law upon publication in the official gazette. In some cases the consent of the Conference of Rulers is required.

---

[57] Art 55(7).

Money Bills are an exception to the above requirements. These must be introduced by a Minister in the *Dewan Rakyat*, and can become law under Article 68 when passed by the House and having received the royal assent. To become law under Article 68 the Bill must be sent to the *Dewan Negara* at least one month before the end of the session, and if not passed by it without amendment within a month, it may be presented for the royal assent, provided the Speaker certifies that the provisions of Article 68 have been complied with. This certificate is conclusive for all purposes and may not be questioned in any court. If the Bill is *not* a money Bill similar rules apply, except that the *Dewan Negara*'s delaying period is maximally one year and one month rather than one month; in other words, a whole session must pass before the Bill can bypass the *Dewan Negara*. By this means the Malaysian Constitution avoids the possibility of a constitutional deadlock between the lower and upper houses, giving the lower house final say over legislation. The presence of this rule has proved sufficient to avoid it ever having to be tested in an actual instance. During the PH government's tenure bills were in general not tabled due to the likelihood of opposition in the *Dewan Negara* and the consequential delay in enacting them.

The role of the *Yang di-Pertuan Agong* in legislation is almost, but not quite, a formality. As a result of a compromise over this issue when it became moot in the 1984 Rulers' crisis,[58] his assent must be given within 30 days of the Bill being presented for assent, otherwise the Bill becomes law automatically. As result of the crisis the Constitution was amended so that the *Yang di-Pertuan Agong* could return a Bill to the *Dewan Rakyat* with his reasons for refusing the royal assent. This latter rule was repealed by a further amendment in 1994, so that only the 30-day rule remains.

Constitutional amendments are in general subject to additional requirements compared to ordinary Bills; these requirements vary according to the constitutional provision sought to be amended, but Parliament is central to the process in all cases.[59] The basic rule is that a Bill to amend the Constitution must be supported at its second and third readings by two-thirds of the total membership of each House. There are, however, several exceptions to the rule, such as an amendment altering the composition of the *Dewan Negara*, admitting a new State to the Federation, altering State boundaries, or changing the Federal capital.[60]

---

[58] See ch 5.
[59] Art 159.
[60] Harding (n 53) 50.

In some cases, in addition to the special parliamentary majorities, the consent of the Conference of Rulers is required (see Chapter 5). This requirement applies to the *Rukunegara* constitutional amendments of 1971 and even ordinary laws passed under those amendments, such as the Sedition Act amendments under Article 10(4), restricting freedom of expression with regard to the sensitive issues. In other cases, where the special constitutional position of Sabah and/or Sarawak is affected by a proposed constitutional amendment, the consent of the respective State Government (but *not* its legislative assembly) is required.[61]

By this means the Constitution, in terms of its *express* provisions, achieves four different levels of entrenchment. We have already noted in Chapter 2 that the entrenchment of the *Rukunegara* provisions could prove problematical in terms of updating the Constitution in light of the issue of *bumiputera* preference.

There is, however, a fifth degree of entrenchment – an *implied* one – which arises from the 'basic structure' doctrine developed by the Supreme Court of India,[62] which has been considered in some Malaysian cases and finally adopted in *Semenyih Jaya*.[63] This doctrine holds that some provisions of the Constitution are impliedly not within the power of constitutional amendment because their amendment would destroy the constitution's basic structure. This doctrine is discussed further in Chapter 8.

The significance of the process for constitutional amendment is much greater in Malaysia than in most countries. For many years the opposition virtually campaigned on the slogan, 'Deny Them Two Thirds', so that preserving the *Merdeka* Constitution unsullied by executive tampering became a rallying point for many parties and for the civil society. Executive over-employment of the amendment process (42 amending Acts and more than 600 individual textual amendments since 1957, but only one since 2008) has had the effect of entrenching the Constitution, and calls for drafting a new constitution are no longer heard.

Moving to parliamentary privilege, we can note that the law in this area has been specifically derived from English law,[64] and accordingly the Constitution provides at Article 63(2) that no person shall be liable to any proceedings in any court in respect of anything said or any vote given by him when taking part in any proceedings of either House or

---

[61] See ch 5.
[62] *Kesavananda Bharati v State of Kerala* AIR 1973 SC 1461.
[63] *Semenyih Jaya Sdn Bhd v Pentadbir Tanah Daerah Hulu Langat* [2017] 5 CLJ 526.
[64] *Teng Chang Khim* (n 51).

any committee thereof, or in respect of anything published by or under the authority of either House. The parliamentary privilege secured by Article 63 is drastically affected by Article 63(4), introduced as one of the *Rukunegara* amendments in 1971. This provides that Article 63(2) shall not apply to any person charged with an offence under a law passed under Article 10(4) (which allows certain restrictions on freedom of speech, assembly and association), or the Sedition Act 1948 as amended by the Emergency (Essential Powers) Ordinance 1970. The same principles apply to the State Legislative Assemblies. This means that not even an MP or assembly member on the floor of the legislature can raise a question relating to policy on any of the 'sensitive issues' (except with regard to implementation), and use parliamentary privilege as a defence to prosecution. The Sedition Act has been used in such instances, for example in the case of *Mark Koding*, in which an MP was convicted of sedition when he advocated in Parliament the closure of Chinese and Tamil schools.[65] The case also shows that these draconian provisions do not simply protect Malay special privileges from criticism; they protect the entire social contract, including the legitimate expectations of other communities (here the legitimate expectation of the Chinese and Tamil-speaking communities to continue to have primary schools using their languages). These legislative amendments are bolstered by Standing Order No 23(2), which allows the Speaker to refuse any parliamentary question which is likely to 'promote feelings of ill-will or hostility between different communities in the Federation or infringe a provision of the Constitution or the Sedition Act'. This power has been widely interpreted, and has been used, for example, to refuse questions asking for statistics concerning the relative position of the various races in Malaysia with regard to scholarships and earnings, and even the numbers of members of the various tribes of *orang asli*. Standing Order No 36(10) also prohibits seditious words and 'words which are likely to promote feelings of ill-will or hostility between different communities in the Federation' being uttered in Parliament. In view of the very broad definition of promoting ill-will or hostility in Malaysia, these rules have in practice prohibited discussion of important but sensitive matters in Parliament.[66] The Sedition Act has been selectively and erratically enforced, and the scope of its application is indeterminate. On taking office in 2018, Attorney-General Tommy Thomas announced, 'no more political prosecutions', a principle that

---

[65] *Public Prosecutor v Mark Koding* [1983] 1 MLJ 111.
[66] See, further, ch 3.

was not followed before, and has not been followed under the subsequent PN government.[67]

There is a Standing Orders Committee, which recommends changes from time to time, but, as with other parliamentary committees, it is dominated by the Government's majority, and even its recommendations (sometimes favourable to the opposition) have not always been adopted by Parliament when they have not found favour with the Government. For example, the Committee recommended that one out of every five days of parliamentary time should be devoted to opposition business, but this has not been followed: in fact under Standing Order No 15(1), on every sitting day Government business has precedence, and there are no days devoted to opposition business as such. Often the *Dewan Rakyat* has been adjourned *sine die*, leaving opposition motions undebated. Private members' business, on the other hand, is allotted 11 days in each session, and the last day before recess is devoted to backbenchers' motions.[68]

## V. PARLIAMENTARY ACCOUNTABILITY

'Di-bakar tak hangus, di-rendam tak basah'

(Scorched but not burned, in the water but not wet)

In most areas Parliament has proved quite ineffective in securing executive accountability. Nonetheless, the mechanisms it affords have been energetically utilised and their terms and details argued over, and therefore kept very much alive by opposition members. Even Government back-benchers have made good use of Parliament to raise citizen or constituent grievances, and sometimes even join forces with the opposition over parliamentary procedure or provision. In general, however, the 'whip' system applies unless specifically lifted; in other words, Government MPs are obliged to vote for the Government and against the opposition, and vice versa.

Apart from budget debates, debates on motions and Bills, and the committee system (for which see below) question-time is the main weapon available. Each day of the Monday to Thursday period that

---

[67] 'I will never charge anyone for political reasons', *The Edge*, 20 September 2020, available at www.theedgemarkets.com/article/i-will-never-charge-anyone-political-reasons-%E2%80%94-ag.

[68] Nurul Izzah Anwar and Nurul Jannah Mohamed Jailani, 'Strengthening Malaysian parliamentary democracy through private members' bills' (2021) 1 *Journal of the Malaysian Parliament* 38.

the *Dewan Rakyat* sits, 90 minutes are allotted for the answering of the hundreds of parliamentary questions per week of which the required 14 days' notice has been given. Given that all Members are entitled to ask oral and written questions, less than half of the questions tabled by the opposition get to be answered orally, and even answers to written questions become available only when the *Hansard* (published parliamentary proceedings) is published some years later. As often happens, question-time becomes a jousting match in which the opposition seeks to ambush the minister (or in Malaysia more usually the deputy minister), and the minister seeks to avoid embarrassment. No specific time is allotted for Prime Minister's questions, and the Government has usually been content to allow itself to be represented by the relevant minister or deputy minister.[69] During the PH Government 2018–20 Prime Minister Mahathir himself turned up regularly to answer questions as if they were Prime Minister's questions.

## VI. PARLIAMENTARY COMMITTEES

'Rumah sudah, pahat berbunyi'

(The house may be finished but the chisel can still be heard. This refers to the reopening of old grievances)

In recent decades parliamentary committees have emerged internationally as a critical part of parliamentary oversight of executive functions, and the Malaysian Parliament has moved rapidly since 2018 to implement committee reforms in line with Commonwealth practice.

Parliamentary select committees, a potentially powerful method of calling the Government to account before Parliament, have, as with other parliamentary mechanisms, until recently been ineffective in Malaysia. In the case of matters due for detailed public investigation of facts there has been in recent years a preference for Royal Commissions of Inquiry (RCI) rather than parliamentary investigation. A prominent example of this is the RCI (July 2011) into the death of Teoh Beng Hock, an opposition party aide, who died in the custody of the Malaysian Anti-Corruption Commission (MACC). While the Commission concluded that Teoh took his own life in response to heavy MACC interrogation (a finding which is hotly disputed), it also made swingeing criticisms of the

---

[69] Shad Saleem Faruqi, *Document of Destiny: The Constitution of the Federation of Malaysia* (Petaling Jaya, The Star, 2008) 522–6.

MACC's interrogation techniques. Another is the RCI that reported in 1999, in relation to the infamous 'black eye' incident, that former Deputy Prime Minister Anwar Ibrahim had been severely beaten in custody by the Inspector-General of Police. This led to the sacking of the Inspector-General of Police and his conviction and prison sentence for assault. More recently a RCI was convened to investigate allegations of over-zealous grants of citizenship to migrants in Sabah.

Nonetheless, parliamentary reform following GE14 has embraced the parliamentary committee system in a thorough-going manner by creating nine new ones. Committees fall into two groups.

The first type are the 'select committees' which are provided for by Standing Orders,[70] and are (somewhat confusingly) in effect *standing* committees that must be appointed with each new Parliament. These are the house committees, dealing with internal parliamentary matters (Selection, Standing Orders, the House and Privileges); and the all-important Public Accounts Committee.

The second type are referred to in Standing Orders as 'special select committees', of which there are now 10. These are not required, but are allowed by, Standing Orders.[71] They are designed to oversee a specific departmental function, or else a topic of general concern. They are the Committees on Budget; Consideration of Bills; Major Public Appointments; Gender Equality and Family Development; Defence and Home Affairs; Federal-State Relations; Elections; International Relations and Trade; Human Rights and Constitutional Affairs; and Science, Innovation and Environment.

These committees are also mirrored in the *Dewan Negara*. Several more committees have been mooted during 2018–20, and it has become usual since 2009 for the opposition to have a front bench 'shadow cabinet', and committees mirroring government departments.

Naturally it is the Public Accounts Committee (PAC) that is the most important of the standing committees in terms of accountability. The PAC has normally been chaired by a Government back-bencher, contrary to the usual Westminster convention, under which the PAC is chaired by an opposition member, although, as a result of recent parliamentary reforms, the PAC is currently chaired by an Opposition member. Opposition members generally sit on it in proportion to seats held in the *Dewan Rakyat*, and currently, and usually, it has 14 members. With the

[70] SO 76–80.
[71] SO 81.

benefit of the annual reports of the Auditor-General,[72] the PAC has often been sharply critical of government expenditure, and its findings, although not formally binding, are in effect regarded as such. Within its remit the PAC is powerful, but its remit does not include many high-spending 'off-budget' executive agencies, such as Petronas, the national oil company, and Malaysian Airlines, the importance of which agencies has been highlighted in Chapter 2. As one commentator has argued, this places many instances of 'lack of financial discipline and dependence; slack financial accountability; a casual and indifferent attitude in decision-making; lack of specific expertise; and weak management' essentially beyond parliamentary correction.[73] This assessment is borne out by the PAC's failure, noted earlier, to bring the Government to account over the 1MDB scandal. The PAC has also been hampered by a three- to four-year time-lag in its scrutiny of public expenditure. Ultimately it has been the publication of the Auditor-General's reports rather than the operation of the PAC itself that has proved more effective.[74]

The committee system represents a notable reform, but reform of parliamentary process can be taken much further, for example with regard to parliamentary services, greater transparency in the legislative process, and scrutiny of members' ethical standards.

## VII. THE *DEWAN NEGARA*

'Di-tindeh yang berat, di-dilit yang panjang'

(Crushed by a heavy weight, bound by long coils)

As we have seen, Malaysia's Parliament is bicameral. Upper houses the world over have been challenged in finding a role that differs materially from that of the lower house, which inevitably enjoys greater electoral legitimacy.[75] In Malaysia the perceived need for an upper house was, as we saw in Chapter 1, deeply related to the federal structure adopted in

---

[72] See also the Audit Act 1957 (Act 62) as amended; and Art 107; Siti Falizah Padlee, 'The practice of Public Accounts Committee in the Parliament of Malaysia' (2021) 1 *Journal of the Malaysian Parliament* 159.

[73] Shad Saleem Faruqi (n 69), 516–22.

[74] Azham Md Ali, '1MDB: The Auditor General Office's questions' (2016) 6(1) *Journal of Public Administration and Governance* 50.

[75] A Harding, 'The Dewan Negara and constitutional reform: Upper houses in comparative perspective' (2021) 1 *Journal of the Malaysian Parliament* 1 (2021).

1948, and the system of electing and appointing members was drawn up to reflect this relationship. Given the brief experience of a unitary state (1946–48) and the strong opposition thereto, guarantees were needed of the autonomy and continuance of the States. This is confirmed also by the fact that the States themselves all have unicameral legislatures. The *Dewan Negara* is smaller than the *Dewan Rakyat*, consisting of 70 members. Of these, currently 26 are elected by the State Legislative Assemblies (two for each State), irrespective of the size or importance of the State. There is, however, no requirement for these members also to be members of the State Legislative Assembly. The other 44 members are appointed by the *Yang di-Pertuan Agong* on the advice of the Government, and must be persons who have rendered distinguished public service or have achieved distinction in the professions, commerce, industry, agriculture, cultural activities or social service, or are representatives of racial minorities or are capable of representing the interests of aborigines (the *orang asli*). Of the appointed members, four are chosen to represent the three Federal Territories (Kuala Lumpur, Putrajaya and Labuan). A Senator's term of office is a single term of three years, renewable once only (reduced from a single term of six years in 1978) and is not affected by a parliamentary dissolution. Therefore, in the case of a change in the Federal Government the executive is likely to be faced with a hostile, opposition-controlled *Dewan Negara*, whose composition it cannot change except slowly as members' three-year terms expire. This indeed was the case during 2018–20; in December 2018 the House rejected a bill that had passed the *Dewan Rakyat* to repeal the Anti-Fake News Act 2018, which had been enacted under the previous government. This was the first time a bill had ever been rejected by the House.

Following GE14 it was argued that appointed Senators should all resign as they were appointed by the previous government, although nothing in the Constitution indicates that they should, as the *Dewan Negara* is not dissolved when the *Dewan Rakyat* is dissolved.[76] Given that Senators do not, in theory at least, represent any party as such, but are appointed from amongst worthy citizens, this argument lacks substance. If the *Dewan Negara* proves to be an obstacle to legislation, the remedy is the general powers of the *Dewan Rakyat*, which include a power to override objections from the *Dewan Negara* on the expiry of

---

[76] S Alagan, *Federal Constitution: A Commentary* (Subang Jaya, Thomson Reuters, 2019) 276.

one year.[77] The episode indicates that a rethink or a clearer understanding of the powers of the *Dewan Negara* is overdue.[78]

Essentially, the choice is between a house guaranteeing States' rights in a Federal system, and a house of second thoughts that can delay legislation and bring different perspectives to the debate. The rationale for the *Dewan Negara* would also determine any changes in its composition. The most common criticism of the current composition of the House is that the appointed members outnumber considerably the members elected by the States, which diminishes the Federal role of the House while also reducing its independence from the Government. It would be possible to reform many aspects of the House without constitutional amendment, and in fact the Constitution envisages that its composition might change radically over time. Article 45(4) allows Parliament to increase the number of State-elected members from two to three for each State; it also provides for the possibility of direct popular election of State members, as well as for the numerical decrease or even abolition of appointed members. The number of appointed members has increased from 16 to 44 since 1957; and since 1964 they have had a majority over the State-elected members. Thus by appointing members who support the Government, the latter can ensure that there will be no effective opposition to its measures in the *Dewan Negara*. The House rarely amends Bills passed by the *Dewan Rakyat*; its debates make little impact on the wider political scene; and its composition ensures that its role in protecting States' rights is very limited. In fact the rapid turnover of Senators, especially since they enjoy only three-year terms, makes the *Dewan Negara* more useful as a source of patronage (a 'parking lot for politicians', as one commentator has it[79]) than for protecting States' rights.

With imagination a positive role for the House could be found in terms of checking constitutionality, making or ratifying appointments, or investigating or considering matters that the *Dewan Rakyat* has no time to investigate. As things stand the *Dewan Negara* has been striking for its lack of impact on legislation, on government, or on the practice of the Constitution. It must be ranked as a 'dignified' element in the Constitution that could, in a new and more democratic era, also become an 'efficient' element. The all-important question is, in what way that objective could be achieved. At the very least, the *Dewan Negara* represents a valuable resource that has not been tapped.

[77] Art 86(1).
[78] Tunku Zain 'Abidin Muhriz, *A New Dawn for the Dewan Negara? A Study of Malaysia's Second Chamber and Some Proposals* (Kuala Lumpur, IDEAS Malaysia, 2012).
[79] Ibid.

## VIII. LEGISLATION AND EMERGENCY POWERS

'Jikalau tidak di-pechah royong, di-mana boleh dapat sagu'
(If the palm-trunk is not broken, how is the pith to be extracted?)

We now look at emergency powers, on the basis that these powers drastically affect the law-making powers of Parliament and also the scope of executive power, as well as potentially suspending the operation of parliamentary democracy, as occurred in 2021. Despite the repeal of all emergency laws and proclamations in 2011, emergency powers have recently become a matter of some importance, with two (geographically limited) emergency proclamations made in 2020, together with one proposal (October 2020) for a general emergency proclamation being rejected and another (January 2021) accepted by the *Yang di-Pertuan Agong*, throwing into relief the potential impact of emergency powers on parliamentary democracy. The 2021 emergency involved Parliament virtually shutting down for about six months.

Although provision for extensive emergency powers overriding certain constitutional provisions is by no means unusual,[80] the operation of the constitutional system in Malaysia has been deeply affected by this regime of exception.[81] Even as the Constitution was being drafted, Malaya was still in the throes of this emergency – in effect a civil war – thereby colouring the entire approach to the constitution-making process regarding parliamentary democracy, rights and judicial powers. More recently the issue of emergency powers has also deeply affected the constitutional role of the Rulers, as will shortly be explained.

The inclusion of Article 149 allowing preventive detention, in addition to Article 150, providing for emergency powers, made it constitutionally possible for the temporary regime of exception to transform into a regime of what could be termed ongoing alternative legality. The state has over time used this regime of exception to suppress criticism of Government policies, along with dangerous speech in Malaysia's fragile public spaces. Emergency and national security powers have therefore operated notably as a major incursion on parliamentary law-making, as well as an inhibition on free speech and an incursion on liberty of the person.

---

[80] V Ramraj and A Thiruvengadam (eds), *Emergency Powers in Asia* (Cambridge, Cambridge University Press, 2009).

[81] CV Das, *Governments and Crisis Powers: A Legal Study on the Use of Emergency Powers* (Kuala Lumpur, Malaysian Current Law Journal, 1996).

From 1948, and especially following the assassination in 1951 of the Governor, Sir Henry Gurney, the Communist Party of Malaya (CPM) pursued a policy of guerrilla warfare, striking suddenly and selectively, and then melting into the inaccessible jungle, assisted by sympathetic rural Chinese. This kind of insurgency proved extremely hard to combat conventionally, and the colonial authorities resorted to some extreme measures. Preventive detention for periods of up to two years was authorised, along with the creation, under the 'Briggs Plan', of 'new villages' to contain the rural Chinese population, cutting off the terrorists from their support systems. In addition, punishments were meted out to whole communities suspected of harbouring terrorists or refusing to cooperate with the authorities.[82] This emergency lasted beyond *Merdeka* up to 1960, and terrorist incidents continued to occur sporadically right up until 1989, when the CPM, by then reduced to a pathetic, half-starved remnant, negotiated a settlement with the Malaysian Government. The emergency was extremely costly in terms of human life, property damage, and damage to normal life – and of course to the rule of law and human rights.

In many ways the 1948–60 emergency set the pattern not only for the conduct of future emergencies, but even, in some respects, for what became regular laws, such as the Internal Security Act 1960 and the Societies Act 1966. Even since *Merdeka*, no less than seven emergencies have been proclaimed: in 1964, 1966, 1969, 1977, two in 2020 and one in 2021, the last three in response to the Covid-19 pandemic. The 1966, 1969 and 1977 proclamations were officially regarded as still in force until they were revoked by Parliament in November 2011 (the Government took the view that the 1964 Proclamation was impliedly revoked by the 1969 Proclamation). There was therefore a legal and general state of emergency in Malaysia continually between 1964 and 2011, in spite of the vastly improved security and public order condition of Malaysia over those last four decades. Thus the rule of regular law had to compete with a system of laws which, although not often invoked, existed as a legal alternative for a range of issues, including criminal prosecutions.

The Constitution confers on the *Yang di-Pertuan Agong*[83] broad powers under Article 150 to proclaim an emergency if he is 'satisfied that a grave emergency exists whereby the security, or the economic life, or public order, in the Federation or any part thereof is threatened'.

---

[82] Ibid 101–07.
[83] On the questions whether he acts on the advice of the government in this capacity, see the discussion below.

The scope of emergency powers under Article 150 was drawn widely by the Privy Council in *Stephen Kalong Ningkan v Government of Malaysia*, stressing that an emergency 'is not confined to unlawful use or threat of force in any of its manifestations … [but] is capable of covering a very wide range of situations and occurrences, including such diverse events as wars, famines, earthquakes, floods, *epidemics* and the collapse of civil government'.[84] Furthermore, in 1981 Article 150 was amended so that a proclamation can be issued before the actual occurrence of the threatened event, by way of preventive action, if the *Yang di-Pertuan Agong* is satisfied that there is imminent danger of its occurrence.[85] The same amendment made it permissible to issue proclamations on different grounds or in different circumstances, regardless of the existence of other proclamations; thus two or more emergency proclamations may validly overlap, chronologically or even geographically, and a later proclamation does not impliedly revoke an earlier one. The result of all this, and of further judicial pronouncements, is a breathtakingly wide power to proclaim and act on an emergency proclamation.[86] This power is not generally subject to judicial oversight, as Article 150(8) precludes judicial review of an emergency proclamation.

The immediate consequence of an emergency proclamation is that the Government obtains the power under Article 150 to legislate by ordinances having the same effect as an Act of Parliament, except when both Houses of Parliament are sitting, and provided the *Yang Di-Pertuan Agong* is satisfied that circumstances exist which render it necessary to take immediate action.[87] This power extends to 'any matter with respect to which Parliament has power to make laws, regardless of the legislative or other procedures required to be followed, or the proportion of the total votes required to be had, in either House of Parliament'. Parliament also has the power to pass emergency laws following a proclamation. The provisions of emergency laws cannot be invalidated on the ground of inconsistency with any provision of the Constitution, except those relating to Islamic law; Malay custom and native custom in Sabah or Sarawak; religion; citizenship; or language.[88] Thus almost the entire

---

[84] *Stephen Kalong Ningkan v Government of Malaysia* [1968] 2 MLJ 238, 241–42. Emphasis added.

[85] Constitution (Amendment) Act 1981 (Act A514).

[86] Das (n 81) ch 5.

[87] See the Emergency (Essential Provisions) Ordinance 1/2021, which had inter alia the effect of preventing any elections being held during its period in force during the first seven months of 2021.

[88] Art 150(6A).

body of fundamental rights is effectively in suspension during an emergency in the sense that any legislation pursuant to the emergency can override them.

Laws passed under Article 150 must eventually be laid before both Houses of Parliament and, if not sooner revoked, cease to have effect if annulling resolutions are passed by both Houses, which is what occurred in November 2011. This is without prejudice to anything previously done by virtue of the proclamation or an executive ordinance, or to the executive power to issue a new proclamation, or promulgate any further ordinances. In practice no such parliamentary resolutions were passed until November 2011, so that emergency laws were still in force unless they could be argued to have lapsed as a result of changed circumstances, an argument which was not resolved by the Malaysian courts before being purportedly pre-empted by the ouster clause in Article 150(8).

Emergency laws were for a long time a constant preoccupation of civil society as well as the Human Rights Commission and international commentators.[89] The notorious Emergency (Securities Cases) Regulations 1975 (ESCAR) were particularly opposed by the legal profession (see Chapter 8). These Regulations amended the procedures for criminal trials involving national security (certified by the Attorney-General to be such) in several respects. Notably they removed judicial discretion in sentencing; provided that multiple accused and offences could be tried together even if not connected; and permitted hearsay evidence, which could be given by anonymous witnesses and awarded the same weight as direct evidence. When a juvenile was given a mandatory death sentence under the then new ESCAR provisions (for possession of a firearm in a situation where national security was not in fact implicated), the Bar convened an Extraordinary General Meeting on 18 October 1977 at which, in an unprecedented step, members resolved to boycott all ESCAR cases because provisions were so clearly 'repressive and against the rule of law'.[90]

Given the great extent and alarming potential of these powers, and the ousting of judicial review, the question arises whether the courts are able to act as any kind of check on their exercise. In 1979 in

---

[89] For a description of actual experience of preventive detention in Malaysia, see Kua Kia Soong, *445 Days Behind the Wire: An Account of the October '87 ISA Detentions* (Kuala Lumpur, Research and Resource Centre, Selangor Chinese Assembly Hall, 1989). For an international response, see N Fritz and M Flaherty, *Unjust Order: Malaysia's Internal Security Act* (New York, The Joseph R Crowley Program in International Human Rights, Fordham Law School, 2003).

[90] [1978] 1 MLJ v.

*Teh Cheng Poh v Public Prosecutor*[91] the Privy Council, in its last and most notable judgment on the Malaysian Constitution, relating to ESCAR, held that once Parliament had sat, the executive power to make regulations under emergency ordinances, as well as the power to enact ordinances, lapsed. Thus all regulations under the 1969 Emergency Proclamation made since February 1971, when Parliament was finally summoned, were invalidated. If it were otherwise, the Privy Council noted, the Cabinet could 'pull itself up by its own bootstraps' simply by calling ordinances 'regulations'. In consequence Parliament passed the Emergency (Essential Powers) Act 1979, retroactively operative from 20 February 1971, to validate all of the emergency regulations, including ESCAR, and all actions taken thereunder, and confer on the Director of Operations all the powers granted under Emergency Ordinance No 1 of 1969, which had effectively given him plenary legislative and executive power. As a result of *Teh Cheng Poh* the Constitution was also amended in 1981 so as to introduce in Article 150(8) the ouster clause referred to above, purporting to deprive the courts of any jurisdiction to challenge or call into question, and to make final and conclusive, the Government's satisfaction with regard to the making of a proclamation and the promulgation or continuance in force of an emergency ordinance. The ouster clause is alarming for its implications for the entire constitutional order. It means that the Government can, unobstructed by threat of legal challenge, proclaim an emergency, make law pursuant to it, and continue to give effect to such laws, irrespective of the situation, the reasons, or any change in circumstances, or any impact on rights or democratic government. Such a drastic power can clearly be abused, and it is therefore important to know what checks there are on its exercise.

The consequence of this position regarding judicial review is that the only check on the executive, and the only safeguard for human rights, was thought to be Parliament itself. Parliament too, however, is ineffective in this regard. Not only does the executive have a majority in Parliament, but since the 1981 amendment to Article 150 there is not even an obligation on the executive to summon Parliament, despite the fact that Article 150(3) requires laying the proclamation and ordinances before both Houses of Parliament. However, in October 2020 the Rulers asserted their power to control emergency proclamations, and did so in an unprecedented manner.[92] When Prime Minister Muyhiddin

---

[91] Discussed further in ch 8.

[92] A Harding, 'Acting (or not acting) on lawful (or unlawful) advice in Malaysia: From Windsor to Kuantan and back again', ICONNect Blog, November 2020, available at

proposed an emergency proclamation in order to avoid spread of the Covid-19 pandemic potentially resulting from a general election, the *Yang di-Pertuan Agong,* following consultation with his brother Rulers, rejected the proposal on the grounds that an emergency was not necessary to deal with the situation. While this decision was widely approved, given the inevitable impact of an emergency on parliamentary democracy, it was unclear on what constitutional basis he had acted. Case law appears to indicate conclusively that in this matter the *Yang di-Pertuan Agong* acts on the advice of the Government.[93] The best explanation is perhaps that in this matter the *Yang di-Pertuan Agong* was exercising reserve powers, which would only very exceptionally be exercised in a constitutional monarchy. For this reason, His Majesty was justified in consulting his brother Rulers, as the matter was controversial and would impact on future holders of his office, and was justified in rejecting the proposal for an emergency proclamation. Apart from the impact on parliamentary democracy it should be borne in mind that the Government did not have a clear majority at that time and had not come into power via an election, so that an emergency proclamation would have avoided any parliamentary process to the Government's detriment. The episode adds force also to the idea that the Rulers' powers are not exhaustively codified in the Constitution (see Chapter 5). On two subsequent occasions in the following two months, however, the *Yang di-Pertuan Agong* did agree to a proclamation limited to districts in which, otherwise, a by-election would have been held following a parliamentary vacancy.[94] And on 12 January 2021 he agreed to a federation-wide emergency that resulted in a virtual shutdown of Parliament and postponement of all elections. The emergency came to an end on 1 August 2021 and there was controversy over the Cabinet's decision to revoke ordinances passed thereunder without apparently presenting the instruments before the *Yang di-Pertuan Agong,* while also not acting on his view that these matters should be debated in Parliament.

Despite the fact that Malaysia has been under emergency law for most of its existence, the beast appears to have been tamed in the sense that the Government does not have carte blanche to control both executive

www.iconnectblog.com/2020/11/acting-or-not-acting-on-lawful-or-unlawful-advice-in-malaysia-from-windsor-to-kuantan-and-back-again.

[93] *Abdul Ghani Ali Ahmad & Ors v Public Prosecutor* [2001] 3 MLJ 561. See also *Teh Cheng Poh v Public Prosecutor* [19801 AC 458, 466; and see Art 40.

[94] 'Malaysia invokes emergency to stop by-elections as covid-19 cases rise', CNA, 16 December 2020, available at www.channelnewsasia.com/asia/covid-19-malaysia-emergency-stop-by-elections-sabah-perak-cases-482026.

and legislative powers absolutely. Emergency laws operate in parallel with the regular constitutional and legal system. This is not to say that Government habitually acted under emergency law and ignored regular law and fundamental rights: quite the opposite. What it does mean is that acting under the rule of ordinary law became optional in some cases. For example, corruption prosecutions could be taken forward under emergency law which was still in force up to 2011.[95]

As if the continuation of emergency powers were not enough, the Constitution at Article 149 also provides for the possibility, *irrespective of any emergency*, of the passing of legislation on such bases as a threat of organised violence; the excitement of disaffection against the Government; the promotion of feelings of ill-will and hostility between different races or other classes of the population likely to cause violence; the procurement of alteration, otherwise than by lawful means, of anything by law established; actions prejudicial to the maintenance or the functioning of any supply or service to the public; or actions prejudicial to public order or security. Any provision of such legislation designed to stop such actions may be valid even if inconsistent with fundamental rights provisions or contrary to the division of state and federal powers. It is under this provision that Parliament passed the now-repealed Internal Security Act 1960, and the Dangerous Drugs (Special Preventive Measures) Act 1985, both of which allow for preventive detention. The Security Offences (Special Measures) Act 2012, which was passed under Article 149 following repeal of the Internal Security Act, provides a more limited power of detention on national security grounds compared to its predecessor.

Internal threats were indeed apparent with violent breakdown in social order in 1969 and potentially occurrence of the same situation in 1987, when heightened ethnic tensions came close to sparking riots; *Operasi Lalang* (Weeding Operation) was mounted to detain those whose were raising tensions, along with a variety of others who were simply opposed to the Government.[96] It now seems clear that both in 1969 and in 1987 there was more than an element of exploitation of inter-ethnic strife by political factions for their own ends. For this many entirely innocent people experienced many months of detention. It is a sign of increased concern about the rule of law that on 24 November 2011

---

[95] Eg Anwar Ibrahim was tried in 1998–99 on five counts of corrupt practices under the Emergency (Essential Powers) Ordinance No 22 of 1970, s 2(1): Wu Min Aun, 'The Saga of Anwar Ibrahim' in Harding and Lee (n 53).

[96] Kua Kia Soong (n 89).

the emergency proclamations were at last revoked by Parliament on the Government's motion, entailing the eclipse of hundreds of emergency laws; and that the rejection of an emergency in 2020 was greeted with widespread relief. Yet still there lurks the possibility of unjustified and uncontrolled use of emergency powers, and Article 150 seems to go far beyond what is strictly necessary.

## IX. CONCLUSION

'Bagai bunga dedap, sunggoh merah, berbau tidak'

(Like the coral flower, it may be red, but it has no fragrance)

It is noticeable, and perhaps not surprising in view of the nature of the political process described in this chapter, that political discussion, as well as the daily round of media coverage of political scandal and turmoil, have not habitually engaged with Parliament as an institution. This has changed somewhat with two changes in government since 2018. There appears not to be a large expectation that the great topics of the day will be ventilated in a serious manner in the legislature, which is seen as a body mainly concerned with legislation and a certain amount of political point-scoring, performing nonetheless some important symbolic and practical functions. Even this function was repeatedly denied in practice during 2020–21 under the PN Government. This does not mean that individual MPs or the Opposition are powerless to affect the implementation of policy or ask questions to ministers. Parliament has increasingly seen lively debate and close questioning of ministers, as with the budget debate in 2020.

Assessed purely in terms of its ability to scrutinise legislation and render the executive accountable for its actions Parliament is clearly lacking in sufficient potency. It needs much more respect for parliamentary institutions on the part of ministers, and several further reforms, before Parliament can be rendered really effective. A critical issue is the existence of the risk of defeat of the Government. Despite the loss of the PH majority in March 2020 and a wafer-thin majority for the PN after that, no Malaysian Government has yet been defeated in a parliamentary vote, with the exception of the constitutional amendment bill in 2019, although the budget for 2021 was passed by only three votes. If and when the political will to reform Parliament returns, however, the present institutions, having become in some sense traditional and accepted, will form a good basis for improving on the reform already undertaken.

## FURTHER READING

AJ Harding, *Law, Government and the Constitution in Malaysia* (The Hague, Kluwer, and Kuala Lumpur, Malayan Law Journal, 1996) ch 6.

Mohamad Ariff Md Yusoff, Roosme Hamzah, and Shad Saleem Faruqi (eds), *Law, Principles and Practice in the Dewan Rakyat (House of Representatives) of Malaysia* (Subang Jaya, Thomson Reuters, 2020).

Shad Saleem Faruqi, Document of Destiny: The Constitution of the Federation of Malaysia (Petaling Jaya, The Star, 2008) chs 35–40.

Kevin YL Tan and Thio Li-ann, *Constitutional Law in Malaysia and Singapore* (3rd edn, Singapore LexisNexis, 2010) ch 5.

# 5

# *Territorial Governance: Monarchy and the State Constitutions*

The Powers and Position of the Rulers – State Government Formation and the Limits of Royal Powers – The Conference of Rulers

## I. INTRODUCTION

'Siapa jadi raja, tangan aku ka-dahi juga'

(Whoever becomes Raja, my hands still go to my forehead)

I N CHAPTER ONE we saw how the ancient Malaysian monarchies are deeply related to the constitutional architecture, in particular to federalism. We also saw how their role in relation to Islam remained intact despite British intervention. In Chapter 2 we saw their role to be of some significance in terms of government appointments and the entrenchment of the social contract. The condition of having a Raja (*kerajaan*) has always been an aspect of Malay governance traditions and, as we will see, it still is in many ways. The Rulers' role in constitutional governance, in religion, and in inter-religious conflict has never been more important at any time during the last 100 years. As a unique and important aspect of both tradition and modern governance the role of the Malay monarchies is deserving of its own chapter in this book.

The monarchies have survived four centuries of colonialism following the fall of Malacca in 1511; constitutional interference with their powers; the intensity of party political competition; and the advent of intrusive news media intent on finding scandal around every corner. In a world in which monarchy has become increasingly rationed, confined and subjected to critical scrutiny, the Malaysian monarchies have gone against the trend, becoming in recent years probably more powerful than they have been at any time since 1945.[1] They constitute nearly a quarter of all the world's existing monarchies. That they have survived is attributable to their centrality in Malay culture and government; their association with Malay nationalism in the 1940s; and their ability to adapt to changing times. Beyond that, the Rulers, along with Islam, are essential to the maintenance of the Malay character of the Constitution and at the same time the need for a multi-ethnic, multi-religious society to have a vivid symbol of unity that lies beyond mere politics and constitutional rules. Malaysian constitutionalism seems to be a unique interweaving of two strands: on the one hand, Westminster-style constitutional structures that require the separation of the head of state from the head of government; and, on the other hand, traditional and symbolic elements that speak of Islam and Malay culture. Historically, the Rulers are identified with both of these strands of constitutionalism. There is also the practical point that in a country with a highly developed sense of protocol,[2] Government leaders can safely leave a good deal of time-consuming official duty to neutral but high-profile figures such as the Rulers and notable members of their sometimes large families. However, as we will see in this chapter, Westminster dualism has not always proceeded smoothly in Malaysia. Recent events detailed in Chapter 2 indicate that the Westminster conventions need to be clearly understood by the actors involved, and also operated and adjudicated upon with some care, having regard to their general currency and problematical precedents in constitutional law. However, as a form of what is essentially customary public law they are not easily transplanted, and inevitably acquire localised understandings and precedents.

Of the 13 States of the Federation, nine have a traditional Ruler as Head of State, and every five years one of their number is chosen as *Yang di-Pertuan Agong* at the Federal level. This involves an election by the Conference of Rulers (for which see below) that in effect rotates the position of *Yang di-Pertuan Agong* between the Rulers; a system that is based on the traditional *adat* constitution of Negeri Sembilan.[3]

---

[1] Kobkua Suwannathat-Pian, *Palace, Political Party and Power: A Story of the Socio-Political Development of Malay Kingship* (Singapore, NUS Press, 2011) ch 1.

[2] For a detailed study of royal protocols, see Adib Vincent Tung, *Titles and Ceremonial Traditions of the Royalty and Nobility of the State of Perak, Malaysia* (Perak Academy, Ipoh, 2018). This book contains 970 pages and is devoted to only one of the nine monarchies – a vivid indication of the extensive and complex nature of the subject.

[3] AJ Harding, *Law, Government and the Constitution in Malaysia* (The Hague, Kluwer, and Kuala Lumpur, LexisNexis, 1996) ch 5.

The *Yang di-Pertuan Agong* can be removed by a majority vote within the Conference of Rulers. The Rulers are all styled 'Sultan' apart from the Raja of Perlis and the *Yang di-Pertuan Besar* or '*Yamtuan*' of Negeri Sembilan.

The other four States (Malacca, Penang, Sabah and Sarawak), due to their colonial history, do not have a Ruler but rather a *Yang di-Pertua Negeri* (Governor), who is appointed by the *Yang di-Pertuan Agong* (acting in his discretion), after consulting with the Chief Minister of the State, to a four-year term, and can be removed only by a two-thirds majority in the State Legislative Assembly. It will be noted that as a result of an invariable practice in appointing *bumiputera* as *Yang di-Pertua Negeri*, all Heads of State in Malaysia to date have been *bumiputera*. However, both Governors and Rulers are constitutional heads, as is required by Schedule 8 of the Constitution, which imposes the Westminster conventions on the State Constitutions (discussed in Chapter 2).

With the McMichael Treaties of 1946 creating the Malayan Union the Rulers supposedly surrendered their sovereignty to the Crown, but in the Federation of Malaya Agreement 1948 their sovereignty revived, and was actually a precondition for the agreement itself. The Constitution of 1957, which was preceded by the Rulers' formal assent and blessing,[4] placed the matter of sovereignty beyond doubt by Article 181(1), which preserves the 'sovereignty, prerogatives, powers and jurisdiction of the Rulers ... within their respective territories as hitherto had and enjoyed'. In addition, Article 71(1) guarantees the right of a Ruler 'to succeed and to hold, enjoy and exercise the constitutional rights and privileges of Ruler of that State in accordance with the Constitution of that State'.[5] Moreover, Article 38, which relates to the Conference of Rulers, provides that legislation directly affecting the privileges, position, honours or dignities of the Rulers may not be passed without the consent of the Conference of Rulers.[6] By securing these provisions the Rulers had rescued their constitutional position from virtual abolition in 1946 to complete constitutional entrenchment in 1957, such that to propose the abolition of the monarchy would now constitute the crime of sedition. Nonetheless they are constitutional heads of state and the constitutional

---

[4] Known as the *Wasiat Raja-Raja Melayu* (Declaration of the Malay Rulers), 5 August 1957.

[5] For discussion of the scope of prerogative powers in Malaysia see RH Hickling, 'The prerogative in Malaysia' (1975) 17 *Malaya Law Review* 207; and contrast AJ Harding, 'Monarchy and the prerogative in Malaysia' (1986) 28 *Malaya Law Review* 345.

[6] For instances of this, see below.

system has sometimes seen a struggle between Westminster norms and the traditional respect and even awe in which the Rulers are held by Malays and non-Malays alike. In this chapter we will consider several examples of this struggle in progress and a remarkable turn-around in the Rulers' fortunes.

## II. THE POWERS AND POSITION OF THE RULERS

'Pagar makan padi'

(The fence eats the crop, equivalent to asking, *'quis custodiet ipsos custodes?'*)

As is the case with the *Yang di-Pertuan Agong*, as we have seen in Chapter 2, the Rulers are subject to the constraints of Westminster-style conventions that are set out explicitly in both the Federal and State Constitutions.[7] In virtually all respects the Rulers' constitutional position at the State level is the same as the *Yang di-Pertuan Agong* at the Federal level. As we also saw in Chapter 2, they have merely the classic Bagehot rights 'to be consulted, to encourage and to warn'. The State Constitutions, although pre-existing the Federal Constitution, are regulated by it. Not only is the Federal Constitution itself supreme law under Article 4, so that any inconsistent law is rendered invalid, but in addition Article 71(4) and Schedule 8 of the Federal Constitution provide that the State Constitutions must include what Schedule 8 calls 'the essential provisions', or else provisions substantially to the same effect. Parliament can if necessary amend the State Constitution to enforce Article 71(4), and under Article 71(3) if it appears to Parliament that State or Federal constitutional provisions are being habitually disregarded in any State, Parliament may by law provide for securing compliance with those provisions. The provisions have, however, not yet seen the occasion for their use. In an extreme case, as occurred in Sarawak in 1966 (see Chapter 6), the State Constitution can be temporarily amended by emergency law.[8] The essential provisions are in effect equivalent to the

---

[7] HRH Raja Azlan Shah, 'The Role of Constitutional Rulers in Malaysia' in FA Trindade and HP Lee (eds), *The Constitution of Malaysia: Further Perspectives and Developments* (Kuala Lumpur, Oxford University Press, 1986); HP Lee, 'Constitutional Heads and Judicial intervention' in Wu Min Aun (ed), *Public Law in Contemporary Malaysia* (Petaling Jaya, Longman, 1999).

[8] *Stephen Kalong Ningkan v Government of Malaysia* [1968] 2 MLJ 238, PC.

Westminster constitutional conventions. Thus, like the *Yang di-Pertuan Agong* at the Federal level, a Ruler is required to act on the advice of the Executive Council (the State's Cabinet).[9] He may act in his discretion only in prescribed circumstances such as the appointment of the *Menteri Besar* (Chief Minister); the withholding of consent to a dissolution of the Legislative Assembly;[10] and the performance of his functions as the Head of Islam. He is also required, as we will see, to assent to Bills passed by the Legislative Assembly.

With regard to legislative powers, before 1984 the *Yang di-Pertuan Agong* had no role to play – and the same was true of the Rulers at the State level – except to signify assent to Bills duly passed by the legislature, and summon and prorogue the legislature as advised by the Head of Government. However, there had been several instances of Rulers simply failing to assent to Bills passed by State Legislative Assemblies, which was usually a way of showing displeasure or disagreement with the State Government. In 1983 the Government, fearing that the next *Yang di-Pertuan Agong* might interfere in federal politics even more deleteriously (in fact he had made a speech saying he would declare an emergency and throw out all the politicians[11]), introduced a controversial constitutional amendment Bill relating to the powers of the Rulers. For Bills passed by Parliament or State Legislative Assemblies the amendment provided for automatic royal assent if assent was not forthcoming 15 days after a Bill's presentation. The Bill also vested the power to proclaim an emergency – exercised hitherto, on Government advice, by the *Yang di-Pertuan Agong* – in the sole hands of the Prime Minister.

The result of this was, ironically, the precipitation of the very mischief the amendment was designed to prevent. The *Yang di-Pertuan Agong*, with the agreement of the other Rulers, refused his assent to the amendment, and the five-month constitutional crisis that followed resulted in an embarrassing climb-down by the Government. A compromise was reached under which the *Yang di-Pertuan Agong* was given the right to refer Bills back to Parliament with his reasons, and the Government

---

[9] By virtue of the Constitution (Amendment) Act 1994, under its amendments to Art 40 and Sch 8, both the *Yang di-Pertuan Agong* and the Rulers at the State level must also *act* on the advice proffered.

[10] Consent to dissolution was refused in two cases: Kelantan in 1977 and Sabah in 1994.

[11] RS Milne and DK Mauzy, *Malaysian Politics under Mahathir* (London, Routledge, 1999) 32.

withdrew the provision concerning emergency proclamations.[12] The Rulers on their part undertook not to withhold their assent to Bills at the State level, although this was not specifically dealt with in the agreed amendment.[13]

As a result of this crisis the Constitution (Amendment) Act 1984 gave the *Yang di-Pertuan Agong* power to send a Bill that had been passed by Parliament back to the House where it originated within 30 days, with a statement of the reasons for his objection to the Bill or any provision in it. If the Bill was passed again by both Houses then it became law automatically if the *Yang di-Pertuan Agong* did not assent to it within another 30 days after it was presented to him. Following a further constitutional amendment in 1994, the position has been greatly simplified, and the powers of the *Yang di-Pertuan Agong* reduced. Now he must assent to a Bill within 30 days, otherwise, on expiry of the 30-day period, it becomes law as if he had assented to it. There has as a result been no further difficulty over the royal assent at either level of government, with the exception of the 1993 crisis, to which we now turn.

The 1983 crisis did not resolve entirely the position of the Rulers, some of whom continued to interfere in politics, occasionally falling out with the *Menteri Besar*. In Kelantan the Ruler even campaigned for the opposition in the 1990 general election. In 1988 the *Yang di-Pertuan Agong* himself was involved in the public furore over the dismissal of the Lord President of the Supreme Court, Tun Salleh Abas (see Chapter 8). Alleged criminal acts by the late Sultan of Johor, both when he was the Crown Prince of Johor and when he was the *Yang di-Pertuan Agong*, were the subject of extensive speculation. An MP listed no fewer than 15 allegations of criminal acts by the Sultan and six by two of his sons. The press highlighted the luxurious lifestyle of the Rulers, and their occasional flouting of the law; in one instance the Sultan of Pahang was criticised for spending RM4000 per day maintaining his horses in a luxurious lifestyle including air-conditioned stables.[14] Allegations of unlawful conduct could not be pursued in the courts because of the Rulers' constitutional immunity from suit. Under Articles 32(1) and 181(2) the *Yang di-Pertuan Agong* and the Rulers were not liable to any proceedings

[12] We saw in ch 2 how important this is as an aspect of cabinet government.

[13] HP Lee, 'The Malaysian constitutional crisis: King, Rulers and royal assent' (1984) 3 *Lawasia* (NS) 22; HF Rawlings, 'The Malaysian Constitutional Crisis of 1983' (1986) 35 *International and Comparative Law Quarterly* 237; S Barraclough and P Arudsothy, *The 1983 Malaysian Constitutional Crisis: Two Views and Selected Documents* (Brisbane, Griffith University, 1985).

[14] Suwannathat-Pian (n 1) 363.

whatsoever in any court. This immunity related to the Rulers acting in their personal capacity and did not of course mean that the Federal or State Government enjoyed legal immunity from acts done in the name of the Head of State. This had been clarified by local cases and in 1980 the Privy Council itself.[15]

Clearly the problem had to be addressed. First, the Government attempted to get the Rulers to agree to act within the law and the Constitution by a self-regulatory Proclamation of Constitutional Principles dated 4 July 1992, which was designed, after some negotiations between the Rulers and the Government, to place the Rulers in a straightjacket of their own making by clarifying the operation of constitutional conventions and affirming the Rulers' intention of acting within the law.[16] However, the document that emerged was itself rather unclear on some points, and was signed only by the *Yang di-Pertuan Agong* and six of the nine Rulers. Moreover, it was clearly not constitutionally binding. Realising that the consensual approach had failed, the Government used an assault by the Sultan of Johor on a hockey coach to signal its intention of hardening its approach and using its two-thirds' majority in Parliament to amend the Constitution.[17]

A Bill to amend the Constitution was tabled in Parliament and was passed by both Houses in January 1993. The Bill removed the immunity of the *Yang di-Pertuan Agong* and the other Rulers from suit when acting in a personal capacity, and gave the jurisdiction in such cases (criminal and civil) to a Special Court consisting of the Chief Justice of the Federal Court (formerly the Lord President of the Supreme Court) as Chairman, the Chief Judges (formerly Chief Justices) of the two High Courts, and two other Judges or former Judges of the Federal Court (formerly the Supreme Court) or the High Court, appointed by the Conference of Rulers. The Bill also conferred parliamentary privilege in respect of anything said during proceedings in Parliament or a State Legislative Assembly concerning a Ruler, except for advocating the abolition of the Ruler's constitutional powers.[18]

---

[15] *Stephen Kalong Ningkan v Tun Abang Haji Openg and Tawi Sli (No2)* [1967] 1 MLJ 46; *Teh Cheng Poh v Public Prosecutor* [1980] AC 458, 467, per Lord Diplock.

[16] See 'Statement by the Keeper of the Rulers' Seal and Proclamation of Constitutional Principles', Suwannathat-Pian (n 1) app 1.

[17] Shad Saleem Faruqi, 'The sceptre, the sword and the Constitution at the cross-road (a commentary on the Constitution Amendment Bill 1993)' (1993) 1 *Current Law Journal* xlv.

[18] M Gillen, 'The Malay Rulers' loss of immunity' (1995) 29 *University of British Columbia Law Review* 163.

However, since legislation affecting the powers and privileges of the Rulers, as we have seen above, requires the assent of the Conference of Rulers (the Government nonetheless disputed this), the Conference met and issued a statement saying that it had unanimously decided not to consent to the Bill, on the grounds that further consultation was required in respect of such an unprecedented measure; that the Bill was unconstitutional as it trespassed on States' rights; and that the Special Court was an unsuitable forum for dealing with matters relating to the Rulers. However, the statement also recognised that 'there cannot be two systems of justice in the country', and that 'no Ruler has the right to hurt or cause harm to another person'. It also suggested, instead of a Special Court, an Advisory Board, which would have power to recommend the removal of a Ruler. Just as in 1983, the inevitable outcome was that an accommodation was reached. In February 1993, following a crucial meeting of the Conference of Rulers, the Rulers and the Government issued a joint declaration saying that an agreement had been reached whereby amendments to the Bill would be returned to the *Dewan Rakyat* by the *Yang di-Pertuan Agong*, and the Rulers would notify at the same time their assent to the amended Bill.[19]

The Bill in its amended form was passed by Parliament in March 1993. It provided for a new Part XV of the Constitution entitled 'Proceedings Against the *Yang di-Pertuan Agong* and the Rulers'. Article 182 provides for a Special Court, constituted as in the original version of the Bill. The Special Court has exclusive jurisdiction (similar to that of the inferior courts, the High Court and the Federal Court), under the Constitution or any Federal law, to try all offences committed in the Federation by the *Yang di-Pertuan Agong* or a Ruler, and all civil cases by or against them, wherever the cause of action arose. However, there are two limitations. First, proceedings may only be taken by or against the *Yang di-Pertuan Agong* or a Ruler in his personal capacity. Secondly, proceedings may not be brought against them except with the consent of the Attorney-General. If the Ruler is convicted of an offence and sentenced to more than one day's imprisonment, he ceases to be the Ruler of the State unless he receives a free pardon. Otherwise, the amendments are in the same terms as the original version of the Bill.[20] Since 1993 there have been only two cases dealt with by the Special Court, both of which were civil cases

---

[19] Ibid; and Harding (n 3) 76ff.
[20] AJ Harding, 'Sovereigns immune? The Malaysian monarchy crisis' (1993) 327 *The Round Table* 305.

against a Ruler. The first in 1996 failed for lack of jurisdiction because the plaintiff was not a Malaysian citizen; the second, in 2008, succeeded, when the Ruler of Negeri Sembilan was ordered to honour the terms of a letter of credit.[21]

If the 1983 crisis was a draw and the 1993 crisis a defeat for the Rulers, they have since that time proved able to reassert the role of the monarchy both in terms of constitutional power and in terms of their influence in society. Partly this has resulted from subsidence of public disquiet concerning outrageous royal actions. This in turn can be attributed to the existence of the Special Court and to a realisation by the Rulers that their public behaviour must be not just lawful, but exemplary.

Since the end of their bête-noir Prime Minister Dr Mahathir's period in office (2003) the Rulers have improved their position in a turn-around even more remarkable than that of the 1940s. Indeed, whereas previously, especially under the Tunku and Mahathir, it was the task of politicians to guard the Rulers 'against weaknesses and follies', it seems now to be, more accurately, the Rulers' perceived role to guard politicians against *their* weaknesses and follies.[22] The ironical result of public anger concerning the Rulers' and their families' behaviour, and the two constitutional amendments that forced them onto the narrow way of the rule of law and constitutional government, has been to improve their behaviour and image beyond recognition. In 2019 the Sultan of Kelantan resigned as *Yang di-Pertuan Agong*, under pressure from the Rulers concerning his treatment for drug addiction and marriage to a Russian model who, it was speculated, might, as a non-Malay non-Muslim become his *Raja Permaisuri* (Queen).[23] Nonetheless, the trend has been the replacement of the Rulers of the previous generation with a new generation of enlightened, highly educated and politically sensitive Rulers and princes, who have gone out of their way to fulfil, or perhaps even over-fulfil, the ideal of the Ruler as the meritorious and politically neutral guardian of the Constitution, morality and justice.

These royals include the Rulers of Perak, Selangor, Terengganu, Perlis and Johor. The signal example, however, and leader of this trend is Sultan Nazrin Shah of Perak, who holds a PhD in political economy

---

[21] HP Lee, 'Malaysian royalty and the Special Court' in AJ Harding and P Nicholson (eds), *New Courts in Asia* (London, Routledge, 2010).
[22] Suwannathat-Pian (n 1) 339–44.
[23] 'Sultan Muhammad V steps down as Malaysia's King', *Straits Times*, 6 January 2019.

and government from Harvard, and is a published academic author.[24] He has in the last few years, in both writing and speeches outlined a version of the monarchy that diverges as far as is perhaps conceivable from its image during the Mahathir era. This ideal sees the Ruler as a check on government and a father-figure for society in general; as a kind of roving ombudsman who will not stop short of sharp criticism of corruption, mismanagement, abuse of power, lapses from religious virtue, and socially destabilising behaviour. Sultan Nazrin has also in his speeches emphasised the importance of constitutional values such as the rule of law and judicial independence.

Kobkua Suwannathat-Pian expresses the new ideal of monarchy in the following words:

> ... the ugly and unacceptable side of the old traditional lifestyle whereby the Rulers and princes could indulge in socio-economic excesses and vices [has] no place in the modern Malaysian world. As Rulers of their individual states, the Malay royalty is required to act responsibly, legally, compassionately, and be racially-blinded in both their private and public capacities. As constitutional monarchs, the [*Yang di-Pertuan Agong*] and the Rulers are expected to be fountains of justice and mercy, and to perform their fundamental duties of advising, warning and being consulted, in a manner which would help to bring balance to the administration of the country, and to safeguard the wellbeing of all Malaysians. The new royal role certainly goes beyond what was understood to be the responsibility and role of a constitutional monarch ever practised in the country.[25]

In performing these functions, we can note that the Ruler is seen as 'racially-blinded' – in other words, combining Malay and Islamic leadership with a role as protector of minorities. There is more than a hint here of learning the lesson of Thailand's King Bhumipol, who reached unassailability through Buddhistic virtue.[26] It also suggests a role as potential mediator in inter-communal disputes. The Rulers have clearly started to take a more active role in Malaysian society. Where in the past they have tended to be remote and sometimes even feared, they are now more likely to be seen in shirtsleeves engaging with the poor and with social problems or religious conflicts. This trend has been marked since

---

[24] Sultan Nazrin Shah, *Striving for Inclusive Development: From Pangkor to a Modern Malaysian State* (Oxford, OUP, 2020).

[25] Suwannathat-Pian (n 1) 383.

[26] AJ Harding and P Leyland, *The Constitutional System of Thailand: A Contextual Analysis* (Oxford, Hart Publishing, 2011) ch 1.

the 2008 elections dented the BN and UMNO's political dominance that goes back to 1955.

The present author has used the term 'Nazrinian' to describe this new, enhanced, monarchy,[27] which sees the traditional Rulers as enlightened and exemplary; serving a community defined by multiculturalism but also Heads of Islam and protectors of the Malays (this is not seen as a contradiction); and not necessarily limited by constitutional texts or Westminster-style conventions. This is despite the fact that an examination of the Malaysian Federal Constitution and the various Malaysian State constitutions would appear to confirm that all we see is a monarchy system defined by these Westminster conventions. In practice, however, Malaysia's monarchy system is more accurately described (following Kumarasingham[28]) as 'Eastminster' than 'Westminster'.

Sultan Nazrin at a conference on 'Royal Revival' at Putrajaya in August 2017 described the Rulers' role in these terms:

> The King is not a monumental ornament – without life – without soul … everything that happens is in the vision and hearing of the King … it is a mistake to think that the role of a constitutional monarch is just like a President, limited to what is written in the constitution. The role of the constitutional monarch is beyond what is contained in the constitution.

In what we might see as a variation on the Nazrinian theme, Sultan Ibrahim of Johor, on the other hand, has mainly relied on Johor's own pre-federation constitutional traditions to legitimise a distinctly anti-federal and anti-Westminster stance. This stance also specifically promotes multiculturalism and religious toleration.[29] In an incident in December 2017, for example, the Sultan severely criticised a Muslim launderette owner who excluded non-Muslims from using his launderette; this stance, to considerable public applause, was backed by a statement of all the Rulers emphasising multi-culturalism and opposition to extremism in religion. During the prolonged crisis over the 1Malaysia Development

---

[27] AJ Harding, '"Nazrinian" monarchy in Malaysia: The resilience and revival of a traditional institution' in AJ Harding and Dian AH Shah (eds), *Law and Society in Malaysia* (Abingdon, Routledge, 2017); AJ Harding, 'The Rulers and the centrality of conventions in Malaysia's "Eastminster" constitution' in H Kumarasingham (ed), *Viceregalism: The Crown as Head of State in Political Crises in the Post-War Commonwealth* (Cham, Switzerland, Palgrave, 2020).

[28] H Kumarasingham, 'Eastminster – decolonisation and state-building in British Asia' in H Kumarasingham (ed), *Constitution-Making in Asia – Decolonisation and State-Building in the Aftermath of the British Empire* (London, Routledge, 2016).

[29] Harding (2020) (n 27) 261, 271–72.

Berhad ('1MDB') scandal (discussed in Chapter 2) it is noteworthy that attention turned to the Rulers in search of leadership that might compel accountability for the missing billions, which neither law nor political process had at that juncture (2015) managed to achieve; in the event 1MDB became an election issue that resulted in a change of government and concerted action to punish culprits and recover assets.[30]

This enhanced Nazrinian role for the Rulers appears to be acceptable in contemporary Malaysian society,[31] one question that seems to arise is whether the Rulers are to enjoy increasing immunity from criticism of the way they perform this role, even as their *legal* immunities are removed.

### III. STATE GOVERNMENT FORMATION AND THE LIMITS OF ROYAL POWERS

'Burong pipit sama enggang, mana boleh sama terbang?'

(Sparrows and hornbills, how shall they fly together?)

Problems in the operation of constitutional conventions with regard to the Rulers' role in government formation and survival at the State level have been a perennial problem in Malaysia, and more so since the 2008 elections, which seem to have given impetus to Nazrinian monarchy in the context of government formation and dismissal. In Terengganu a constitutional crisis erupted following the 2008 election when the Ruler rejected the BN's sitting candidate, who had overwhelming BN support, after the BN won the State election. Another BN Assemblyman was appointed by the Ruler, the Prime Minister complaining that the appointment was unconstitutional. Amidst threats of dissolution of the Assembly and support for the *Menteri Besar* from PAS, who were actually in opposition in the Assembly, the Prime Minister backed down, and the *Menteri Besar* survived. In these instances the Ruler did not even feel obliged to explain his preference. In both Selangor and Perak the appointment of the Member of the Assembly proffered by the PR coalition, which was

---

[30] Ibid 261.

[31] A research project by the Institute of Southeast Asian Studies in Singapore in 2017 found that 75% of Johor residents approved of occasional interventions in politics by the Ruler: Norshahril Saat, 'Johor survey 2017: Attitudes towards Islam, governance and the Sultan', *Perspective*, Issue 2017/ 83 (Singapore, ISEAS, 2017).

successful in the election, was not automatically endorsed but was the subject of searching inquiry by the Ruler.[32]

In one instance arising from the political convulsion of 2008 the matter is particularly instructive in the light of the new politics and Nazrinian monarchy, and eventually went to the highest court. The State Constitution in those States that have a Ruler as Head of State usually requires the *Menteri Besar* to be Malay (in Penang, by contrast, the Chief Minister has usually been Chinese). The Ruler is, however, empowered, in his discretion, to override any provisions in the State Constitution restricting his choice of *Menteri Besar* if, in his opinion, it is necessary to do so in order to comply with the duty to appoint whoever has the confidence of the Assembly. This issue arose in Perak in March 2008, but instead of asking the Ruler to override the constitutional provision regarding the appointment of the *Menteri Besar* by appointing the leader of the party with most seats, which would have meant appointing a Chinese *Menteri Besar*, the PR proffered a Malay PAS Member, Datuk Nizar, who was acceptable to all three parties in the PR, even though PAS had the least number of seats. Nizar took office but was soon in trouble with the Ruler when he purported to transfer a religious official without consulting the Ruler, who is the Head of Islam in the State.

As is explained above, the Constitution of Perak, along with the other State Constitutions, provides for the operation of Westminster-style conventions. Under Article 16(2)(a), in the context of appointment of the Executive Council:

> His Royal Highness shall first of all appoint as *Menteri Besar* to preside over the Executive Council a member of the Legislative Assembly who in his judgement is likely to command the confidence of a majority of members of the Assembly ...

Article 16(6) goes on to state:

> If the *Menteri Besar* ceases to command the confidence of the majority of the members of the Legislative Assembly, then, unless at his request His Royal Highness dissolves the Legislative Assembly, then he shall tender the resignation of the Executive Council.

There is no express provision for the dismissal of the *Menteri Besar*.

In a 59-member Assembly, the PR held 31 seats, while the BN held 28 seats. In February 2009 three PR Assemblymen apparently

---

[32] Suwannathat-Pian (n 1) 388–90.

announced their resignations from the assembly, leaving the assembly apparently deadlocked at 28:28. The three defectors then switched sides to the BN. Nizar approached the Ruler on 5 February 2009 for a dissolution 'to resolve the deadlock' in the Assembly. The Ruler refused the request, but before informing Nizar of his decision he had met with 31 assemblymen and satisfied himself that these 31 members (including the three defectors) supported the BN leader, Datuk Zambry, as the *Menteri Besar*. Accordingly, the Ruler, immediately following his refusal of a request for dissolution, informed Nizar that he no longer commanded the confidence of a majority of the Assembly and asked for his resignation. This was not forthcoming, but later the same day the Ruler's office issued a press statement stating that the office of *Menteri Besar* had fallen vacant and that Zambry had been appointed as he commanded the confidence of a majority in the Assembly. Thus Nizar was ousted without any vote being held in the Assembly. He sued Zambry for declarations to the effect that he, Nizar, was still the *Menteri Besar* of Perak. The courts had to decide whether the Ruler had power in effect to dismiss the *Menteri Besar* by declaring the office vacant and appointing another Member, there being no express power of dismissal in the Constitution; and whether such power, if it existed, could be exercised on the basis of events occurring outside the Assembly, there having been no motion of no confidence or similar event in the Assembly.

The case caused considerable excitement across the country. A High Court decision in favour of Nizar was appealed to the Court of Appeal successfully by Zambry, who again succeeded on a further appeal by Nizar to the Federal Court.[33] The outcome was that the courts read into the Constitution a power to declare the office of *Menteri Besar* vacant, and found it was constitutionally valid for the Ruler to take such action even without a vote in the Assembly. The decision breaks new ground in allowing the Ruler considerable latitude, which is not apparent in the constitutional text or in general understandings of constitutional conventions, to reach his own judgement as to the issue of the legislature's continued confidence in the head of government. It is not only a highly problematical understanding of the notion of

---

[33] *Datuk Nizar Jamaluddin v Datuk Seri Zambry Abdul Kadir* [2010] 2 MLJ 285. For an extensive critique and discussion of the Perak crisis, see A Quay (ed), *Perak: A State of Crisis* (Loyarburok, Kuala Lumpur, 2010).

confidence and the proper role of the head of state in a Westminster-style constitution, it also appears to be contrary to Malaysian precedent, which suggests that confidence can only be ascertained on the floor of the legislature.[34] This proposition has now been dented by the way in which a change of government at the Federal level was effected in March 2020, as discussed in Chapter 2, and by continuing speculation as to the PN Government's majority since that time. It also conjures up the possibility of royal interference in the operation of the Constitution at both state and federal levels, and of the monarchy becoming a political football as party political competition continues to intensify.

Despite the difficulties with this case, the Malaysian courts have at least, as in this example, usually been both willing to exercise jurisdiction in political cases involving conventions, and also willing to pronounce clearly on the role of the head of state. For example, in 1985 they intervened in a constitutional crisis in Sabah to quash an appointment of a Chief Minister.[35] The State elections had produced a close result, PBS gaining 25 out of the 48 seats, USNO 16, and Berjaya, which had been the State Government since 1976, six. PBS had an overall majority, even if a small one, and its Leader, Datuk Joseph Pairin Kitingan, expected to be appointed Chief Minister. However, at about 3.40am on the night of the announcement of the election results, Tun Mustapha Harun and Harris Salleh, the Leaders of USNO and Berjaya, visited the residence of the *Yang di-Pertua Negeri* (Governor), Tun Adnan, and prevailed upon him to appoint Tun Mustapha as Chief Minister on the basis that USNO and Berjaya had 22 seats, but with the appointment of an additional six members who had to be nominated by the *Yang di-Pertua Negeri*, they would have an overall majority in the Assembly. Tun Adnan had not been officially made aware of the election results. He was shown a piece of paper which said 'we have no confidence in you and will remove you', which he interpreted as a threat to his life. At about 5.30am he swore in Tun Mustapha as Chief Minister. At 2.30pm the same day Tun Adnan wrote to Tun Mustapha revoking his appointment, and informed Datuk Pairin of this. At 8pm he swore in the latter as Chief Minister. Tun Adnan had never given Tun Mustapha the usual Instrument of Appointment.

---

[34] *Stephen Kalong Ningkan v Tun Haji Openg and Tawi Sli* [1966] 2 MLJ 187.
[35] *Tun Datu Haji Mustapha bin Datu Harun v Tun Datuk Haji Mohamed Adnan Robert and Datuk Joseph Pairin Kitingan (No 2)* [1986] 2 MLJ 420.

Tun Mustapha challenged the validity of the revocation of his appointment and of Datuk Pairin's appointment, seeking declarations that he himself had been validly appointed, and was still the Chief Minister. In the meantime the Assembly passed two votes of confidence in Datuk Pairin. The defendants (Tun Adnan and Datuk Pairin) objected that the court had no jurisdiction over the questions at issue, because they concerned the manner of exercise of discretion by the Head of State and raised political questions which should be, and had been, dealt with by the legislature and not by the courts. The Judge held that although the court had no jurisdiction to question the manner of exercise of discretion by the Head of State, it did have jurisdiction to consider whether there had in law been an appointment, which, in view of the defendants' reliance on allegations of conspiracy, misrepresentation, fraud and duress, was in issue. The questions involved were legal, constitutional, ones within the jurisdiction of the court and were distinct from the political question of the confidence of the Assembly. The defendants appealed to the Supreme Court, which upheld the Judge's decision, and the matter was sent back for trial.

In an unimpeachable decision the Judge held that the Head of State had not exercised his judgement on the issue of confidence because he had not received the official results of the election, and because the appointment of Mustapha had been the result of the cumulative effect of the pressure and threats operating on his mind, and that accordingly the swearing-in was null and void. It was also held that in exercising his judgement the Head of State had to consider the position when, following a general election, the nominated members had yet to be appointed: they could only be appointed on the advice of the Cabinet, which could itself only be appointed after the appointment of the Chief Minister. Finally, he held that the appointment of a Chief Minister had to be signified by a signed Instrument of Appointment under the Public Seal, a matter required by unbroken convention in Sabah.

These are not the only occasions on which constitutional conventions have given rise to uncertainty, even though they are written into the Federal and State Constitutions. Happily this very fact has enabled the courts to take custody of conventions and treat them as justiciable. While the Sabah case is reassuring as evidence of the courts' willingness to enforce the spirit as well as the letter of the Constitution, the Perak decision seems to be a high-water mark for expansion of the Ruler's constitutional powers and creates some uncertainty as to where this kind of reasoning could lead. Indeed, as we saw in Chapter 2, such uncertainty led to a hotly disputed appointment of Malaysia's eighth Prime Minister in 2020, when the *Yang di-Pertuan Agong* resorted to extensive extra-parliamentary evidence to make his decision as to majority support.

## IV. THE CONFERENCE OF RULERS

'Yang tegak di-sokong'
(What is already upright is buttressed)

In 1897, meetings of the Rulers or Durbars were instituted. This led to the creation of the Conference of Rulers under the Federation of Malaya Agreement 1948, and its retention in the *Merdeka* Constitution as an expression of the Rulers' resistance to any erosion of their sovereignty, where they saw some strength in numbers and constitutional entrenchment. A distinction needs to be drawn between two kinds of function performed by the Conference.

First, it discusses questions of national policy. Here the Rulers meet with the *Yang di-Pertua Negeri* of the four States without a Ruler, as well as the *Yang di-Pertuan Agong*, the Prime Minister and the *Menteri Besar* or Chief Minister of each State. The Heads of State act on advice in this capacity. The Constitution requires that the Conference be consulted before any change in policy affecting administrative action under Article 153 (special privileges: see Chapter 2). In practice the Conference is primarily a useful means of discussing federal–state relations outside the glare of publicity, and without confrontation, as it has no actual powers in this regard.

Second, it performs functions of a constitutional nature, in relation principally to the monarchy itself and religion; but here the Conference consists only of the nine Rulers and each Ruler acts in his discretion. These functions include the election of a *Yang di-Pertuan Agong*; giving consent to any law altering State boundaries or affecting the privileges of the Rulers; and giving advice on any appointment which requires the Conference's consent or where the Conference is required to be consulted. This latter function includes, most importantly, the appointments of the Chief Justice of the Federal Court, the President of the Court of Appeal, the Chief Judges of the High Court in Malaya and the High Court of Sabah and Sarawak, the Judges of the High Court, the Auditor-General, and the Chairmen and members of the Public Service Commission and the Election Commission. In relation to religion the Conference can extend religious observances to the whole Federation, and can also give rulings on some religious issues: in one instance it was forceful in reminding the Islamic Development Department that it had no power to issue a fatwa on the propriety of Muslims participating in yoga.[36]

The Conference has also begun in recent years to assert itself in relation to judicial appointments, on one occasion successfully rejecting the Prime Minister's nominee for a senior judicial appointment even though its role is stated as merely that of being consulted.[37] Moreover in 2018 the Rulers initially objected to the appointment of a non-Malay / Muslim as Attorney-General, even though there is no such restriction of the choice of Attorney-General and the Rulers have no constitutional role in relation to the appointment.[38] The Prime Minister's choice of Attorney-General was eventually confirmed by the *Yang di-Pertuan Agong*.

One significant power that falls under this second type of function relates to the *Rukunegara* amendments, as a result of which Article 159, which deals with constitutional amendments, was amended to impose the requirement of consent to the passing of constitutional amendments and ordinary laws relating to the 'sensitive issues': citizenship, the special privileges of Malays and natives of Sabah and Sarawak, the national language, and the Rulers themselves; and laws governing the questioning of policy on those issues.[39] In effect, the Conference of Rulers has been given the task of policing any attempt to reverse the *Rukunegara* amendments, as though the social contract itself is entrusted to the Rulers collectively. This indicates how the Rulers fulfil the dual role of being guardians of Malay rights and also protectors of the legitimate interests of non-Malays. This dual role can also be seen in the intervention of the Sultan of Selangor in the DUMC church-raid issue, where he appeared both to protect Muslims from attempts to convert them from Islam while at the same time encouraging Christians to assert, but realise the limits of, their religious freedom.[40] In practice the Conference has indeed provided evidence that it sees itself as the guardian of the social contract,

---

[36] Suwannathat-Pian (n 1) 398.

[37] Ibid 387–88. For a positive construction of what is meant by consultation in this and other contexts, see JC Fong, *Constitutional Federalism in Malaysia* (Petaling Jaya, Sweet and Maxwell Asia, 2008) ch 9.

[38] 'Agong consents to appointment of Tommy Thomas as Attorney-General', *New Straits Times*, 5 June 2018.

[39] See ch 3.

[40] Sultan: Insufficient Evidence for Prosecution in JAIS Raid', *Free Malaysiakini*, 11 October 2011, www.freemalaysiakini.com/?p=16355.

as it reminded everybody in a sternly worded 'Special Press Statement' dated 16 October 2008.[41]

## V. CONCLUSION

'Gajah masok kampong'

(An elephant enters the village – used especially of a visit by the Raja)

We have seen in this chapter how even debates about the position of Malaysia's monarchies bring us ineluctably back to the nature of governance, basic freedoms and the role of religion and ethnicity in a situation of conceptually fraught and contested democracy. There are clearly advantages and disadvantages in the rejuvenated twenty-first century monarchy. Malaysians themselves seem not to have made up their minds at this early stage of monarchy renewal whether they actually approve of the development. Most would welcome the distinct improvement in royal behaviour, making the Rulers into exemplary figures. Some would see the monarchy as an antidote to the arrogance and unethical behaviour of some politicians, and also as a recourse when all else fails, especially in inter-religious matters. However, it is uncertain whether the majority are content to see the Rulers going beyond the strict confines of the constitutional text in the way the royal house of Perak appears to envisage. Whether this version of the monarchy is merely a by-product of a situation where the BN is no longer seen as a protector,[42] but the opposition also has limited power, remains to be seen. It is especially noteworthy that the Rulers were widely entreated to resolve the situation created by the 1MDB scandal, when it appeared that political leadership was the cause of, rather than the solution to, a major issue of kleptocracy.

### FURTHER READING

AJ Harding, 'The Rulers and the centrality of conventions in Malaysia's "Eastminster" constitution' in H Kumarasingham (ed), *Viceregalism: The Crown as Head of State in Political Crises in the Post-War Commonwealth* (Cham, Switzerland, Palgrave, 2020).

---

[41] Suwannathat-Pian (n 1) app 3.

[42] Chandra Muzaffar, *Protector? An Analysis of the Concept and Practice of Loyalty in Leader-Led Relationships within Malay Society* (Penang, Aliran, 1979).

AC Milner, *Malaysian Monarchy and the Bonding of the Nation* (Bangi, Penerbit UKM, 2011).

V Sinndurai (ed), *HRH Sultan Azlan Shah: Constitutional Monarchy, Rule of Law and Good Governance – Selected Papers and Speeches* (Kuala Lumpur, Professional Law Books, and Petaling Jaya, Sweet and Maxwell Asia, 2004).

Kobkua Suwannathat-Pian, *Palace, Political Party and Power: A Story of the Socio-Political Development of Malay Kingship* (Singapore, NUS Press, 2011).

# 6

# Territorial Governance: Federal, State and Local Government

Character of Malaysian Federalism – Federal and State Powers – Federal and State Finance – Special Position of Sabah and Sarawak – Local Government

## I. INTRODUCTION

'Jamah lubah jampat datai, Berumban bemalam rantau jalai'

(In the spirit of federalism, this is a Sarawakian proverb: 'If you are patient you will arrive soon enough, if you are in a hurry you will spend the night half way'. More haste, less speed – a good way, perhaps, to embark on the federal project.)

I N CHAPTER ONE we saw how the adoption of a federal structure was a necessary condition for independence and also a necessary consequence of opposition to the Malayan Union, which was followed by the Federation of Malaya Agreement 1948, and later the Malaysia Agreement 1963, which added three new States (Singapore left the federation in 1965) to the Federation on special terms.[1] We have also seen in Chapter 5 how federalism is deeply related to the status and continuance of the Malay monarchies. Any attempt to abolish either monarchy or the federal structure, both of which were beyond even Mahathir at the

---

[1] Tan Tai Yong, *Creating 'Greater Malaysia': Decolonization and the Politics of Merger* (Singapore, Institute of Southeast Asian Studies, 2008). For detailed discussion of this constitutional history from the aspect of federalism, see JC Fong, *Constitutional Federalism in Malaysia* (Petaling Jaya, Sweet and Maxwell Asia, 2008); Kevin Tan, 'The Creation of Greater Malaysia: Law, Politics, Ethnicity, and Religion' in AJ Harding and Dian AH Shah (eds), *Law and Society in Malaysia: Pluralism, Religion and Ethnicity* (Abingdon, Routledge, 2017).

height of his ascendancy in the 1990s, seems bound to be foiled by the profound cultural linkage of the States with their Rulers. Anyone who has been in a State capital in Malaysia at the time of the Ruler's accession or birthday will understand that this link is unbreakable. This is the point the colonial government was rudely reminded of in 1946. However, the constitution-making process followed only a few years after Malaya had proved indefensible before a concerted Japanese attack in 1942, and took place in the midst of a bloody and vicious civil war (the 'emergency' of 1948–60). Therefore, although federalism was a necessary element the focus was nonetheless on creating a strong central government with only 'a measure of autonomy' (to use the Reid Commission's expression) being given to the States. The imperatives of the developmental state for six decades of BN rule tended to accentuate a centripetal tendency in the practice of federalism in Malaysia, and so it is the strong central government rather than the rigid maintenance of States' rights that has prevailed.[2] The constitution-making process of 1956–57 also ensured, however, that, unlike in India, the States maintained their own written constitutions, based on constitutional monarchy, an elected, unicameral state legislature, and a Westminster-style constitution as mandated by the Federal Constitution at Schedule 8 (the 'essential provisions' of State Constitutions). In Chapter 5 we saw how the Westminster conventions operate at the State level.

The question arises whether federalism serves any useful purpose other than the cultural one of supporting the unique system of constitutional monarchy and providing a sense of identity. The answer appears to be that it does. It is necessary to consider, first of all, that in 1963 Malaysia adopted a 'two-tier' or asymmetric Federal system (in which not all States exercise the same powers) with the accession of Sabah and Sarawak on superior terms to the existing 11 States. Malaysia is therefore in a sense a Federation of *three subjects* (Malaya, Sabah and Sarawak), one of which (Malaya) is itself a Federation. For this reason, federalism operates most importantly at this higher level, where the monarchy is in no sense relevant; Sabah and Sarawak each have a Governor, not a Ruler – nonetheless, as we shall see, there are cultural and societal reasons for maintaining real autonomy. However, unlike Sabah and Sarawak, Malaya has no regional government separate from that of the Federal Government itself. It exists only as a kind of legal fiction in that it has its own

---

[2] FE Hutchinson, 'Malaysia's federal system: Overt and covert centralisation' (2014) 44(3) *Journal of Contemporary Asia* 422.

High Court, legal system, legal profession, legal history and a number of important statute laws that apply only to it, such as the National Land Code 1965 and the Local Government Act 1976. This might be argued to be a design fault in that it necessarily places the Federal Government – as the Federal Government for Malaya as well as the whole of Malaysia – in a superior position to Sabah and Sarawak, which were supposed to be equal partners with Malaya, not subordinate to it (see below).

One major reason for federal structures is that they are a means of accommodating ethnic difference. This is often assumed to be relevant in Malaysia but it is in fact only a marginal factor, because almost all ethnic groups, even the indigenous *orang asli*, are spread across most or all of the States. Even strongly Malay populations, like those of Kelantan and Terengganu, have quite large Chinese minorities concentrated mainly in urban areas. On the other hand, some ethnicities are concentrated more in some States than others: Sabah and Sarawak with their indigenous groups,[3] such as the Iban and the Kadazan, have demographies quite different from the States of Malaya and from each other. More obvious are considerable differences in culture, history and economy. Kelantan is more Malay/Muslim, while Penang is more Chinese; Selangor is ethnically mixed but more urbanised and more middle class. Malacca has a rich colonial history recognised by UNESCO, and a uniquely complex ethnic mix, while Negeri Sembilan clings to its unique matrilineal *adat* (customary) laws and constitution.[4] Johor and Kelantan have a highly developed sense of their own autonomy, having shown the greatest reluctance of all in joining the Federation, while Sabah claims to be swamped by migrants and is intermittently claimed by the Philippines as part of the old Sulu Sultanate.[5] Sarawak was carved out of the Brunei Sultanate and ruled by the 'white rajahs' (the Brooke family) for a century before World War Two. There are also geographical considerations. Sabah and Sarawak are very large with vast tracts of jungle, and are separated from Malaya by the South China Sea, making communications with '*semananjung*' (the peninsula) particularly troublesome. Penang, Malacca and the Federal Territory of Kuala Lumpur are effectively city-states, and Perlis is also tiny, while Penang alone amongst the States is an

---

[3] The Constitution, Art 161A(7) specifies 28 different groups, including Malays, as natives of these States.

[4] For Malacca, Negri Sembilan and customary land holdings, see Art 90.

[5] For Sulu insurgency into Sabah at Lahad Datu in 2013, see Law Yew Meng, 'Malaysia's security concerns: A contemporary assessment' in M Weiss (ed), *The Routledge Handbook of Contemporary Malaysia* (Abingdon, Routledge, 2014) 391ff.

island. Kedah produces rice, and Pahang and Johor produce palm oil. Selangor people drive along multi-lane highways to their vast residential estates while Sarawakians trudge through impenetrable jungle to their longhouses. There is, in short, no single, special logic that explains the differences between the States; they are just all different from each other along different axes, and have very different needs, especially as between West and East Malaysia, that would exist regardless of whether there were a federal structure. Apart from the modes of difference listed, a federal structure also provides a welcome form of political ventilation in what has become a highly centralised system of government. The State governments exercise agency, and intergovernmental relations change with changes in political authority at the State level.[6]

At root, however, it is still the cultural factor that maintains the federal structure. One might pass insensibly the boundary between Johor and Negri Sembilan, barely marked by a signboard and an unrelieved scene of oil-palm plantations. Yet it would be a brave proposition that would reduce in any way the significance of their identities: Johor's proud history of independence, or Negri Sembilan's unique *adat* constitution. When in 1994 it was proposed to relieve Johor of its Royal Johor Military Force, a private army under the direct control of its Sultan and the only one of its kind (a reasonable measure, one would think, in a federal system of government), the Parliamentary Bill giving effect to this had to be hastily withdrawn in the face of Johor UMNO members' opposition, even though there were genuine concerns about the actual and possible use of this force.[7] The Johor royal family has been especially assertive of what it calls Johor's historic 'sovereignty'; in this conception the existence of a Federal Government and a Federal Constitution are only grudgingly acknowledged.[8]

The question of utility also raises the inevitability of a downside to federalism, in particular when there is also local government to consider as an additional layer of governance. If federalism is an immovable fact, is it still the case that Malaysia with its population of 32 million needs *three* levels of government, let alone three levels of *elected* government?

---

[6] T Yeoh, *Federal-State Relations under the Pakatan Harapan Government* (Singapore, ISEAS Publishing, 2020).

[7] *Far Eastern Economic Review*, 29 September 1994, 28.

[8] AJ Harding, 'The Rulers and the centrality of conventions in Malaysia's 'Eastminster' constitution' in H Kumarasingham (ed), *Viceregalism: The Crown as Head of State in Political Crises in the Post-War Commonwealth* (Cham, Switzerland, Palgrave, 2020).

Inefficiencies and lack of coordination arise when different governments are responsible for overlapping, inter-locking, gap-creating, or sometimes contradictory, functions, as was revealed during the Covid-19 pandemic. While Malaysia's response to the pandemic received mixed assessments, it revealed different policy preferences at Federal and State levels, and five non-PN-governed States' leaders were excluded from a critical Covid-19 meeting in March 2020.[9]

Most areas of State action require coordination. Obvious examples are provided by foreign investment and environmental management. Foreign investment approval is given by the Federal Government; but land has to be obtained from the State Government; and the local authority's permission is required to build a factory. Environmental regulation is another case where powers are spread across all three levels of government, leading to complexity in environmental policy and decision-making,[10] and confusion over water supply, water resources and drainage.[11] We will see that the efficient secret that allows this system to work quite well, by and large, and irrespective of who is in power at Putrajaya, is in practice its flexibility, and its reliance on institutionalised forms of cooperation. Litigation on Federal and State powers, for example, has been relatively rare compared to most federal systems. A study of Federal-State relations under the PH Government, 2018–20, reveals how state governments were treated fairly by the Federal Government even when controlled by opposition parties.[12]

In this chapter the focus is on Federal–State relations, but we will also look at the conditions of territorial governance at the State and local government levels. Since East Malaysia does not otherwise feature heavily in this book, and federalism tends to take on a different aspect according to where one is standing, the topic will be approached with Sabah and Sarawak very much in mind, and a section is devoted to their special position within the Federation.

---

[9] Azmil Tayeb and Por Heong Hong, 'Malaysia: Improvised pandemic policies and democratic regression' in V Ramraj (ed), *Covid-19 in Asia: Policy Responses and Contexts* (Oxford, Oxford University Press, 2020) 327–28.

[10] Maizatun Mustafa, *Environmental Law in Malaysia* (Alphen-aan-den-Rijn, Netherlands, Kluwer Law International, 2013); and see *Ketua Pengarah Jabatan Alam Sekitar v Kajing Tubek* [1997] 3 MLJ 23; and Fong (n 1) 56–57.

[11] Rasyikah Md Khalid, Faridah Jalil, and Mazlin Bin Mokhtarin, 'Fifty years of water resources management in Malaysian federalism: A way forward', in A Harding and J Chin (eds), *50 Years of Malaysia: Federalism Revisited* (Singapore, Marshall Cavendish, 2014).

[12] Yeoh (n 6) vii.

## II. FEDERAL AND STATE POWERS: A MEASURE OF AUTONOMY

'Bertepok tangan sa-belah tak 'kan berbunyi'
(Clapping with one hand cannot make noise)

Bestowing on States a mere measure of autonomy implies that most legislative and executive powers are vested in the Federation rather than the States. This is confirmed by an examination of Schedule 9 and Articles 74 and 80 of the Constitution. Schedule 9 contains three lists, pertaining to Federal, State and concurrent powers. Concurrent powers can be exercised by either State or Federal authorities, and any residual powers not mentioned belong to the States. The lists designate both legislative and executive powers. If there is any inconsistency between Federal and State law, Federal law prevails.[13] Schedule 9, in the main the work of Sir Ivor Jennings, is riddled with complexity and succeeds in delineating almost every detail of Federal and State powers. It has required remarkably little adjustment since 1957. However, there is a strong body of contemporary opinion that more powers need to be devolved to the States.[14]

As one would expect, the Federation deals with all of the larger issues affecting the country as a whole, such as external affairs, defence, energy, the legal system and citizenship. Trade, industry and transport are also Federal powers, as well as social issues such as health care and education. Most importantly, finance and general taxation are Federal matters.

State powers are largely limited to Islamic law and custom, land, agriculture, forests and natural resources; however, local government and therefore all of its functions are also under State control. The concurrent powers such as social welfare, planning and public health, are in general exercised by the States. Sabah and Sarawak have powers over immigration, as well as over native customary law and personal law, and some other functions such as harbours and posts. They also have power to impose a sales tax but have not usually exercised it.[15]

It is immediately apparent that the Federation has much more power than the States, and that Sabah and Sarawak have much more power than the Peninsular Malaysian States. Sabah and Sarawak's control over immigration, not only from outside Malaysia but also from the rest of the country, is very unusual in a Federal system. The most expensive

---

[13] Art 75.
[14] See eg A Harding and J Chin, 'Fifty years of Malaysia: Reflections and unanswered questions' in Harding and Chin (n 11).
[15] One exception to this is mentioned below: the sales tax on Petronas in Sarawak.

functions too, such as defence, police, health care and education, lie with the Federal power. On the other hand, the States are in charge of many functions that impact directly and visibly on the lives of communities. It will be noted that most of these relate to the physical environment. Local government too has significant functions such as building and development control, housing, public health and market regulation.

The exclusive arbiter over the constitutional division of powers is the Federal Court. It is also the exclusive arbiter of disputes of any kind between States or between the Federation and a State.[16] Although the Federal Court has on occasion decided disputes of this kind, it has only rarely struck down a statute as being unconstitutional,[17] and in one case it laid down definitively the applicable criteria.

In *Mamat bin Daud v Government of Malaysia*[18] the plaintiffs were charged under an amendment to the Penal Code, section 298A, which created a new offence of doing an act on the ground of religion which was likely to cause disunity or affect or prejudice harmony between people professing the same or different religions. They were charged with acting as unauthorised Bilal, Khatib and Imam at Friday prayers. They sought declarations that section 298A was ultra vires Article 74, which guarantees the division of State and Federal powers, because in pith and substance it dealt with Islam, a State matter, and was therefore beyond the power of Parliament to enact. The apex court decided, by a majority of three to two, that the acts prohibited by the section had nothing to do with public order, a Federal matter, but were directly concerned with religion. Two of the majority formulated the following test, with which the dissenting judges also agreed:

> it is the substance and not the form or outward appearance of the impugned legislation which must be considered ... no amount of cosmetics used in the legislative make-up can save legislation from being struck down for pretending to be what it is not. The object, purpose and design of the impugned section must therefore be investigated for the purpose of ascertaining the true character and substance of the legislation and the class of subject-matter of legislation to which it really belongs.

---

[16] Art 128(1).

[17] In *City Council of Georgetown v Government of Penang* [1967] 1 MLJ 169, two State laws were struck down as inconsistent with Federal law. In *Noordin Salleh v State Legislative Assembly of Kelantan* [1993] 3 MLJ 344, a State party-hopping law was struck down because it violated Art 10 of the Constitution which gave the power to regulate freedom of association to Parliament only.

[18] *Mamat bin Daud v Government of Malaysia* [1986] 2 MLJ 192.

This test was endorsed unanimously in *Iki Putra bin Mubarrak v Kerajaan Negeri Selangor* in which the Federal Court struck down a state enactment creating the Islamic offence of *liwat* (unnatural sex) on the ground that the subject matter fell within the federal legislative power over criminal law.[19]

The division of Federal and State powers also has to be read against provisions that give the Federation even greater powers than appear in Schedule 9. Under Article 76, the Federal Parliament is empowered to legislate in respect of matters on the State list in three situations.

First, it may legislate for the purpose of implementing international agreements. Here it cannot legislate with respect to Islamic law or Malay custom, which are quintessentially State powers; and not in any case without consulting the State Government.

Secondly, it may legislate to promote legal uniformity between two or more States; in this case as well as for the first situation, the law only takes effect when passed by the State legislature, when it becomes State law. Additionally, Parliament is given a specific power to legislate for ensuring uniformity of law and policy in relation to land and local government; but in this instance the law does not have to be passed by the State legislature and remains Federal law. The Constitution also recognises the importance of creating uniformity in relation to these issues by creating a National Land Council and a National Local Government Council.[20] These provisions concerning land and local government do not apply to Sabah or Sarawak.[21]

Thirdly, Parliament can legislate where simply requested to do so by a State legislature.[22] The National Land Code 1965 is a good example of the use of this power. Like the Local Government Act 1976, discussed later in this chapter, it is a Federal law dealing with a State matter; it was passed at the request of all the States rather than under the special powers mentioned above for land and local government. The two statutes mentioned here were passed following agreement between the Federation and the States in their respective national councils. But again, they do not

---

[19] *Iki Putra bin Mubarrak v Kerajaan Negeri Selangor* [2021] 2 MLJ 323.

[20] Arts 91, 95A. See also Arts 83 and 92 on land acquisition and development plans.

[21] Art 95D.

[22] See also Art 76A, which gives States limited powers to pass laws on Federal matters; and Arts 83 and 85–88 which allow the Federation to acquire State land in the national interest and to declare an area a development area, which gives Parliament power to pass laws otherwise prohibited by Art 74. In practice development areas have often been simply absorbed into the Federal Territory (eg Putrajaya), or declared as special economic zones, eg the Iskandar Development Region in Johor.

apply to Sabah or Sarawak, which, as on many other issues, have their own laws.

Although executive powers follow legislative powers, Article 80 provides similar flexibility to Article 76 by allowing Federal law to confer executive authority on a State. A good example is the Immigration Act 1959, as amended in 1963, which gives the Governments of Sabah and Sarawak control over immigration in their respective States. It is also permissible for State and Federal authorities to exercise executive powers on behalf of each other. State powers must also be exercised so as to ensure compliance with Federal laws, and not so as to impede the exercise of Federal powers.[23] These provisions, taken together, compel the conclusion that Malaysia has a system of cooperative federalism.[24]

This structure has the merit of channelling the preponderance of power to the centre without reducing States to the position of mere agents of the Federal power and without creating too much structural rigidity. If there is a difficulty with the division of power it lies in the under-resourcing of State and local governments. The division of power outlined above has not required any significant adjustment since 1957, in spite of the constitutional changes made to the Federal structure in 1963, which indicates that on this issue the Reid Commission successfully reconciled the aspiration for State Government autonomy with the needs of national development and nation-building. The single significant amendment to Schedule 9 relates to the issue of tourism, which was added to the Federal List in 1994; this was slipped into a major constitutional amendment relating to other issues and without consultation with the State Governments, which had their own tourism initiatives.[25] However, States have not been prevented, in practice, from promoting tourism, and more recently the Federal Government agreed to share tourist taxes equally with State governments.[26]

Nonetheless, it would be too much to claim that this design has prevented all difficulties between States and the Federal power, or reduced all inefficiencies to a vanishing point, as we will see in the next section. The structure is also tested by a post-dominant-coalition politics in which some State Governments are controlled by Federal opposition parties.

---

[23] Art 81.
[24] R French, 'Cooperative federalism' in C Saunders and A Stone (ed), *Oxford Handbook of The Australian Constitution* (Oxford, Oxford University Press, 2018).
[25] Constitution (Amendment) Act 1994 (Act A885).
[26] *New Straits Times*, '2019 budget: Tourism tax revenue to be shared with state government', 2 November 2018.

## III. FEDERAL AND STATE FINANCE

'Biar sepeh, tumbang jangan'

(Chip the tree if you like, but don't fell it)

In fulfilment of the idea of a strong central Government with limited powers for the States, the Reid Commission placed financial matters firmly in the hands of the Federal Government. They refused on grounds of efficiency to give States the power to tax income, as a result of which the imbalance between Federal and State finances is marked. The total expenditure of all of the States combined in 2018 was around RM12 billion, and Federal transfers amounted to about RM8 billion; this may be compared with Federal expenditure of around RM234 billion in the same year.[27] In other words, if we judge by expenditure, the Federal Government spends about 20 times the amount spent by all of the State Governments, who are hard pressed to avoid an operating deficit. Development funding normally has to come from Federal sources.[28] The problem therefore was, and is, how to resource the execution of State powers. For a Federal system this represents a very low degree of autonomy for the States: Thailand, a unitary state, transfers about 30 per cent of its revenue to its provinces.[29]

The solution adopted in 1957 was to enable the States to draw on Federal resources while exploiting the possibilities for maximising their own revenue. To avoid annual battles over the amount of Federal funding, States are entitled under the Constitution to certain grants, which are calculated according to fixed formulae.[30] These mandatory grants are as follows:

First, there is a *Capitation Grant*, which is based on the annual population projection for the State, as assessed by the Federal Government, and, being graduated, favours States with a small population. The amounts payable are amended from time to time by Parliament according to inflation and population increase, but Parliament may not reduce the grant to less than 90 per cent of the previous year's grant.

Second, there is a *State Road Grant*. Maintenance of State roads is an important function and a large expenditure. This grant is calculated

---

[27] Malaysian Treasury, *Economic Report 2017/18*, 4: Public Finance.

[28] Fong (n 1) ch 5.

[29] A Harding and Rawin Leelapatana, 'Possibilities for decentralisation in Thailand: A view from Chiang Mai', 1:1 *Thai Legal Studies* 76.

[30] Art 109; for details as to how this works, see Fong (n 1).

by multiplying an average maintenance cost per mile by the number of miles of road the State has, and so favours those States with extensive highways and therefore high maintenance costs. Arguably this leaves States that need infrastructural *development* at some disadvantage; however, since this argument applies principally to Sabah and Sarawak whose development needs are dealt with by other means, this system does not seem to have given rise to a problem of entrenched underdevelopment.

These grants are constitutionally guaranteed and set out in detail in Schedule 10, so that there is no element of discretion involved. In theory, therefore, State finance does not depend on Federal approval; but in practice the situation tends to be otherwise. Mandatory grants are in general terms barely sufficient for State Governments to operate, and they have often been run on deficit funding which is then made up by the Federation.[31] In order to take development initiatives, however, States need finance over and above the mandatory grants, and they will be dependent on discretionary Federal grants. A principle of not following political preference in this matter appears to be becoming part of political practice, unlike in previous decades. Nonetheless, Governments still continue to give priority in funding to constituencies where their own MPs are incumbent.[32]

Nonetheless, States also have sources of revenue based on their own powers, which are similarly guaranteed by the Constitution.[33] They can, for example, charge rents on State property, impose licence fees, and charge water rates. In practice the most important elements are the royalties and other revenue derived from land and natural resources, such as tin, petroleum, oil, minerals and timber; however, Parliament may restrict the levying of royalties or similar charges made in respect of mineral concessions.[34] In 2017 these sources amounted to 76 per cent of all State revenues.[35]

The need for States to obtain royalties on natural resource exploitation has given rise to conflict between States that have such resources (principally Sabah, Sarawak and Terengganu) and the Federal Government.[36] States have attempted to claim the right to royalties on

---

[31] Yeoh (n 6) 24, 30.
[32] Yeoh (n 6) 26.
[33] Art 114.
[34] Art 110.
[35] Malaysian Treasury (n 27).
[36] Fong (n 1) 98–103.

the exploitation of resources (oil and gas, for example) found under the continental shelf adjacent to, but beyond, territorial waters; areas that, in their view, belong to the State, but in the view of the Federal Government belong to the Federation. This conflict was initially resolved by the Petroleum Development Act 1974, sections 2–4, under which all oil and gas rights were vested in the Federation in the form of Petronas, the national oil company, in return for 'such cash payment as may be agreed between the parties'. Petronas is one of the notable government-linked companies examined in Chapter 2. In 1975 the payment was agreed with Sabah, Sarawak and Terengganu at 5 per cent of the price of oil and gas found and sold by Petronas,[37] although this has been a continuing source of dissatisfaction on the part of these three States. However, Sabah and Sarawak are also the recipients of the largest amount of development funding from the Federal Government. As a former Attorney-General of Sarawak comments, this outcome only shows the dependency of these States on Federal development funds.[38] It is highly arguable that the 5 per cent payment is far below what is reasonable, and in 2018 Prime Minister Mahathir indicated 20 per cent was appropriate, as the PH manifesto had set out. However, the outcome was a dispute between Sarawak and Petronas over the Sate's imposition of a RM1.3 billion sales tax. This was disputed unsuccessfully in the High Court at Kuching, but subsequently Petronas agreed to pay RM2 billion to Sarawak and withdrew an appeal against the decision.[39] It seems that such matters, albeit settled fairly in the end, are essentially in practice within the Federal Government's discretion.

One other possible way of raising revenue was explored by the Government of Kelantan in the 1960s, and also led to conflict with the Federal Government. Although State Governments are prohibited from borrowing except from, or with the consent of, the Federal Government, Kelantan attempted in effect to achieve the opposite result by obtaining pre-payment of mining royalties from a mining company. On a reference to the then Supreme Court by the Federal Government it was held

---

[37] Under Tripartite Agreements of 1975, involving the Federal Government and the Governments of Sabah, Sarawak and Terengganu.

[38] Fong (n 1) 103, n 24.

[39] Yeoh (n 6) 19; a similar dispute involving Terengganu ran from 2000–2008; see 'Terengganu drops Petronas suit', *The Edge*, 23 April 2012, available at www.theedgemarkets.com/article/terengganu-drops-petronas-suit; and *Petroliam Nasional Bhd v State Government of Terengganu* [2004] 1 MLJ 8.

that this constituted a valid source of revenue; it was not a loan, because no interest was payable. However, this position was then reversed by a constitutional amendment extending the definition of the word 'borrow' in Article 160.[40] This indicates once again how real power rests ultimately with the Federal Government.

It can be seen that a successful federal fiscal arrangement, which Malaysia by and large can claim to have, requires a good deal of negotiation and compromise. This is achieved through the mechanism of the National Finance Council (NFC),[41] whose main task is to iron out difficulties of a fiscal nature arising in the federal context. It consists of the Prime Minister, such Ministers as the Prime Minister shall appoint, and one representative from each State. It must meet at least once every 12 months, and is summoned, as often as he considers necessary, by the Prime Minister, who presides (or else by three or more State representatives). The Federal Government is under a constitutional duty to consult the NFC in respect of matters such as the making of Federal grants to the States; the assignment to the States of Federal taxes or fees; and the making of loans to the States. Parliament is required annually to pay into a State Reserve Fund such sums as are deemed by it, after consultation with the NFC, to be necessary; and the Federation may from time to time make payments out of the Fund to the States for the purposes of development or to supplement revenues. All matters of potential controversy are dealt with by the NFC, and it is interesting to note that open fiscal controversy between a State and the Federation, or between States (with the exception of the issue of oil revenues, as above), is rare.

As JC Fong writes,

> The financial arrangement between the Federation and the States ... has enabled Malaysia to maintain financial stability, economic progress and transformation ... it may not be perfect, but it has proved to be one which seems to be best suited for the Federation.[42]

Whether this will continue to be true in the era of opposition-controlled State Governments remains to be seen.

---

[40] *Government of Malaysia v Government of Kelantan* [1968] 1 MLJ 129; and see Constitution (Amendment No 2) Act 1971 (A31), s 8.
[41] Art 108.
[42] Fong (n 1) 120.

## IV. ASYMMETRY AND THE SPECIAL POSITION OF
## SABAH AND SARAWAK

'Dekat tak berchapai, jauh tak berapa entara'

(Near, but not to be grasped; far, but no great distance)

The Tunku's grand design for decolonisation, which was consonant with British policy too, was to incorporate the remaining Southeast Asian territories under British control, namely, Singapore, Sabah, Sarawak and Brunei, into a larger Federation spanning Malaya and Borneo.[43] The only realistic options for the Borneo territories were to become independent separately, form their own federation with Brunei, or join Sukarno's increasingly unstable and hostile Indonesia. Communist insurgency determined this issue for the majority of people in these territories. At the same time there was unease about the possibly deleterious effects of joining the Federation. A Memorandum of the Malaysia Consultative Committee, a Committee of the Commonwealth Parliamentary Association, consisting of representatives of the Governments of Britain, Malaya, Sabah and Sarawak, supported the federation of Sabah and Sarawak with Malaya and Singapore in its Memorandum of February 1962. Brunei ultimately declined to join Malaysia. The Cobbold Commission, consisting of representatives of the British and Malayan Governments, visited Sabah and Sarawak in 1962 and reported that the majority supported federation with Malaya, provided due regard was had to the special position of Sabah and Sarawak, the ethnic implications, the physical distances involved, and these territories' political immaturity compared to Malaya and Singapore.[44]

The Legislative Assemblies of both territories voted in favour of federation subject to appropriate safeguards. An Inter-governmental Committee was then set up, comprising representatives from the same four Governments, to thrash out constitutional safeguards for Sabah and Sarawak, reporting in February 1963. Negotiations with Singapore proceeded separately, and a referendum in Singapore also supported federation. The Malaysia Agreement was eventually signed on 9 July 1963 by all the Governments concerned, and Malaysia came into being on 16 September 1963. This was effected not by a new Federal Constitution,

---

[43] Poh-Ling Tan, 'From Malaya to Malaysia' in AJ Harding and HP Lee (eds), *Constitutional Landmarks in Malaysia: The First 50 Years, 1957–2007* (Kuala Lumpur, LexisNexis, 2007); Harding and Chin (n 11).

[44] The Commission's Report, *The Report of the Commission of Enquiry: North Borneo and Sarawak, 1962*, was published by the Colonial Office as Cmnd 1794/1962 (HMSO).

but simply by the admission of new States to the existing but renamed Federation under Article 1 of the Constitution, and by numerous amendments to the Constitution giving effect to the negotiated settlement that was embodied in the Malaysia Agreement.[45]

The principal point of concern was the possible effect of migration on land, commerce, and the employment and professional opportunities of East Malaysians faced with competition from more qualified people from Malaya and Singapore. In this connection a draft Bill on immigration was appended to the Malaysia Agreement and promptly passed into law as the Immigration Act 1963 a few days before Malaysia came into being. However, there was also concern about other issues: financial arrangements and development; the special position of natives of Sabah and Sarawak; the national language; religion; the legal system; representation in the Federal Parliament; and of course how these States would be protected from future constitutional changes affecting any of these issues. Between them Sabah and Sarawak have about 60 per cent of Malaysia's land area and a superabundance of natural resources, but only about a fifth of its population. They saw their priority as the need for protection against more powerful neighbours. The Cobbold Commission had stressed the need for a sense of equality and partnership in the new federal scheme. According to Lord Cobbold it was to be a 'partnership', not a 'takeover'.[46]

Sabah and Sarawak were thus placed in a position that was not available to the States that formed the Federation of Malaya in 1948, in that they were able to negotiate their part in the Federal scheme. These States were both resource-rich and under-developed. Accordingly, they have the benefit of special grants and other fiscal privileges, adding to the asymmetrical nature of federalism.[47]

First, unlike the other States, they may borrow money with the consent of Bank Negara (the Central Bank of Malaysia). Second, Schedule 10 also provides for special grants for Sabah and Sarawak, over and above the Capitation Grant and the Road Grant (see above), the bases of which were negotiated at the time of their accession. The object of these is to ensure that State revenue is adequate to meet the cost of existing State services, with reasonable provision for their expansion. Third, Sabah and Sarawak are allowed eight further sources of revenue not allowed to the

---

[45] See, generally, Harding and Chin (n 11).
[46] The Commission's Report (n 44) para 237.
[47] Art 112.

other States. Fourth, the restrictions on the proportion of export duty on minerals mentioned above do not apply to Sabah and Sarawak.

Quite apart from the central issue of immigration, Sabah and Sarawak have substantially more powers than the other States, as we have seen. Parliament's powers to legislate for land and local government do not apply to Sabah and Sarawak; this allows these States exclusive legislative control over these two matters.

Crucially, the Governments of Sabah and Sarawak also have special powers to veto constitutional amendments affecting their States, and in this respect they have a considerable advantage over the other States, which have no such powers.[48] As we saw in Chapter 1, Kelantan failed to secure a constitutional right to be consulted over the creation of Malaysia in 1963. Under Article 161E(2) no amendment shall be made to the Federal Constitution without the concurrence of the Government of Sabah or Sarawak, as the case maybe (yet oddly, one can note, *not* the concurrence of the legislative assembly), if the amendment is such as to affect the operation of the Constitution with regard to: Malaysian citizenship and the equal treatment of persons born or resident in the State; the constitution and jurisdiction of the High Court of Sabah and Sarawak, and the appointment, removal and suspension of its judges; the State's legislative and executive powers and financial arrangements between the Federation and the State; religion and language in the State, and the special treatment of natives of the State;[49] and the quota of MPs allocated to the State in proportion to the total number of MPs.[50]

The reference to the judiciary is an unusual one. The object here was to preserve the separation of the High Court and the legal profession serving it. This was designed to guarantee judicial enforcement of the law in Sabah and Sarawak, bearing in mind that essentially each of these States had its own legal history, statute laws, legal system and legal profession, and to protect its legal profession from being swamped by lawyers from Malaya seeking to practise before its courts. Since the jurisdiction of the High Court in Sabah and Sarawak enjoys the protection indicated in the last paragraph, this entails that there is doubt whether, for example, the separation of Syariah from civil jurisdiction effected by the constitutional amendment of 1988 (see Chapter 9) has any application in

---

[48] This was demonstrated by the Kelantan case: see ch 1.

[49] See also Art 161A.

[50] Over-representation of Sabah and Sarawak was guaranteed only up to 1970, but after that the issue is whether their representation is equal to other States: see ch 4.

these States.[51] In any event the judiciary in the two States has remained largely unaffected by turbulent developments regarding the judiciary in Peninsular Malaysia;[52] however, the joining of the two systems at the Federal level via the umbilical cord of appeals to the Court of Appeal and the Federal Court mitigates this factor to some extent.

The balance of power between the Federation and the two Borneo States received a severe test soon after Malaysia came into being.[53]

By 1966 tensions had developed between the Federal and Sarawak Governments. The ruling party in Sarawak, SNAP, was a member of the Alliance, which ruled at the Federal level; however, the Chief Minister of Sarawak, Stephen Kalong Ningkan, pursued an independent policy of protecting native land rights that irritated Federal leaders. Constitutional chicanery followed as the Federal Government undermined Ningkan's position. A letter, signed by 21 of the 42 members of the Council Negri, the State Legislature, was sent to the *Yang di-Pertua Negeri* (Governor) saying that the signatories no longer had any confidence in Ningkan as Chief Minister. On the basis of this letter the *Yang di-Pertua Negeri* asked for Ningkan's resignation, and when this was not forthcoming – Ningkan having asked that 'the matter be put to the constitutional test' – he dismissed Ningkan by publishing a declaration in the Gazette that Ningkan had ceased to hold office, and appointed another member of the Council Negri as Chief Minister. These events are strikingly similar to those in the more recent Perak crisis of 2009, discussed in Chapter 5. As in Perak, there had been no motion of no-confidence, and Ningkan refused to accept his dismissal, commencing proceedings in the High Court for declarations that he was still the Chief Minister.

The issue was whether a power to dismiss the Chief Minister could be implied into the State Constitution, and, if so, whether it had been properly exercised. Article 7(1) of the State Constitution, in line with Westminster-style conventions said: 'If the Chief Minister ceases to command the confidence of a majority of the members of the Council Negri, then, unless at his request the [*Yang di-Pertua Negeri*] dissolves the Council Negri, the Chief Minister shall tender the resignation of the members of the Supreme Council [State Cabinet]'. The High Court

[51] Fong (n 1) 143.

[52] See ch 7.

[53] HP Lee, 'The Ningkan saga: A Chief Minister in the eye of a storm' in Harding and Lee (n 43).

held that even if there was a power to dismiss the Chief Minister, the term 'confidence' implied a vote in the legislature, not a letter, even leaving aside the ambiguous mathematics of the case.[54] The dismissal was therefore unlawful and Ningkan resumed office. This decision is at odds with the decision in Nizar's case discussed in Chapter 5.

The extraordinary response from the Federal Government was to proclaim, on the ground of a threat to the security of Sarawak, an emergency, under which the Federal and State Constitutions were temporarily amended by the Emergency (Federal Constitution and Constitution of Sarawak) Act 1966 so as to give the *Yang di-Pertua Negeri* power to dismiss the Chief Minister, and to summon the legislature without receiving government advice to that effect. However, there was no real security threat, as the real reason for the proclamation was the existence of a constitutional crisis which offered no immediate resolution in favour of the Federal Government's interests. The Council Negri was duly summoned; Ningkan lost the vote on the ensuing no-confidence motion and was dismissed from office.

This was not quite the end of the story. Ningkan challenged the emergency proclamation in the courts, alleging, plausibly, a fraud on the Constitution. He took his case eventually to the Privy Council, but without success.[55]

The problem with this episode from the perspective of the States, and of Sabah and Sarawak in particular, is that it means there are ultimately no legal or even, probably, political limitations, on the power of the Federation to interfere with the State Constitution, State Government or the division of State and Federal powers. The Privy Council, considering in *Stephen Kalong Ningkan* the meaning of 'emergency' in Article 150(1), stressed the breadth of the concept that

> it is not confined to unlawful use or threat of force in any of its manifestations ... the natural meaning of the word itself is capable of covering a very wide range of situations and occurrences, including such diverse elements as wars, famines, earthquakes, floods, epidemics and the collapse of civil government ...[56]

The reference to epidemics is of interest in the light of an emergency proclamation related to the Covid-19 pandemic and affecting the entire

---

[54] *Stephen Kalong Ningkan v Tun Abang Haji Openg and Tawi Sli* [1966] 2 MLJ 187, [1967] 1 MLJ 46.
[55] *Stephen Kalong Ningkan v Government of Malaysia* [1968] 2 MLJ 238.
[56] Ibid.

Federation, in January 2021, discussed in Chapter 3. Emergency laws continued in force in Sarawak after the end of the emergency on 1 August 2021, as State elections were due there.

In some cases even more hidden methods have been used to interfere with the State Government. Sabah provides a good example.[57] Following the February 1994 State elections in Sabah, PBS, under Datuk Joseph Pairin Kitingan, was returned with 25 of the 48 seats in the State Legislative Assembly, with the BN under Tan Sri Haji Sakaran Dandai taking 23 seats. After a rather unseemly delay, during which he remained in his car, parked outside the Istana (Governor's residence) for two days, Pairin was appointed Chief Minister, and shortly afterwards his Cabinet also received their appointments. Immediately on Pairin's resumption of office, moves began to unseat him. He soon learned of the defection of three PBS assemblymen, which turned his majority of the elected members into a minority; attempting to forestall what seemed inevitable, he requested that same day a further dissolution of the Assembly. This was refused by the *Yang di-Pertua Negeri*. He then learned of a petition to the *Yang di-Pertua Negeri*, signed by 30 members of the Assembly, saying they had no confidence in him and demanding his resignation. Less than one month after taking office, Pairin resigned, without there having been any motion of no confidence in the Assembly. By this time, he commanded only 21 votes in the Assembly, as against 27 for the BN. Sakaran was then appointed Chief Minister.[58]

Unfortunately, paying assemblymen to switch parties has happened on many occasions, and the courts have struck down anti-hopping laws (see Chapter 3) designed to prevent this occurring on the ground that they contravene freedom of association under Article 10 of the Constitution.[59] Although such episodes are not exclusive to Sabah and Sarawak, three leading instances of manipulation of State Government have occurred in these States, which are supposed to have special protection under the Constitution. The opposition, too, has tried to manipulate State politics in its favour. Following the 2008 election,

---

[57] AJ Harding, 'When is a Resignation not a Resignation? A Crisis of Confidence in Sabah' (1995) 335 *The Round Table* 353; see also AJ Harding, 'Turbulence in the Land Below the Wind: Sabah's Constitutional Crisis of 1985–6' (1991) XXIX *Journal of Commonwealth and Comparative Politics* 86.

[58] Even so, a member of Pairin's Cabinet brought a case, unsuccessfully, to have Pairin's resignation held inapplicable to Cabinet members: *Datuk Amir Kahar Tun Mustapha v Tun Mohamed Said Keruak* [1994] 3 MLJ 737.

[59] W Tay and J Neo, 'Political stability and anti-hopping laws: Comparative perspectives and reflections' [forthcoming].

a plot was hatched under which a number of Sarawak MPs would defect to the opposition and a government of national unity would be formed. The plot failed when information reached the Prime Minister, and 40 East Malaysian MPs were sent to Taiwan by a backbenchers' club 'to study agriculture'.[60]

Although the Federation has not sought to alter the balance of legislative powers in its favour, the underlying reality of Federal politics means there are limits to States' political autonomy, even where they receive special constitutional protection. Of particular concern here is that the use of emergency powers (for which see Chapter 3) can side-step the consent of the State Government, which is the main guarantee against abuse of the power of constitutional amendment. Another device has been what has been called 'organisational duplication',[61] for example with regard to religion (see Chapter 9).

Concern regarding the nature of federalism as seen from East Malaysia has been growing considerably in the last decade or so, reaching a level that can be described as intense frustration. Some groups even aim for secession. The desire for autonomy is variously expressed in demands for recognition of the special status of these States within the Federation; for greater autonomy or 'devolution' within the existing Federal system; for transfer of specific powers, regarding for example health, education and police, to these States; and for full implementation of the Malaysia Agreement.[62] The demand for greater autonomy has been recognised, in principle at least, by the last two Federal Governments, but neither the PH nor the PN has taken any very significant steps towards acting on such recognition, beyond setting up committees to look into the matter. However, a bill to amend the Constitution was introduced in 2019, which if passed would merely have amended Article 1 to list Sabah and Sarawak separately from the other States to acknowledge their special status. The amendment, purely symbolic as it was, narrowly failed to get the

---

[60] 'Vox-Pop: Our MPs won't learn anything in Taiwan', Malaysiakini, 9 September 2008, available at www.malaysiakini.com/news/89324. The 'Sheraton move' episode of 2020 (see ch 2) is yet another example of the manipulation of factions to undermine a government – on that occasion at the Federal level.

[61] Hutchinson (n 2).

[62] A Harding, 'Devolution of powers in Sarawak: A dynamic process of redesigning territorial governance in a federal system' (2017) 12(2) *Asian Journal of Comparative Law* 1; Harding and Chin (n 11).

required two-thirds majority in the *Dewan Rakyat*, being opposed by some members as a matter of principle, and by others because it did not go far enough.[63]

What appears to be necessary in order to resolve this issue is a recalibration of Malaysian federalism to devolve more powers to the States, and especially to Sabah and Sarawak, taking account of the commitments in the Malaysia Agreement, and the notion of a partnership, not a takeover. These commitments have not in general been observed over the last six decades, and Sabah and Sarawak suffer from a serious development deficit, which is all the more troubling in the light of their command of vast natural resources.[64] It is suggested that devolution of substantial powers may be achievable without constitutional changes, but it may be that such devolution fails to satisfy the demand for real autonomy that seems to be supported by a majority of residents in those States. The price of failure to address this problem may be the emergence of serious separatist movements in Sabah and Sarawak. East Malaysians on their part have ample possibilities through the political process to make demands for autonomy, having extensive representation in the Dewan Rakyat, the Dewan Negara, the Cabinet and the Federal government and civil service, as well as their own institutions at State level. The Territorial Sea Act 2012, for example, was passed by Parliament with little or no objection from Sabah or Sarawak until after the event.

## V. LOCAL GOVERNMENT

'Dapat puncha-nya sahaja sampai-lah ka-hujong-nya'

(Just give me one end of the fishing line and I can get to the other)

Malaysian local government along its present lines can be traced back to the British occupation of Penang, which later formed, with Malacca and Singapore, the colony of the Straits Settlements. In 1801 a Committee of Assessors was established there to supervise urban development. Local authorities were then established gradually in the Straits Settlements, and later in the Malay States, but only as and when it appeared necessary in a particular urban setting. As independence loomed after 1945, experimentation with democracy was undertaken at the level of urban

---

[63] Yeoh (n 6) 13.

[64] J Chin, 'Federal-East Malaysia relations: Primus-inter-pares?' in Harding and Chin (n 11).

local government. By 1957 there were no fewer than 289 local authorities in Malaya, and major city councils were elected.

Two major changes have been made to local government since *Merdeka.*[65]

First, in 1965, local government elections were suspended as an emergency measure, and have not since then been reinstated.[66] At the same time a Royal Commission of Inquiry on Local Authorities was established, which reported in 1968 (the Nahappan Report) recommending the continuance of local elections and a reduction in the number of local authorities. Unfortunately the proposed reforms were overtaken by the 'May 13' episode in 1969. In 1971 the Development Administration Unit (DAU) of the Prime Minister's Department rejected the Nahappan Report's recommendation for reinstating local elections, arguing that elected local government, which facilitated the domination of the haves over the have-nots, and provided for 'over-democratised over-government at the local level', was no longer consonant with the objectives of a developmental state.[67]

The passing of the main statute, the Local Government Act 1976 (LGA), was the second major reform, designed to implement the other main recommendation of the Nahappan Report. The LGA, preceded in this by the Local Government (Temporary Provisions) Act 1973, regularised local authorities in Malaya, which had grown in number from 289 in 1957 to an unwieldy 373 in 1976, in no less than five different categories. With implementation of the legislation during 1976–88, and an equivalent exercise in Sabah and Sarawak, the total number of local authorities in the whole of Malaysia was eventually reduced to 138 and the categories to three: municipal councils, city councils, and district councils. At present there are 156 local authorities, of which 94 are District Councils, 38 are municipal councils, and 18 are city councils led by a *Datuk Bandar* (Mayor). There are also six statutory development agencies under Federal jurisdiction but carrying out local-authority

---

[65] For the reforms of the 1970s, see MW Norris, *Local Government in Peninsular Malaysia* (Farnborough, Gower, 1980).

[66] Elections were suspended by the Emergency (Suspension of Local Government Elections) Regulations 1965. The Local Government (Temporary Provisions) Act 1973 abolished all elected local authorities and gave the power to appoint local authorities to the State Governments; see now Local Government Act 1976, s 15; and see P Tennant, 'The decline of elective local government in Malaysia' (1973) 13 *Asian Survey* 347.

[67] J Saravanamuttu, 'Act of betrayal: The snuffing out of local democracy in Malaysia', *Aliran Monthly 2000*, available at aliran.com/archives/monthly/2000/04h.html; Lim Mah Hui, *Local Democracy Denied: A Personal Journey into Local Government in Malaysia* (Petaling Jaya, SIRDC, 2020).

functions. There are three Federal Territories (Kuala Lumpur, Putrajaya and Labuan). Currently more than two-thirds of Malaysians live in urban areas, and these correspond to Malaysia's 'local government areas', that is, those areas that have local authorities as defined by the LGA. Rural areas are under the authority of District Councils, which are still administered with respect to local functions by the colonial system of District Officers (DO), who are appointed by, and are responsible to, either the State Government or the Federal Government, depending on the State in which the authority lies. The DOs are Presidents of the District Councils, which are advised by various committees of specialists. The districts have never had representative local government; indeed they are not even regarded as being part of the system of local government as such under the LGA. Nonetheless, they perform the same functions as municipal and city councils.

Local government is the lowest level of Malaysia's multi-levelled system of government, employing only 7 per cent of public employees. Nonetheless, local government functions such as development control, public housing, parks and public places, and public health and public nuisances, are an extremely important aspect of urban living and the environment. Local councils consist of between 8 and 24 persons and are appointed by the State Governments from amongst prominent citizens resident in the locality,[68] and they therefore tend to reflect the interests of the party or coalition in power at the State level. With regard to Kuala Lumpur, since it is a Federal Territory the *Datuk Bandar* is appointed by the Federal Government for a period of five years, and the Dewan Bandaraya Kuala Lumpur (KL City Council) is placed under the Prime Minister's Department.[69] There is a persistent demand for Kuala Lumpur to have its own elected council, as it is the only capital city in Southeast Asia not to have one.[70] The National Local Government Council, comprising Federal and State appointees and set up under Article 95A of the Constitution, coordinates policy for the 'promotion, development and control of local government' and the administration of local government law.

---

[68] LGA, ss 3, 13.
[69] Federal Capital Act 1960, rev 1970, ss 4, 7.
[70] 'Time for KL to be run by elected officials as a state, says think tank', *Free Malaysia Today*, 31 January 2021, available at www.msn.com/en-my/news/national/time-for-kl-to-be-run-by-elected-officials-as-a-state-says-think-tank/ar-BB1dfKcy?ocid=msedgntp.

Local authorities derive their revenue from rents, fees for services, and licences (about 32 per cent); State and Federal Governments by fiscal transfers, for example, for road maintenance or development projects (about 17 per cent); and local taxation in the form of property assessments or the equivalent (about 51 per cent). Fiscal transfers in the form of equalisation grants are made to local authorities by the Federal Government, but in general according to statistics of the Ministry of Housing and Local Government, these represent only about 10 per cent of the shortfall in revenue against local authorities' assessed needs.[71] Local authorities are also empowered to borrow money from State and Federal Governments and financial institutions. The result of lack of adequate resourcing has been an understandable emphasis on maintaining services rather than on development and response to changing needs. Privatisation has been undertaken in some areas. There is consequently a deficit in effective enforcement of relevant laws, authorities seemingly unable in many ways to fully utilise their powers. One particular problem that seems capable of being easily addressed is that, since local government employees do not form part of the public service as such, but are simply employees of the local authority in question, they cannot simply be transferred to other local authorities. Thus meritorious employees can get stuck at middle levels of promotion for years, there being few opportunities for promotion, and may leave the service for better prospects elsewhere; mediocre employees on the other hand tend to remain where they are.[72]

Another problem with the local government system is its secrecy. In February 2006 even a federal minister was moved to call local government authorities 'secret societies' because of

> the lack of transparency and accountability, highlighted by public concern over mismanagement, wastage of public funds on overseas junkets under the pretext of study tours, approvals for deforestation of land causing untold damage to the environment, lack of enforcement, bribery and corruption in local townships.[73]

---

[71] UNESCAP, 'Country Paper: Malaysia', *Local Government in Asia and the Pacific: A Comparative Study* (1999).

[72] Ibid.

[73] Cited in PG Lim, 'Elected Government Should be Considered Again by Malaysia', *City Mayor Politics*, 20 February 2006, available at www.citymayors.com/politics/malaysia_locdem.html.

Even though the meetings of local authorities are open to public scrutiny, they have the option to make the minutes secret. Committee meetings are even more inaccessible because there is a presumption of secrecy.[74] A study of public participation in the preparation of Petaling Jaya's Structure Plan in 1996 revealed that even during a process of statutory public consultation, so little information was actually released that it was difficult for the public to produce strong and constructive criticisms.[75] The lack of a substantive right to demand information and the existence of laws that actually limit access to information are serious concerns in local government, and indeed other, contexts. Hopefully the current trend towards freedom of information will go some way to alleviating these difficulties.

Without either elections or access to information regarding local authority decision-making, it is extremely difficult for members of the public to determine whether local authorities are acting in the public interest. Since many urban concerns (particularly public nuisances and planning issues, but also the provision of environmental services) are under the control of local government, the State Governments' attitude towards local government becomes an important factor. The absence of electoral or any form of accountability other than judicial review, and the general fiscal weakness of local authorities, indicate that the State Governments regard local authorities as minor instruments of policy rather than as the dynamic and autonomous development agencies they could be.

This position is disappointing when it is considered that the suspension of local elections was implemented initially only because of the Indonesian confrontation with Malaysia in 1964–65: the Royal Commission had actually recommended not only the retention of local government elections, but their extension to *all* local government areas. The May 13 incident in 1969 led to the permanent (as opposed to emergency) abolition of local government elections by the Local Government (Temporary Provisions) Act 1973. In view of social, economic and political changes since that time, one would have thought the case for reinstatement of local elections to be overwhelming; and indeed the case for restoring them has never fallen silent. It seems that the

---

[74] LGA, ss 23, 27.
[75] AJ Harding and Azmi Sharom, 'Access to Environmental Justice in Malaysia (Kuala Lumpur)' in AJ Harding (ed), *Access to Environmental Justice: A Comparative Study* (Leiden, Martinus Nijhoff, 2007).

Government has not considered that local politics might act as a safety valve releasing tensions in national politics; and that it can produce innovations that would be beneficial when generally adopted. In any event the lack of accountability ensuing from lack of elections is great. For example, even now most local authorities do not produce annual public financial accounts or activity reports.

In spite of this public participation in local government matters has been on the rise, and was given a large boost by the decision of the Court of Appeal in the 'Kiara Green' case in Kuala Lumpur in 2021.[76] In that case the court struck down the Mayor's decision on a planning application relating to a 'green-lung area'. He had failed to take account of the structure plan and local objections, when granting permission for a major development on the city's only green lung, a place where rare hornbills nested. In addition, there was a conflict of interest, the Mayor himself being a party to the relevant joint-venture contract, and there was no evidence that the residents' extensive concerns had in fact been taken into account. For good measure, the court added that the Mayor was also in breach of his implied duty to give reasons, at the relevant time, for his decision. The legal position set out in this case changes at a stroke the entire situation of public participation in local government, and more widely, in several respects. It is to be hoped that the Federal Court will affirm this very important decision.

The conclusion of Tennant as long ago as 1973 that 'elective local government was a late colonial intrusion which did not flourish in the Malaysian political system'[77] seems as almost as apposite now as it was almost 50 years ago; but perhaps not for much longer. Opposition parties in 2008, 2013 and 2018 campaigned for reinstating elections, or at least more local democracy in some form. In power the PH Government in 2018 initially promised to reinstate local government elections in some areas, and was examining various models for local elections; however, Prime Minister Mahathir expressed himself as being against local elections, which he claimed would create inter-ethnic problems, and no progress had been made when the PH Government lost power in March 2020. Some State Governments have clearly wished to reinstate local elections. In Penang there was an attempt to 'consult' votes regarding the

---

[76] *Perbadangan Pengurusan Trellises & Ors v Datuk Bandar Kuala Lumpur & Ors* [2021] 2 CLJ 808. An appeal was heard in the Federal Court on 14 June 2021.

[77] Tennant (n 66) 365.

'appointment' of local councillors. However, the court ruled that they had no power to organise what was in effect an election, and Federal legislation would be required to do so. The demand for local elections simply keeps resurfacing.[78]

## VI. CONCLUSION

We have seen in this chapter how the 'measure of autonomy' that the Constitution affords the States, although not overtly altered by constitutional amendment, has been subject to political control and even manipulation by the Federal government. The opportunities for standardisation of the law across the Federation have also been fully exploited, and even in administrative and financial affairs the Federation holds sway. The States are, as a result, only just able to maintain their measure of autonomy under the prevailing federal system. This applies even to the States with asymmetric powers, that is, Sabah and Sarawak. As a result, Malaysia, Southeast Asia's only federation, is also, paradoxically, one of its most centralised systems of governance.

The seemingly ineluctable domination of territorial government by a highly centralised state seems, however, to be waning. Territorial governance has been ventilated and re-examined in leading States such as Selangor and Penang in recent years. If local elections are reinstated at least in urban areas, then the answer to the question, can Malaysia sustain three levels of democratic government, seems to be: yes for urban areas, but probably no for rural areas. If so, then a release of energy and participation at all three levels seems the likely outcome.

### FURTHER READING

JC Fong, *Constitutional Federalism in Malaysia* (Petaling Jaya, Sweet and Maxwell Asia, 2008).

A Harding and J Chin, *50 Years of Malaysia: Federalism Revisited* (Singapore, Marshall Cavendish, 2014).

---

[78] See, further, 'Local democracy in a multi-layered constitutional system: Malaysian local government reconsidered' in A Harding and M Sidel (eds), *Central-Local Relations in Asian Constitutional Systems* (Oxford, Hart Publishing, 2015); Danesh Prakash Chacko, *Reintroduction of Local Government Elections in Malaysia* (Petaling Jaya, Bersih & Adil Network Sdn Bhd, 2021).

A Harding, 'Local democracy in a multi-layered constitutional system: Malaysian local government reconsidered' in A Harding and M Sidel (eds), *Central-Local Relations in Asian Constitutional Systems* (Oxford, Hart Publishing, 2015).

A Harding, 'Devolution of powers in Sarawak: A dynamic process of redesigning territorial governance in a federal system' (2017) 12(2) *Asian Journal of Comparative Law* 1.

FE Hutchinson, 'Malaysia's federal system: Overt and covert centralisation' (2014) 44(3) *Journal of Contemporary Asia* 422.

Poh-Ling Tan, 'From Malaya to Malaysia' in AJ Harding and HP Lee (eds), *Constitutional Landmarks in Malaysia: The First 50 Years, 1957–2007* (Kuala Lumpur, LexisNexis, 2007).

# 7

# *Human Rights:*
# *A Struggle over Ambiguity*

Asian values and Human Rights – Human Rights and International
Law – The Right to Individual Liberty – Preventive Detention – The
Human Rights Commission – An Indigenous Perspective

## I. INTRODUCTION

'Ada-kah pernah telaga yang keroh mengalir ayer-nya jerneh?'
(Will you ever get clear water from a dirty well?)

THIS CHAPTER DOES not seek to present an exhaustive analysis of
each right provided in the Constitution, which would require a
book in itself.[1] Instead, it attempts to paint a picture of human
rights as a contested concept in the context of the constitutional system
as whole. Reference has been made to equality before the law, socio-
economic rights, and restrictions on freedom of expression in Chapter 2.
In Chapter 8 we examine the judiciary, including its process of constitutional interpretation of fundamental rights; and in Chapter 9 we will
look at freedom of religion. In this chapter, as a means of gauging the
concept and actual experience of human rights in Malaysia, we will take
three different approaches.

First, we will examine the fate of a particular fundamental-rights
provision, Article 5, which provides for the right to life and personal
liberty, especially in the light of attempts to curtail individual liberty
on the basis of national-security considerations. This has been the most

---

[1] The reader is referred to Kevin Tan and Thio Li-ann, *Constitutional Law in Malaysia
and Singapore* (3rd edn, Singapore, LexisNexis, 2010) chs 11–19; S Alagan, *Federal
Constitution: A Commentary* (Subang Jaya, Thomson Reuters, 2019); Lim Wei Jiet,
*Halsbury's Law of Malaysia, Volume 3(3): Constitutional Law* (2019 Reissue, Petaling
Jaya, LexisNexis, 2019).

frequently litigated right, and is in several ways the most basic of human rights, as well as the most indicative of the value attached to human rights in the Malaysian context.

Secondly, we will examine human rights from an institutional perspective by looking at Suhakam (the National Human Rights Commission) as a major initiative in the development of human-rights awareness and social entrenchment.

Thirdly, we will examine human rights from a minority, non-metropolitan perspective by looking at the rights of Malaysia's indigenous people, where we go beyond the fundamental-right provisions of the Constitution, presenting a more positive and holistic picture of imaginative application of human rights in an area where ethnic pluralism and human rights meet head on.

## II. ATTITUDES TOWARDS HUMAN RIGHTS

Human rights have always been a matter of some ambiguity in Malaysia. While many reject human rights as a Western imposition, Malaysia also has a very strong legal profession and Bar Council with a very active Human Rights Committee[2] and equally strong, diverse and well-organised civil society and social movements, many of which advocate for human rights.[3] In recent years the judiciary has become more protective of the Constitution's bill of rights, and more expansive in its interpretation: one writer identifies 1996 as a watershed year in terms of a sea-change in judicial attitudes to fundamental rights.[4] To some extent the more contested politics post-2008 has prevented further erosion of constitutional protection, following 50 years in which human rights tended to be marginalised in favour of development, a tendency that was reinforced by appeal to national security and public order in the wake of the May 13 riots in 1969, discussed in Chapter 2.

During his first period in the office of Prime Minister, Tun Mahathir argued strenuously against Malaysia's adoption of Western liberal democracy in a manner that spoke directly, and negatively, of human rights. He emphasised the claims of stability and authority over those

---

[2] See https://malaysianbar.org.my/list/about-us/committees/human-rights.

[3] AR Govindasamy, 'Social movements in contemporary Malaysia: The cases of BERSIH, HINDRAF, and Perkasa' in M Weiss (ed), *The Routledge Handbook of Contemporary Malaysia* (Abingdon, Routledge, 2014).

[4] Lim Wei Jiet (n 1) 27.

of democracy and individual rights, painting the West as both in thrall to extreme individual licence, and making use of human rights to establish a form of hegemony over the developing world. In contrast, he presented Malaysia as both culturally attuned to stricter social values and as requiring efficient implementation of development as a priority over human rights.[5]

Many commentators have since then followed this view, especially amongst the religious right and adherents of Malay supremacy.[6] Quite apart from civil-society organisations and the legal profession, Mahathir's own Deputy Prime Minister at the time and now PKR leader, Anwar Ibrahim, took and continues to take a contrary view of human rights, identifying them as both universal and evident in all cultures, including Islamic ones.[7] Now that Malaysia is no longer regarded as a developing country, the logic of the Asian values argument should lead to some version of human rights featuring as part of national ideology, rather than their rejection, but the Asian-values argument is still quite persistent. Opponents of international human rights nonetheless stress Malaysia's adherence to some human-rights principles and the extent of its compliance in practice. Tun Mahathir emerged in his second term as a converted believer in multi-party democracy and civil liberties, especially press freedom. In fact, in September 2018 he announced in the UN General Assembly that Malaysia would ratify the human-rights covenants: a promise that was surprising but not in fact, as it turned out, fulfilled.[8] While the PH government had set out a human-rights agenda in the *Buku Harapan*, the PN government has not stated any clear general position on the matter. However, the Covid-19 pandemic through 2020–21 naturally laid emphasis on social responsibility and prompted some to see human rights as a form of hyper-liberalism that works against the communal interest.

As a country front and centre in the 'Asian values versus international human rights' debate, Malaysia has generally received quite a bad press from international bodies such as the UN Human Rights Committee

[5] AJ Langlois, *The Politics of Justice and Human Rights: Southeast Asia and Universalist Theory* (Cambridge, Cambridge University Press, 2001) chs 1–2; Khoo Boo Teik, *The Paradoxes of Mahathirism: An Intellectual Biography of Mahathir Mohamad* (Shah Alam, Oxford University Press, 1995) 42–47.

[6] John Liu, 'Civil liberties in contemporary Malaysia: Progress, retrogression, and the resurgence of "Asian values"' in Weiss (n 3) 292 ff.

[7] Anwar Ibrahim, *Asian Renaissance* (Kuala Lumpur, Times International, 1996).

[8] '[Speech text] Dr Mahathir at 73rd UN General Assembly', *New Straits Times*, 29 September 2018, available at www.nst.com.my/news/nation/2019/09/415941/speech-text-dr-mahathir-73rd-un-general-assembly.

in its universal periodic reviews, the International Commission of Jurists, Amnesty International, and Human Rights Watch. Criticism has abounded of its official stand on human rights in general, and for its actual practice of human rights with regard to, for example, preventive detention and other restrictions on civil liberties; failure to take tough action on international issues such as human trafficking; and, more recently, for restrictions on freedom of religion (for which, see Chapter 9). Moreover, unlike many comparable Asian countries, it has not, in spite of Mahathir's speech to the UN, acceded to widely accepted international instruments, such as the International Covenant on Civil and Political Rights, the International Covenant on Economic, Social and Cultural Rights, and the International Convention on the Elimination of Racial Discrimination (ICERD). This position has usually been justified on the basis of the Asian-values argument, or on the basis that the rights contained in these instruments are already guaranteed under Malaysian law. The reality is more that there is strong popular disagreement, especially among Malay/ Muslim groups, with signing the covenants. There is also an official view that the covenants are acceptable but should only be signed when Malaysia is in complete compliance with them; since this is not yet the case, any other stand would be hypocritical.

Undoubtedly, the Asian-values debate has affected adversely and probably delayed the improvement of human rights in Malaysia, especially during the first Mahathir period. His successor, Abdullah Badawi, had previously, as Foreign Minister, stated the Asian-values argument at the 1993 Vienna Conference on Human Rights, saying that the rights of the individual were 'certainly not in splendid isolation from those of the community', and that excessive individualism was an agent of moral decay which weakened the social fabric.[9] At the same time he did not reject the need to 'continuously strive for the upholding of human dignity, and the essential worth of the human person'. Subsequently the 1993 Bangkok Declaration, signed by 34 Asian countries including Malaysia, decried the emphasis on civil liberties and emphasised the importance of the basic needs of Asian peoples in terms of socioeconomic rights.[10] The Convention on the Elimination of all Forms of Discrimination Against Women, on the other hand, was ratified

---

[9] 'Statements by Representatives of Asian Governments at the Vienna World Conference on Human Rights' in James TH Tang (ed), *Human Rights and International Relations in the Asia-Pacific* (London, Pinter, 1995) 213, 236.

[10] Thio Li-ann, 'Panacea, placebo or pawn? The teething problems of the Human Rights Commission of Malaysia (Suhakam)' (2008–2009) 40 *George Washington International Law Review* 1271, 1286.

by Malaysia as early as 2005,[11] and a constitutional amendment that included gender discrimination as an explicitly prohibited form of discrimination under Article 8 had already been enacted in 2001.[12] This is in fact the only constitutional amendment to date that has actually expanded fundamental rights, apart from the reduction of the voting age to 18, referred to in Chapter 4.

The next Prime Minister, Najib Razak, in relation to the first Bersih rally in July 2011 also made statements reflecting the Asian-values argument, indicating that such protests (in fact peaceful and orderly) could not be afforded as they would create chaos on the streets.[13] Nonetheless, he presided over the repeal of emergency laws that restricted human rights. As we will see in a later section, the Human Rights Commission of Malaysia (for which the Malay acronym is 'Suhakam'), as the official arm of the state responsible for human rights, has also given some emphasis to socio-economic rights in its practical human rights work; as Whiting points out, this is a logical response to the privileging of development over civil liberties, which is a general preference of those who advocate an Asian-values approach to human rights.[14]

From 2018 the PH Government did, as we have seen, evince an intention to sign the covenants, and moreover announced abolition of the death penalty as well as repeal of oppressive laws such as the Sedition Act 1948, and other legislation that severely inhibits freedom of expression. Matters began promisingly, as, immediately on embarking on his period in office in 2018, an event marked by controversy, the new Attorney-General Tommy Thomas, a long-time human-rights advocate, announced that there would be 'no more political prosecutions', which was a reference to the previous use of laws restricting freedom of expression being used against the Government's political opponents. He also instructed his lawyers not to resist leave applications in judicial review cases and not to

---

[11] However, Malaysia has derogated from some provisions due to conflict with the Constitution and Islamic law. It has however also ratified the Convention on the Rights of the Child.

[12] Art 8(2); in *Noorfadilla bt Ahmad Saikin v Chayed bin Basirun* [2012] 1 MLJ 832 compensation was given to a woman dismissed because she was pregnant, and in this and several other cases the courts have stressed the international nature of the obligation to honour rights under CEDAW and other instruments. See, further, Lim Wei Jiet (n 1) 49ff.

[13] 'Political affray in Malaysia: Taken to the cleaners', *The Economist*, 14 July 2011, available at www.economist.com/node/18959359.

[14] A Whiting, 'In the shadow of developmentalism: The Human Rights Commission of Malaysia at the intersection of state and civil society priorities', and Thio Li-ann, 'Taking development seriously: Beyond the statist rhetoric of the human right to development in ASEAN States', both in C Raj Kumar and DK Srivastava (eds), *Human Rights and Development: Law, Policy and Governance* (Hong Kong, LexisNexis, 2006).

raise technical objections to citizens' claims against the state.[15] As with many of its commitments in the human-rights area and elsewhere, the PH Government failed to act concertedly or with dispatch on its express promises, and in many cases simply reneged on them. With regard to ICERD, however, the Government faced a strong backlash and demonstrations by groups that feared (irrationally, according to Suhakam[16]) the denting of Malay supremacy and abolition of the bumiputera-preference system (discussed in Chapter 2), and reversed its stand.[17] On the death penalty, the Government changed its stand to one of opposition to mandatory death penalties, but in the event no changes were made before the PH Government fell.[18] Unfortunately, this example is typical of what occurred with most of the PH Government's governance reforms.

The prevailing theory of human rights in Malaysia therefore remains uncertain, oscillating between on the one hand a refusal, for the time being at least, to accept the international bill of human rights as a set of binding norms, and maintaining on the other hand that human rights are well understood and respected in Malaysia, albeit differently defined from the West, their fulfilment in practice being a governmental objective, as evidence by the creation of Suhakam. It is clear, however, that Asian-values are less stridently advocated than in 1990s, and the advent of the ASEAN human-rights mechanism[19] has also dampened the initiative for a distinctively Asian-values-based approach, which has in any case been abandoned by some of Malaysia's natural allies in this area, such as Indonesia.

## III. ORIGINS OF CONSTITUTIONAL RIGHTS

A lack of real enthusiasm for human rights was apparent even from the beginning. In drafting the *Merdeka* Constitution the Reid Commission

---

[15] 'Transcript of *The Edge* and *Malaysiakini*'s joint interview with AG Tommy Thomas' (Putrajaya, Attorney-General's Chambers of Malaysia, 2018). For an example, see *Public Prosecutor v Azmi bin Sharom* [2015] 6 MLJ 751. See also T Thomas, *My Story: Justice in the Wilderness* (Petaling Jaya, SIRDC, 2021) chs 26, 45.

[16] *Suhakam Annual Report 2018*, available at https://suhakam.org.my/2019/12/annual-report-2018.

[17] 'Why Malaysia backpedalled on ICERD ratification', *New Straits Times*, 24 November 2018, available at www.nst.com.my/news/nation/2018/11/434078/why-malaysia-back pedalled-on-icerd-ratification.

[18] 'A call to abolish the death penalty', *The Star*, 12 October 2020, available at www. thestar.com.my/opinion/letters/2020/10/12/a-call-to-abolish-the-death-penalty.

[19] The ASEAN Intergovernmental Commission on Human Rights, for which see https:// aichr.org.

proceeded on the rather unhelpful basis that, while fundamental rights were firmly entrenched in Malaya, there were 'vague apprehensions about the future' and there was 'no objection' to including them in the Constitution.[20] By the standards of the 1950s, with India's Constitution looming large as the state-of-the-art version of human-rights protection, and in light of the Commission's unwillingness to look carefully at this issue, it was hardly surprising that the *Merdeka* Constitution simply, for the most part, adopted a somewhat attenuated version of the Indian provisions. Even now constitutional law texts and court judgments make extensive use of Indian case law on fundamental rights. As we saw in Chapter 1, the debate that followed concentrated on judicial review rather than on the actual content of the human rights provisions. As a result, the definition of human rights in Malaysia struggles even now to catch up with evolving international human-rights standards.

The fundamental liberties in Part II of the Constitution include the right to life and personal liberty; freedom from slavery and forced labour; protection against retrospective laws and double jeopardy; equality before the law; the right of freedom of movement; freedom of speech, assembly and association; freedom of religion; and the right to property.[21] The Indian Constitution provided for judicial review of any legislative restriction on freedom of expression, assembly and association on the basis that such restrictions had to be reasonable. Article 10 of the *Merdeka* Constitution made no such provision, merely listing a series of broad grounds upon which Parliament may restrict these rights if it 'deems it necessary or expedient'. These grounds include security of the Federation, public order, morality, and incitement to any offence.[22] As a result the Constitution substantially restricted judicial review of legislation, at least as concerns freedom of speech, assembly and association, and it has been specifically held that 'reasonableness' cannot be imported into Article 10 as a restriction on parliament's power to restrict the rights contained therein.[23] We have seen in Chapters 2 and 4, and will see in Chapter 9, instances where these Article 10 rights have been restricted in practice. However, the recent espousal of the 'basic structure doctrine' in Malaysia, which is discussed in the next chapter, implicates fundamental rights in that the essence of these rights should be seen as part of the basic structure of the Constitution, which in

---

[20] *Federation of Malaya Constitutional Commission, 1956–7 Report* (Kuala Lumpur, Government Printer, 1957) paras 161–62.
[21] Arts 5–13.
[22] Art 10(2).
[23] *PP v Azmi bin Sharom* (n 15).

turns means that this essence may not be abridged either by constitutional amendment or by ordinary legislation, even if such legislation is passed on the basis of one of the permitted types of restriction listed above.[24]

The Constitution was also drafted during the emergency of 1948–60, a context which deeply affected the perceived relevance of human rights at the time and therefore subsequently too. Emergency powers were provided for under Article 150 as a basis for allowing exception in an emergency to most of the human rights provisions. In addition, Article 149, in providing for special powers against subversion, gave justification for substantial restrictions on human rights even under *normal* circumstances.[25] Taken together, these special powers, already drawing human rights narrowly even by the standards of 1957, barely begin to fulfil present-day expectations. They also amount, almost, to the entrusting of human rights to the mercy of the executive power. It was inevitable that the rights set out in the Constitution would be eroded over time as the developmental state increased its power. Indeed, with most of the provisions of Part II one finds that the opposite of rights is the result: for example, equality becomes in practice discrimination, while freedom becomes in practice prohibition. The fundamental rights provisions hardly even needed to be amended to achieve this result, so broad were the permissible restrictions. A notable exception is Article 10 itself which, as discussed in Chapter 2, while providing for potentially large restrictions, was in fact also drastically amended by the *Rukunegara* amendments to restrict public speech even further than was already allowed by Article 10, with regard to the so-called 'sensitive issues', and resulted in a severe tightening of the laws on sedition.

## IV. INDIVIDUAL LIBERTY AND PREVENTIVE DETENTION

'Baharu bertunas sudah di-petek'

(The tree had barely produced shoots when they were plucked.)

In this section, against the background of national security laws, we look at individual liberty as provided for under the Constitution. Here the question is: how does such a guarantee work in practice in light of all these overriding laws?

---

[24] See p 163.
[25] See ch 3, and above.

Article 5(1) provides that '[n]o person shall be deprived of his life or personal liberty save in accordance with law'. Article 5 goes on to protect the life and liberty of the person by providing for rights in the criminal process: the right to habeas corpus; to be informed of the reasons for arrest and have access to counsel; and to be brought before a court within 24 hours of arrest.[26] Yet as with many other Malaysian fundamental rights provisions, Article 5 in effect takes away with one hand what is proffered with the other. As is indicated above, the Constitution provides the Government and Parliament with the means to circumvent Article 5 (in addition to most other rights) where a threat of organised violence (Article 149) or an emergency (Article 150) is in question. Both of these latter provisions allow Article 5, as well as other fundamental rights provisions, to be overridden, and in practice it has been overridden by a number of pieces of legislation such as the Internal Security Act 1960 (ISA) and the Emergency (Public Order and Prevention of Crime) Ordinance 1969.

At the time of writing the Emergency (Essential Provisions) Ordinance 2021 is in force pursuant to the proclamation of 12 January 2021. The Ordinance mainly affects the right to property, but regulations made thereunder may potentially affect Article 5 rights, and at section 7(1) it provides for the armed forces, during the emergency, 'to have the authority to arrest and detain, and possess the right of a police officer under the Criminal Procedure Code ... as well as the authority vested in them under the Armed Forces Act 1972'. This is a very large extension of state powers over individual liberty.

These ISA and all existing emergency laws along with emergency proclamations and two oppressive, although much less used laws – the Restricted Residence Act 1933 and the Banishment Act 1959 – were repealed by 2013. These laws were often criticised for their negative impact on fundamental rights, especially in that they allowed for preventive detention, as well as for their vague expressions and openness to executive abuse. For example, the ISA had been 'invoked or threatened to be invoked in respect of those alleged to have spread rumours, forged passports, cloned hand phones, breached copyrights, counterfeited coins and documents', as well as 'to stifle legitimate opposition and silence lawful dissent'.[27] The repealed laws are replaced by the Security Offences (Special Measures) Act 2012 (SOSMA). SOSMA was an improvement on

---

[26] Art 5(2)–(4).
[27] Johan Sabaruddin and S Dhanapal, 'The rule of law: an initial analysis of the Security Offences (Special Measures) Act 2012' (2015) 23 *IIUM Law Journal* 1, 3–4.

the ISA but has also been criticised on similar grounds.[28] SOSMA has been used for both legitimate and illegitimate purposes. For example, it was used to detain 104 Filipino insurgents during the Lahad Datu insurgency in Sabah in 2013, but in addition was used to detain Bersih activists, and even citizens wearing yellow tee-shirts supporting Bersih, during its rally, also in 2013. SOSMA, at section 4, reduces the period allowed for administrative detention in respect of security offences defined under the Act, to 28 days, in place of the two years, renewable, provided under the ISA. It also provides that '[n]o person shall be arrested and detained under this section [section 4] solely for his political belief or political activity'. However, it is supplemented by a 2012 amendment to the Penal Code, section 124, which provides for a number of offences in connection with actions designed to undermine parliamentary democracy, and by the Prevention of Offences against Terrorism Act 2015 (POTA), and amendments to the Prevention of Crime Act 1959 (POCA), under which a person can be detained without trial, ultimately for a period of two years, as with the ISA. At the end of all this, Malaysian citizens are hardly any better protected from arbitrary detention without resource to court process except for habeas corpus, than they were before 2012. The only further protection they now have is that in the case of preventive detention there has to be a recommendation of detention from a board established under the relevant statutes allowing for detention, rather than the minister being empowered to act alone. But this new regime also means that the extensive and beneficial case law on Article 5 is still applicable.

The most important issue arising under Article 5 in practice has been whether Article 5(2) (the right to habeas corpus) and other rights in Article 5 can be used to challenge a preventive detention order. For most of post-1960 Malaysian history the ISA was the main area of tension in which the judiciary was caught between the authoritarian state, on the one hand, and an outraged civil society (many of whose members had direct experience of preventive detention) on the other. Accordingly most of the relevant habeas corpus cases have occurred under the legal regime of the ISA.

The approach generally taken by the judiciary in habeas corpus cases has been to eschew direct challenge to the Government on the issue of substantive justification for the detention, while implementing a high level of scrutiny with regard to the procedure adopted. This is understandable, as the substantive conditions under POCA and POTA are, like

---

[28] Ibid.

the ISA, expressed in vague terms, referring generally to national security, while the procedure is quite detailed. For example, section 19(A) of POCA[29] states:

> The Board may, after considering the report of the Inquiry Officer submitted under section 10 and the outcome of any review under section 11, direct that any registered person be detained under a detention order for a period not exceeding two years, and may renew any such detention order for a further period not exceeding two years at a time, if it is satisfied that such detention is necessary in the interest of public order, public security or prevention of crime.

A good example of the extensive use of such powers, on this occasion under the ISA, is Operasi Lalang in October 1987. Following the escalation of acute racial tensions in Kuala Lumpur over the issue of Chinese education, 109 persons of different political and ethnic groups, including notable opposition figures, were detained for periods of several months or longer. The incident caused an outcry both in Malaysia and internationally. It was said that the Government had used racial tensions, which undoubtedly existed, to crack down on its opponents regardless of their responsibility in the matter. At the same time many Malaysians considered this crackdown as the only alternative to serious racial riots, and the spectre of 'May 13' was, as on other occasions, invoked to justify the crackdown.[30] Fortunately no major episode of this kind has occurred since then, but preventive detention powers have nonetheless continued to be used on occasion.

The courts heard numerous habeas corpus applications arising from *Operasi Lalang* and other invocations of the ISA and emergency legislation couched in similar terms to the replacement statutes. In general they have refused to investigate the allegations of fact relied on by the Government, as well as the sufficiency of those facts in justifying the decision to detain. This was established in the seminal case of *Karam Singh* in 1969,[31] and reaffirmed in *Theresa Lim Chin Chin* in 1988,[32] where Salleh Abas LP stated that

> the court will not be in a position to review the fairness of the decision-making process by the police and by the Minister because of the lack of

---

[29] Cf POTA 2015, s.13, which is in similar terms except for a requirement that the detainee be engaged in terrorist activities. The Emergency (Essential Powers) Act 2021, enacted pursuant to the proclamation of emergency of January 2021, is designed to deal with pandemic-related issues and does not contain any power of detention.

[30] Kua Kia Soong, *The Malaysian Civil Rights Movement* (Petaling Jaya, SIRD, 2005) ch 7.

[31] *Karam Singh v Minister for Home Affairs* [1969] 2 MLJ 129.

[32] *Theresa Lim Chin Chin v Inspector-General of Police* [1988] 1 MLJ 293.

evidence since the Constitution and the law protect them from disclosing any information and materials in their possession upon which they based their decision …

a result which was described by him as adopting a 'subjective' as opposed to an 'objective' test of ministerial satisfaction. In another case decided at about the same time, the apex court drew a distinction between the grounds for the detention and allegations of fact, stating that the former but not the latter were reviewable.[33] In *Tan Sri Raja Khalid*[34] it was alleged that, acting as Managing Director of a consultancy company and as a member of the loans committee of a bank in which large numbers of members of the armed forces had an interest, the detainee had caused substantial losses to the bank, thereby causing feelings of anger and agitation among members of the armed forces. It is hardly surprising that habeas corpus was granted in this case, but what is surprising is that, in view of the case law, the decision was based on the absence of any actual evidence that the detainee had acted in any manner prejudicial to security; in effect the court applied the objective test. To similar effect is an important case in a plural society, the case of *Jamaluddin Othman*, where the court held that the ISA could not be used to detain a person who was attempting to convert Muslims to Christianity.[35]

However, the issue was not completely resolved by these cases. A notable Singapore Court of Appeal case in 1989[36] established an *objective test* of ministerial satisfaction under Singapore's ISA, following which the statute was amended in such a way as to prevent judicial review. The Malaysian Parliament followed the example of Singapore's Parliament in passing the Internal Security (Amendment) Act 1989, substituting a new section 8B – an ouster clause, which prohibited judicial review of any act or decision of the *Yang di-Pertuan Agong* or the minister in the exercise of their powers under the Act, save in regard to compliance with any *procedural* requirement in the Act governing such act or decision.

As a result of this amendment, in considering habeas corpus applications both under the ISA and other laws providing for administrative detention, the judiciary has concentrated on procedural defects. They

---

[33] *Minister for Home Affairs v Karpal Singh* [1988] 1 MLJ 468.
[34] *Re Tan Sri Raja Khalid bin Raja Harun* [1988] 1 MLJ 182.
[35] *Minister for Home Affairs v Jamaluddin bin Othman* [1989] 1 MLJ 418.
[36] *Chng Suan Tze v Minister for Home Affairs* [1989] 1 MLJ 69.

have taken the view that, where the liberty of the subject is involved, the statute must be construed strictly with regard to procedure.[37] On the whole they have indeed been very strict. Procedural issues have been held to include such defects as: a break of nine and a half hours in the chain of authority to detain; failure to interview the detainee during a 60-day period of detention; failure to inform the detainee properly of his right to make representations by inadequate translation of the forms into Tamil; failure to detain the detainee in the place specified in the order; refusing access to a lawyer or members of the detainee's family; and even failure to serve two copies of the detention order on the detainee, rather than one. However, there are limits even to this degree of scrutiny: a detainee cannot obtain release due to a mere typographical error in the order.[38]

In contrast with the strictness of their approach to procedural issues, the courts have been less sympathetic with detainees who suffered actual mistreatment, even though such detainees, by definition, are being detained for security reasons and not because they have committed an offence or merit punishment. Here they have held that the conditions of detention do not go to the legality of the detention itself.[39] Exemplary damages have, however, been awarded in one case of mistreatment during detention.[40]

One of the difficulties with legislation as broad in substantive scope as those referred to above is that there is potentially no limit to the types of cases that can be regarded as coming under it. Although the ISA was designed to combat communist insurgency following the ending of the 1948 emergency, even the courts have recognised, in *Theresa Lim Chin Chin*,[41] that it is not confined to such general threats. In practice, not only has the principle of administrative detention been applied in legislation against drug-trafficking and drug addiction,[42] it has also been used against people forging documents, defrauding banks and spreading Shi'ite Islamic teachings. In 1995 the IGP even suggested it be used

---

[37] *Re Datuk James Wong Kim Min* [1976] 2 MLJ 245.

[38] In order to avoid excessive citation of cases supporting these simple propositions, the reader is referred to Shad Saleem Faruqi, *Document of Destiny: The Constitution of the Federation of Malaysia* (Petaling Jaya, The Star, 2008) 226–32.

[39] *Morgan Perumal v Ketua Inspektor* [1996] 3 MLJ 281; *Rajeshkanna Marimuthu v Tuan Haji Abdul Wahab* [2004] 5 MLJ 155.

[40] *Abd Malek bin Hussin v Borhan bin Haji Daud* [2008] 1 MLJ 368.

[41] *Theresa Lim Chin Chin* (n 32) 296.

[42] Drugs Dependants (Treatment and Rehabilitation) Act 1983; Dangerous Drugs (Special Preventive Measures) Act 1985.

against persons spreading rumours of vampires.[43] The temptation to see literally any social problem through the lens of the special legal regime, irrespective of individual human rights, seems to have proved irresistible. Only the courts stand between the citizen and such executive overreach, on which detention boards have rarely acted as any kind of check and balance. Fortunately, they have proved increasingly willing to provide a bulwark for the citizen in relation to habeas corpus and other matters arising under Article 5.

There are indeed even broader implications for individual liberty than habeas corpus contained within Article 5. The Malaysian courts have, for example, considered the meaning of the right to 'life and personal liberty' under Article 5(1), as well as the meaning of the phrase 'in accordance with law'. In relation to the latter they have ruled that 'law' includes reasonable, fair and just procedure, as well as substantive fairness, and this includes the principle of rule of law.[44] They have refused, despite many ingenious arguments to the contrary, to hold that a mandatory death sentence is constitutionally invalid under Article 5(1) or otherwise.[45] Nonetheless, the right to life has been given an astonishingly broad construction. It has been held to include the rights to dignity, privacy and a livelihood, including by exercise of native customary land rights; the right to live in a healthy, pollution-free environment; the right to one's reputation; the right not to experience delay in carrying out a death sentence; and the right to seek judicial review of an administrative decision. It has also been used to impose a duty to investigate custodial deaths.[46]

One striking case indicating recent engagement with acute social issues is one affecting transsexuals. The appellants were Muslim males who had been repeatedly detained, arrested and prosecuted by the religious authorities in Negeri Sembilan for cross-dressing, which was an offence under the Syariah Criminal (Negeri Sembilan) Enactment 1992, section 66. Having suffered constant humiliation and being perpetually at risk of arrest and prosecution, they sought a declaration that the law was void for being inconsistent with Article 5(1) and various other constitutional rights. The Court of Appeal invalidated the law, holding

---

[43] Kevin Tan, 'The law and practice of preventive detention: Recent developments in Malaysia and Singapore' in Wu Min Aun (ed), *Public Law in Contemporary Malaysia* (Petaling Jaya, Longman, 1999) 309.

[44] *Tan Tek Seng @ Tan Chee Meng v Suruhanjaya Perkhidmatan Pendidikan & Anor* [1996] 1 MLJ 261; *Sivarasa Rasiah v Badan Peguam Malaysia* [2010] 2 MLJ 333, para [17].

[45] Eg in *Public Prosecutor v Lau Kee Hoo* [1984] 1 MLJ 110.

[46] For details and citations, see Lim Wei Jiet (n 1) 26ff.

that section 66 directly affected the appellant's right to live with dignity as guaranteed by Article 5(1), as well infringing their right to equality under Article 8(1).[47]

Although one can say on the evidence of the case law referred to in this section that on the whole the judiciary affords fairly good protection, nonetheless reports of police conduct remain extremely worrying. A Royal Commission on the Police reported in 2005 recommending a raft of fundamental reforms, but no substantial reforms have actually been implemented. The lack of government action on this agenda contributed to the resignation of Abdullah Badawi as Prime Minister in 2009. Since then little has been done to address the recommendations, which included the setting up of an independent police complaints body.

Concern has been repeatedly expressed, including by Suhakam and the Bar Council, over deaths in prisons, rehabilitation centres, police lockups and detention centres for illegal immigrants; yet instances of police being accountable or punished in relation to these instances remain very few. There have also been cases involving other enforcement agencies such as the very controversial and tragic case of Teoh Beng Hock, a young DAP party worker who died in 2009 after being questioned while in the custody of the Malaysian Anti-Corruption Agency (MACA). His body was found in the street below the MACA offices. A vocal civil-society campaign was set in motion to challenge the official story that he took his own life. A Royal Commission looked into the matter and reported in the same fashion, but found that Teoh had been 'subjected to aggressive and relentless questioning'. Nonetheless an open verdict was reached by the Coroner and questions still remain. The case was ordered to be reopened for investigation in November 2020.[48]

Civil society organisations such as Proham and Hakam remain as vocal as they ever were in demanding reforms in the human rights area. In 2018 it briefly looked as though such reforms would occur, but unfortunately, as with many other reforms, the political situation since GE14 has set back reform considerably. Nonetheless, there have been improvements in terms of Government actions, judicial oversight and rising awareness of human rights issues in government and amongst the public.

---

[47] *Muhamad Juzaili bin Mohd Khamis & Ors v State Government of Negeri Sembilan & Ors* [2015] 3 MLJ 513; the decision was overturned on other grounds by the Federal Court: [2015] 6 AMR 248.

[48] See the Bar Council press statement at www.malaysianbar.org.my/article/about-us/president-s-corner/pressstatements/press-comment-the-malaysian-bar-welcomes-the-decision-to-reopen-investigations-in-the-teoh-beng-hock-case-and-calls-for-the-enactment-of-a-coroners-court-act-in-malaysia.

Much of this awareness can be attributed to civil society organisations and to Suhakam, to which we now turn.

## V. SUHAKAM: THE HUMAN RIGHTS COMMISSION

'Bergurindam di-tengah rimba'

(Reciting poetry in the middle of the forest)

The setting up of Suhakam represents the most significant positive development in the field of human rights in Malaysia since 1957. Following the Vienna Conference in 1993 a number of Asian states decided to set up a national institution with responsibility for human rights. In Malaysia the result was the Human Rights Commission of Malaysia Act 1999. Coming as it did during the highly charged political tumult resulting from the arrest and trial of former Deputy Prime Minister Anwar Ibrahim, matters started on the wrong foot as the Bill to create Suhakam was announced only two months before it was introduced in Parliament and was not made public until it was passed. Far from applauding this human-rights initiative, civil society organisations expressed dismay at the lack of public participation and suspicion as to what the real motives for the Act were.[49]

As with the general run of such national institutions, the functions of Suhakam are to promote awareness of human rights; advise and assist the Government in relation to legislation and administrative procedure; make recommendations to the Government with regard to accession to international human rights instruments; and inquire into complaints.[50] Suhakam's specific powers include advising the Government of complaints and recommendation of measures to be taken; studying and verifying infringements of human rights; visiting places of detention; conducting public inquiries into human rights violations; and issuing public statements.[51] It will be noted that none of these powers enables Suhakam to take direct enforcement action, or even to litigate, on human rights issues. Its functions are entirely secondary or indirect.

Given the 'Asian values' ideology frequently propounded in the 1990s by Government leaders in opposition to international human rights, a pertinent question is: how are human rights defined for Suhakam's

---

[49] S Sothi Rachagan and Ramdas Tikamdas (eds), *Human Rights and the National Commission* (Kuala Lumpur, Hakam, 1999).

[50] Human Rights Commission of Malaysia Act 1999, s 4(1).

[51] Ibid s 4(2).

statutory purposes? The 1999 Act defines human rights as the 'fundamental liberties as enshrined in Part II of the Constitution'. On the other hand, regard is to be had to the UN Declaration of Human Rights 1948 'to the extent that it is not inconsistent with the Federal Constitution'. It seems therefore that the practical standard is Malaysian law but this does not preclude Suhakam from arguing for adoption or adherence to international norms as a matter of development of law and practice, or to investigate rights which simply fall outside the fundamental rights provisions of the Constitution. Suhakam's own elaboration of human rights in its published materials and programmes[52] takes a universalist rather than a relativist or culturally specific position in explaining and defining human rights, referring to a range of international instruments including ones Malaysia has not yet ratified. It adopts a practical definition of human rights that in several respects does indeed go beyond the list of fundamental liberties set out in the Constitution. Examples are native land rights; the right to housing; the right to privacy; the rights of persons with disabilities; and lesbian and gay rights. Suhakam has even investigated water privatisation on the basis that access to water supply is an internationally recognised human right.

A related issue is how Suhakam's activities relate to judicial review. The 1999 Act is quite clear on this. It cannot investigate a matter that is before the courts or where it has already been determined by the courts.[53] In *Vythilingam v Human Rights Commission of Malaysia*, the High Court refused to compel Suhakam to hold an inquiry into a serious incident (the Kampong Medan riots, in which a number of Indian villagers were killed or injured); however the court also facilitated human rights monitoring by deciding that Suhakam can nonetheless hold a watching brief in an appropriate case before the courts, where it suspended its investigation due to expected legal proceedings.[54]

Commissioners are appointed by the *Yang di-Pertuan Agong* on the recommendation of the Prime Minister for a period of three years, which term is renewable once.[55] The Act does not indicate with any specificity the kind of persons to be appointed, except to say that the Commissioners should be appointed from amongst 'men and women of various religions, political and racial backgrounds, who have knowledge

---

[52] See www.suhakam.org.

[53] Human Rights Commission of Malaysia Act 1999, s 12.

[54] *Vythilingam v Human Rights Commission of Malaysia* [2003] MLJU 94.

[55] Human Rights Commission of Malaysia Act 1999, s 5, substituted by National Human Rights Commission (Amendment) Act 2009 (A1353), s 2. Prior to this the period was two years with no restriction on reappointment.

of, or practical experience in, human rights matters'.[56] Following an amendment to the Act in 2009, and in a nod towards independence in the process of appointing the Commissioners, paralleling the judicial appointments process (for which see Chapter 8), the Prime Minister must now consult a Committee comprising the Chief Secretary to the Government (the Chair); the Chair of Suhakam; and 'three members of civil society who have knowledge of practical experience in human rights, to be appointed by the Prime Minister'. The Committee members may include former judges and former Commissioners but not active participants in politics or current or former enforcement officers.[57] The Act provides for appointment of up to 20 Commissioners. The actual number of Commissioners has varied between 18 and seven over the years since 2000, and there are currently nine, including the Chair. The backgrounds of the current Commissioners are in law, academia, religion, civil society, public service and diplomacy; in terms of human rights they cover wide areas of expertise, from the UN periodic review and development economics to women's and children's rights, migrant workers and indigenous peoples. Four are women and five men, and they are also ethnically mixed.

The reduction in the number of Commissioners arguably reduces the amount of energy and the breadth of expertise that are brought to bear in the fulfilment of a very broad and complex remit, which currently embraces no less than 22 different areas of activity. The Commissioners fulfil their duties part-time with allowances but (except for the Chair) without remuneration.[58] Suhakam currently employs 93 staff, mainly at its head office in Kuala Lumpur, with offices also in Sabah and Sarawak. Its information and services are readily available to the public. The 1999 Act also provides that the Government shall provide Suhakam with adequate funds to enable it to discharge its functions under the Act.[59] In other words Suhakam does not enjoy budgetary independence; the adequacy of funding is clearly a matter to be judged by the Government in light of its overall commitments and policies. Therefore, in the matter of both appointments and budget Suhakam cannot be said to enjoy any real measure of independence from the Government. Nonetheless

---

[56] Human Rights Commission of Malaysia Act 1999, s 5(3), substituted by 2009 Act, s 2. Before the amendment s 5 referred to 'prominent persons'.

[57] Human Rights Commission of Malaysia Act 1999, s 11A, added by 2009 Act, s 3; and amended by Human Rights Commission (Amendment) (Amendment) Act 2009 [sic] (A1357), s 2.

[58] Human Rights Commission of Malaysia Act 1999, s 8.

[59] Ibid s 19(1).

Suhakam enjoys a ranking of 'A' for its compliance with the 1992 Paris Principles, granted by the Global Association of National Human Rights Institutions. Commencing its operations in 2000, under the chairmanship of Tan Sri Musa Hitam, a former Deputy Prime Minister and former Chair of the UN Human Rights Commission, Suhakam was almost immediately involved in the storm over the Anwar Ibrahim sodomy prosecution. Investigating allegations of human rights violations at a mass demonstration related to the Anwar case at the Kesas Highway near Kuala Lumpur, it issued a report severely criticising the authorities for their handling of the demonstration and found many violations of human rights.[60] Their Report was airily (and puzzlingly given the backgrounds of the Commissioners) dismissed by Prime Minister Tun Mahathir as resulting from a 'Western bias'.[61] According to an early assessment of Suhakam, it 'surprised and alarmed the government by taking its mandate seriously and issuing public statements, investigatory reports (including several reports on visits to places of detention) that were critical of executive action, police behaviour and repressive laws. It also strongly recommended accession to important international human rights treaties'.[62] Alarm bells were set off when two key Commissioners associated with the Kesas investigation were not reappointed.

Since then, however, the human rights situation in Malaysia has become somewhat less a matter of controversy, and approval of Suhakam's performance has grown, especially following two public inquiries into the disturbing disappearance of four religious figures in 2019. Disturbingly, the reports on these inquiries implicate State agents in the disappearances.[63]

In recent years Suhakam has received between 1000 and 2000 complaints annually, although many have been found to be outside its jurisdiction. Complaints have focused overwhelmingly on police powers, specifically with respect to inaction, excessive use of force, abuse of powers, and preventive detention. In Sabah and Sarawak, however, the focus has been mainly on land issues, especially encroachments on indigenous land.[64] Suhakam has a number of Divisions indicating their main

---

[60] *Inquiry on its own Motion into the November 5th Incident at the Kesas Highway* (Kuala Lumpur, Human Rights Commission of Malaysia, 2001).
[61] Thio Li-ann (n 10) 1332.
[62] Whiting (n 14) 389.
[63] The two Reports appear at www.suhakam.org.my.
[64] See the *Report on the National Inquiry into the Land Rights of Indigenous People* (Kuala Lumpur, Suhakam, 2013).

areas of activity. These relate to Education and Training; Promotion and Outreach; Complaints and Monitoring; Law Reform and International Treaties; International Cooperation and Media Relations; Publication and Documentation; and Corporate Services. It also established an Office of the Children's Commissioner in 2019. Its annual reports present an impressive picture of activity designed to create awareness and improvement of human rights in the broadest sense of the term and by the broadest possible means.

The real problem with Suhakam, however, has been constantly, not so much poor performance, as a lack of action following its work and its pronouncements. Suhakam has repeatedly requested closer engagement with Parliament, in terms of reporting to it, having the commissioners appointed via parliamentary process, engaging with the legislative process, and the creation of a select committee on Suhakam. With some Commissioners resigning 'or declining to have their terms renewed because this official indifference has persuaded them that they are engaging in an exercise in futility', wrote Mahadev Shankar, a former Commissioner who is also a former appeal court judge, 'there is a growing sense of public disquiet that [the annual reports'] ultimate fate is to become fodder for the termites that must lurk in the parliamentary archives'.[65] The problem goes further than lack of interest in Suhakam's reports. The Government has also failed to act on most of its specific recommendations. For example, an eminently sensible and well-argued case presented in 2002 for a National Human Rights Action Plan, placing human rights at the centre of development and aimed at practical programmes to deliver human rights, especially for the most vulnerable groups, was rejected with the somewhat obtuse statement that human rights were already guaranteed under the Constitution and the law; however, by 2018 the Human Rights Action Plan (NHRAP) was published. The thrust of NHRAP is the balancing of international obligations with Islamic principles. The plan was roundly criticised by human rights organisations for its omissions and its failure to ensure compliance with international norms, being described variously in responses as 'cosmetic', 'unambitious in aims and unchallenging in aspirations', and needing 'to be completely rewritten'. NHRAP was not published in English, and has been little discussed since 2018 despite embracing 294 plans relating to 83 priority issues.

---

[65] M Shankar, 'Suhakam: The National Human Rights Commission' in A Harding and HP Lee (ed), *Constitutional Landmarks in Malaysia: The First 50 Years, 1957–2007* (Kuala Lumpur, LexisNexis, 2007) 243, 251.

In terms of reporting, Suhakam reports to Parliament (section 21 of the Act), but is in effect controlled by the government (section 5). Suhakam itself favours increased independence and desires to report only to a select committee of Parliament, and indeed in July 2018 the PH government included such reform in a list of bodies whose reporting arrangements would be altered to create great independence.[66] Suhakam also sees a need to engage with religious organisations as well as State Governments over such matters as religious rights, child marriage, and indigenous land rights. In recent years Suhakam has highlighted issues in relation to fragile communities such as children, indigenous people, refugees, stateless persons, migrant workers, and transgendered people. Its Report on the Land Rights of Indigenous People was published in 2013, but, as with other initiatives this has not received much attention from government.

The de facto minister for law stated, revealingly, in 2006 that Suhakam was 'never meant to have teeth'.[67] It has been assumed that, if Suhakam was never meant to have teeth, it was invented merely to provide the government with an alibi, to give the impression that human rights were being addressed. However, the minister was literally correct in that it is a facilitative, advisory, body without any actual powers of enforcement. Suhakam cannot unilaterally, for example, award compensation, or set up a body to monitor police conduct. There is clearly still misunderstanding as to Suhakam's role. An example is provided by a long-term Suhakam Chair, Tan Sri Hasmy Agam:

> When we told the police we wanted to monitor [an illegal assembly for a candlelight vigil against the ISA] the first reaction wasn't good ... They thought we wanted to join the protesters. I think many among the police don't understand Suhakam's basic function. They probably thought that since it was an illegal assembly, we had no right to observe it.[68]

As often happens with reforms of this kind, the rot sets in when it comes as a shock for the reformers to realise that their motives are taken literally by appointees who attempt to fulfil their stated remit conscientiously. Nonetheless a survey of Suhakam's work over two decades reveals that it has in fact achieved much in terms of ventilating a wide range of issues, inculcating language and sometimes practice implicit in human rights

---

[66] 'Nine agencies to begin reporting to new Parliament', *The Star*, 15 July 2018.

[67] 'Govt: We don't intend to give Suhakam teeth', *Malaysiakini*, 27 March 2006, available at www.malaysiakini.com/news/48965.

[68] 'Suhakam chief: We're an independent agency', *The Nutgraph*, 30 August 2010.

awareness. Of particular importance is Suhakam's support for vulnerable groups, to one of which we now turn.

## VI. HUMAN RIGHTS: THE INDIGENOUS PERSPECTIVE

'Dulu gajah menyerang kita. Sekarang pembangunan yang menyerang kita'
(In the past, we were attacked by elephants. Today we are attacked by development)[69]

Malaysia's indigenous communities provide a useful case study on human rights for a number of reasons. First, the topic of human rights is appropriate for the introduction of this important strand of Malaysia's ethnic diversity amounting to about 12 per cent of the population; the indigenous communities themselves are not a group, but are culturally and ethnically very diverse, with different modes of subsistence and levels of integration and education. Secondly, these communities span both West and East Malaysia, being mainly concentrated in Sabah and Sarawak and in the jungle; this enables us to view human rights from a distinctively non-metropolitan perspective. Thirdly, the Constitution and the law have been thoroughly tested by the problems of these vulnerable communities, some of which result from over-development (incursion on traditional land), while others arise from under-development (socio-economic issues such as health and education). We will see here a much more positive aspect than in some other areas of human rights, showing some real potential for development of human rights in the constitutional context. Fourthly, indigenous rights have been strongly advocated by Suhakam in recent years and have become an area of significant activity both in Suhakam and in the courts. Currently there are estimated to be more than 150 native land claims in the Malaysian courts.[70]

In Malaysia the word 'indigenous' is an ambiguous one.[71] The native people settled in what is now Malaysia before the Malays, but the Malays were first to organise a state as opposed to living tribally. The Malays also lay claim to indigenous status in Malaysia, as is implied in the common use, in both legal and everyday contexts, of the word '*bumiputera*', and of course the name of the country itself. Under the Malaysian Constitution, as we have seen in Chapter 2, *bumiputera* – that

---

[69] The author is indebted to Cheah Wui Ling for this quotation: see below (n 75).

[70] The author is indebted to two lawyers, Yogeswaran Subramaniam and Bah Tony Hunt, for information on the native and *orang asli* peoples.

[71] R Bulan, 'Native status under the law', in Wu Min Aun (n 43).

is, the communities defined in the Constitution as 'Malays and natives of Sabah and Sarawak' – are entitled to certain special privileges amounting to a constitutionally entrenched affirmative action programme.

The natives of Sabah and Sarawak[72] comprise a large number of tribal people indigenous to those two Borneo states, including the Iban, Murut, Kadazan, Kenyah, Penan and many other groups. The Iban constitute 30 per cent of Sarawak's population, while the Kadazan-Dusun are the largest group in Sabah, also at about 30 per cent. Taken altogether the indigenous peoples at around 3.1 million constitute about half of the population of these two States. In general, these communities live in longhouses and live off cash crops or the produce of the sea and the jungle, but development has introduced other forms of employment in the logging, oil, gas and palm-oil industries. However, the considerable economic development has largely left the native communities behind; indeed, development in the form of logging, construction and new dams often threatens their land and their traditional way of life.

In addition to these groups there are the several indigenous peoples of the Malayan peninsula. These are known collectively as the '*orang asli*' (aboriginals), and number around 217,000. They are, illogically, and unlike the natives of Sabah and Sarawak, *not* officially fully classified as *bumiputera* despite the fact that they have lived in Malaya for more than 40,000 years, which is a matter of grievance on their part.[73] Nonetheless there are many programmes benefiting the *orang asli*. The *orang asli* are not one community but 18 distinct communities, having different geographical origins, languages, cultures and modes of subsistence. The generic term *orang asli* was coined for administrative and strategic purposes during the colonial period, and, since the Aboriginal Peoples Act 1954, it is in effect a term that also has legal consequences. Most of them live in about 7,000 remote mountainous villages, but some are semi-nomadic, some live in fishing villages, and a few have now joined the urban economy.

From a human rights perspective, the indigenous people as a whole

suffer disproportionately from preventable diseases, have higher infant and maternal mortality rates, are poorly provided with basic services and utilities, and have lower levels of education ... the great majority ... continue to

---

[72] The term 'native' is used here, in accordance with the convention in Malaysian law and the Constitution to denote the Indigenous peoples of Sabah and Sarawak, *only*.

[73] 'Speaker shoots down motion on Orang Asli's *bumiputera* status', *Malaysia Today*, 19 October 2010. See Arts 8(5)(c), 45(2), 160(2) for the different legal status of native and *orang asli* peoples.

suffer widespread and persistent poverty, high rates of illiteracy, and limited access to medical care.[74]

*Orang asli* do not have the full benefit of *bumiputera* status, and unlike the natives of Sabah and Sarawak, do not have official legal recognition of their customs. Again, unlike the natives of Sabah and Sarawak, they do not (or did not until recently) enjoy land rights as such, but only what we might call land concessions, unlike all other Malaysian citizens, who have property rights protected by the Constitution at Article 13. They were regarded as 'wards of the government' and their land rights amounted to being 'tenants-at-will'.[75]

The Constitution does recognise the special needs of the *orang asli* in some respects. It provides for the validity of 'any provision for the protection, well-being or advancement of the aboriginal peoples of the Malay Peninsula (including the reservation of land) or the reservation to aborigines of a reasonable proportion of suitable positions in the public service'.[76] The Constitution also provides for appointed members of the *Dewan Negara* [Senate] to include 'representatives of racial minorities' and those who 'are capable of representing the interests of aborigines'.[77] The emergence of activists and advocates for the *orang asli* community, and for the natives of Sabah and Sarawak, has been a critical factor leading to the ventilation of the land rights issue in the courts, and other human rights issues before State Governments and Suhakam.

Historically the *orang asli* have been successively ignored, resettled, controlled, treated as an opportunity for religious proselytisation (both Christian and Muslim), and exploited economically. The very definition of the *orang asli* as a group is the result of the colonial government's need to prevent them from helping communist insurgency during the Malayan Emergency (1948–60),[78] or to recruit them behind government efforts to end it. The 1954 Act, passed at the height of the emergency, contained some extraordinary provisions that transformed the situation of the *orang asli* overnight from complete separation to complete governmental

---

[74] SR Aiken and CH Leigh, 'Seeking redress in the Courts: Indigenous land rights and judicial decisions in Malaysia' (2011) 45(4) *Modern Asian Studies* 825, 83; Suhakam report (n 64).

[75] Cheah Wui Ling, '*Sagong Tasi* and *Orang Asli* land rights in Malaysia: Victory, milestone or false start' (2004) 2 *Law, Social Justice and Global Development Journal* 5, available at warwick.ac.uk/fac/soc/law/elj/lgd/2004_2/cheah.

[76] Art 8(5)(c).

[77] Art 45(2).

[78] J Leary, *Violence and the Dream People: The Orang Asli in the Malayan Emergency 1948–1960* (Athens, CIS, Ohio University, 1995).

control. The Government was empowered to appoint village headmen, to remove *orang asli* communities from their designated areas and reserves, and to reacquire such land from them at any time without appeal or compensation (other than for crops and dwellings but not for actual land values[79]), or any alternative provision. The recognition, definition and entrenchment of their land rights is tenuous at best; in practice compensation has been very small and very slow in being granted. Only around 25 per cent of land officially recognised as *orang asli* land has been gazetted as aboriginal reserve, leaving them largely unprotected from compulsory government land acquisition or third-party encroachment.[80] Even this figure does not take account of lands claimed by them. Between 1992 and 2002 gazetted *orang asli* lands in the State of Selangor were drastically reduced as the Kuala Lumpur conurbation spread rapidly, embracing the Multimedia Super Corridor and Malaysia's information technology capital Cyberjaya, Kuala Lumpur International Airport, the new administrative capital of Putrajaya, and all the attendant infrastructural and residential development, involving in this case extensive highways and a new dam.

All these developments had an adverse impact on the *orang asli*, for whom the land question is of enormous significance. They have deep spiritual and emotional ties to the land, and they have continuously depended on it, for thousands of years, for their livelihood and their sense of wellbeing. Thus, while economic development is of great importance, not just for urbanites but for the *orang asli* too, there has to be some means of accommodating and mediating between development and traditional land rights. The Constitution and the laws providing for the rights of the *orang asli* can be a means of laying down the most basic matters which should be assumed in seeking the solutions to their problems. Of particular importance is the assertion that the *orang asli* have land *rights* (not merely concessions) which must be respected, and that they have a right to be heard and to be represented in the relevant decision-making processes. These problems are quintessentially human-rights issues.

The Malaysian courts have not usually been supportive of public interest litigation,[81] and have not always adopted socially progressive

---

[79] *Koperasi Kijang Mas Bhd v Government of Perak* [1991] 1 CLJ 486.

[80] Cheah Wui Ling (n 75); and see 'Ismail Sabri: 80pc of needs of *orang asli* community fulfilled', *Malay Mail*, 4 March 2018.

[81] See eg *Government of Malaysia v Lim Kit Siang* [1988] 2 MLJ 12; Tey Tsun Hang, 'Public interest litigation in Malaysia: Executive control and careful negotiation of the

interpretations of fundamental rights provisions or advanced the interests of vulnerable groups. In the present instance it took several years of patience and extremely hard, unremunerated legal work and factual research by a number of lawyers and NGO advocates to get indigenous customary land rights legally recognised. In *Director-General of Environmental Quality v Kajing Tubek*, for example, in 1997, the Court of Appeal even cast doubt on whether representatives of 10,000 natives of Sarawak had standing to challenge the environmental impact assessment for a dam that would flood their traditional lands and deprive them of their livelihood.[82] Along with the legal resistance to indigenous claims went a general hostility towards activism by indigenous groups or any recognition of their rights.

The decisive breakthrough came in 1997 when 52 *orang asli*, whose land rights were affected by development in the State of Johor, succeeded in a representative action against the Government of Johor in securing the recognition of their land rights in terms that were unequivocal. In this case, *Adong bin Kuwau v Government of Johor*[83] the Court of Appeal referred to a line of similar cases in different jurisdictions culminating in well-known Australian and Canadian[84] cases. The Court rejected the notion that native peoples had no rights except those granted by the subsequent conqueror or discoverer, and affirmed the notion that their land rights, in the form of 'usufructuary' rights (rights to harvest the produce of the land), remained in force at common law except where clearly and specifically extinguished by legislative or executive action. A wide interpretation was given to the constitutional right to property (Article 13) and to adequate compensation for its deprivation, as applied to indigenous land rights.

A similar line of decisions became apparent in East Malaysia. In Sarawak, native customary land rights, under the Sarawak Land Code 1957,[85] had been frozen as of 1 January 1958, with some limited

---

frontiers of judicial review' in Po Jen Yap and Holning Lau (eds), *Public Interest Litigation in Asia* (London, Routledge, 2011).

[82] [1997] 3 MLJ 23; see Gurdial Singh Nijar, 'The Bakun Dam case: A critique' (1997) 3 *MLJ* ccxxix.

[83] *Adong bin Kuwau v Government of Johor* [1997] 1 MLJ 418, affirmed by the Court of Appeal in [1998] 2 MLJ 158; see MB Hooker, '"Native Title" in Malaysia: *Adong's Case*' (2001) 3(2) *Australian Journal of Asian Law*.

[84] Especially *Mabo v State of Queensland* (1992) 66 ALJR 408; *Calder v A-G of British Columbia* (1973) 34 DLR (3d) 145.

[85] Laws of Sarawak, c 81, ss 2, 5. For Sabah, see the decision in *Sipadan Dive Centre Sdn Bhd v State Government of Sabah* [2010] 1 LNS 1218; and A Doolittle, *Property and Politics in Sabah, Malaysia (North Borneo): A Century of Native Struggles over Land Rights, 1881–1996* (Seattle, University of Washington Press, 2005).

opportunities for creating such rights after that date. In *Nor Anak Nyawai v Borneo Pulp Plantation Sdn Bhd* in 2000[86] an impressive judgment in the High Court of Sabah and Sarawak adopted the same reasoning as in *Adong*, following the Australian and Canadian cases as well as *Adong* itself in establishing the legal nature of the customary land rights in Sarawak. Furthering the tendency to look also at international norms, the Judge referred to the Draft Declaration on the Human Rights of Indigenous People. This decision offered further encouragement to customary land claims, and the *Adong* case was then affirmed and extended in the High Court of Malaya and the Court of Appeal in 2005 in the apex case of *Government of Selangor v Sagong Tasi*.[87]

This case related to the Temuan people who had for generations occupied land, some of which had been gazetted as aboriginal land under the Aboriginal Peoples' Act 1954. Part of this land was compulsorily acquired for the construction of the main highway between Kuala Lumpur and the new Kuala Lumpur International Airport. The Temuan were 'evicted rather unceremoniously and left to fend for themselves and their families'. They sued the Selangor State Government for statutory compensation and trespass. Whereas the *Adong* case had asserted that the *orang asli* had usufructuary rights over their designated land, *Sagong Tasi* went much further. It decided that the *orang asli* have not just usufructuary rights but 'customary community title' at common law, and that their property is constitutionally protected. The Land Acquisition Act 1960, which provided only a power to grant compensation was modified in its application to accord with Article 13 of the Constitution, which states that 'no person shall be deprived of property save in accordance with law' and that 'no law shall provide for compulsory acquisition or use of property without adequate compensation'. The Court of Appeal affirmed *Adong* in deciding that the State authorities owe a fiduciary duty to the *orang asli*: 'a duty to protect the welfare of the aborigines including their land rights, and not to act in a manner inconsistent with those rights, and further to provide remedies where an infringement occurs'. It held also that their rights extended to land which had erroneously not been gazetted by the defendant State Government. For good measure the court awarded the plaintiffs full

---

[86] *Nor Anak Nyawai v Borneo Pulp Plantation Sdn Bhd* [2001] 6 MLJ 241. An appeal succeeded on the facts but the Court of Appeal affirmed the law as stated in the High Court: [2005] 3 CLJ 555.

[87] *Government of Selangor v Sagong Tasi* [2002] 2 MLJ 591, [2005] 5 MLJ 289.

costs and exemplary damages reflecting the brutal manner in which they had been treated.[88]

Again the same principles have been extended to the natives of Sabah and Sarawak in *Madeli Salleh v Superintendent of Lands and Surveys, Miri Division*.[89] In a 2011 case *Andawan bin Ansapi v Public Prosecutor*,[90] six natives were convicted of criminal trespass when they cultivated rice padi in a forest reserve. The High Court overturned the conviction on the basis that they were exercising customary land rights that pre-existed the reservation, and that the exercise of their customary rights was guaranteed by the right to life under Article 5(1).

Since the *Sagong Tasi* case, courts, especially in Sabah and Sarawak, have been flooded with native land claims. The outcome of the cases is still not satisfactory in terms of full recognition of native customary land rights, and the State has, according to one writer 'demonstrated remarkable resolve in contesting the recognition of the full gamut of *Iban* customs relating to land through the courts'.[91] However, these developments take the human rights of indigenous peoples beyond land rights, and even beyond the right to life, as there are undoubtedly many other issues to be addressed. What the cases have done apart from establish native customary land rights is to establish indigenous rights more generally as a matter of concern rather than resistance. Even so, as Zainun Ali FCJ in her dissent in *TR Sandah* pointed out, 'there is no reason why [customary rights] should be excluded from any understanding of what "law" is'.[92] As a result of these cases, in 2008 the State Government of Selangor not only withdrew the appeal against the decision in *Sagong Tasi* but established an Orang Asli Land Task Force to protect native land. Suhakam too in 2010 established its first National Inquiry Committee, which investigated the land rights of indigenous peoples, and led to its important report on the subject in 2013 mentioned above.[93]

---

[88] MB Hooker, 'Native Title in Malaysia continued – *Nor's Case*' (2002) 4(1) *Australian Journal of Asian Law* 92.

[89] *Madeli Salleh v Superintendent of Lands and Surveys, Miri Division* [2008] 2 MLJ 677.

[90] *Andawan bin Ansapi v Public Prosecutor*, Suit No KK-41-128-2010, High Court, Kota Kinabalu.

[91] Yogeswaran Subramaniam, '"Legal pluralism" in Malaysia: The case of Iban native customary right sin Sarawak' in A Harding and Dian AH Shah (eds), *Law and Society in Malaysia: Pluralism, Ethnicity and Religion* (Abingdon, Routledge, 2017); and see *Director of Forests, Sarawak & Anor v TR Sandah anak Tabau & Ors and other appeals* [2017] 2 MLJ 281, FC.

[92] Ibid para [131].

[93] See also R Bulan (with A Locklear), *Legal Perspectives on Native Customary Land in Sarawak* (Kuala Lumpur, Suhakam, 2008).

Suhakam has also established offices in Sabah and Sarawak to provide access to its services for native people, and has mounted initiatives in aboriginal education and towards the recognition of aboriginal customary law. In 2010 it also investigated and referred to the police allegations of long-term sexual abuse of Penan women and girls by timber workers in Sarawak.[94] In 2019 the Federal Government took the unprecedented step of suing a State Government on the basis of breach of fiduciary duty towards the *orang asli*. All this tends towards establishing the rights of indigenous people in Malaysia in a way that is envisaged both by notable judgments from other Commonwealth countries and by international instruments. As the Judge in a Sarawak case said:[95]

> Finally, given that natives are the original inhabitants of the country it might be questioned whether it is entirely correct to treat claims for NCR by looking at them only from the standpoint of ownership of the lands. Rather such claims should be looked differently, namely, that the natives are part of the land as are the trees, mountains, hills, animals, fishes and rivers ... The fruits on the wild trees, the fishes in the river, the wild boars and other animals on the land are their food for survival.

## VII. CONCLUSION

'Di-mana bumi di pijak, di-situ langit di junjung'

(On whatever soil we stand, there we carry the weight of the sky)

This chapter gazes beyond the constitutional provisions relating to human rights, looking not just at issues of civil liberties, especially the right to life and liberty of the person in relation to national security, but also institutional arrangements to bridge the gap between aspiration and delivery in the human rights context. In the last section we have looked at human rights from the aspect of disadvantaged indigenous communities for whom the struggle for human rights has begun only recently. The imperatives of human rights were hardly taken seriously by the Reid Commission when they considered the entrenchment of human rights in the *Merdeka* Constitution. More attention to how to define and guarantee human rights in the Malaysian context might have made it harder for human rights to be eroded as they have been under

---

[94] Suhakam press statement, available at http://www.suhakam.org.my/wp-content/uploads/2014/01/penan-210710.pdf.
[95] *Agi Anak Bungkong v Ladang Sawit Bintulu Sdn Bhd* (2010) 1 LNS 114.

the strictures of an authoritarian developmental state that took 'Asian values' as its guide to human rights. However, there are some positive aspects to this story.

Human-rights discourse has never disappeared, even when the intervention of the state has been at its most invasive and when the Asian-values argument has been most evident; if anything, the human-rights discourse has gained in prominence over time. The reason for this is that the Bar and civil society have proved able to maintain their own freedom to operate and speak about human rights issues, even under the most difficult of circumstances. Indeed, compared with their equivalents in many developing countries, they have been heroic and often successful. This success has taken the form, initially, of resisting very deep incursions on human rights by the state, and, latterly, the embracing of human rights as an ideal of some description even by the state itself. Clearly human rights discourse also resonates with a substantial proportion of the electorate, and prompted government towards an uncertain, open-ended path of reform during 2018–20. There is no reason of course to suppose that the struggle for human rights in Malaysia is anything other than a work in progress. However, constitutional rights, despite their narrow formulation, have been an important reference point. Litigation is not, as we have seen, the entire story of human rights, and has produced patchy outcomes, but it remains the principal method of defining the content of human rights in the Malaysian context, and often the only effective method of enforcing them. Suhakam has proved a very useful addition to the human-rights apparatus, but does not have the powers either to accomplish or to command enforcement of human rights. Many human rights issues not dealt with here remain to be addressed, but there are means to address them.

In the result there can be no doubt that human rights have truly arrived in Malaysia. Their accomplishment as a matter of law, habit and policy remains a project for the future. An excellent start was the repeal of all the oppressive national security and emergency laws which cast a spell over all aspects of human rights. Experience in Malaysia has shown that the ability to speak of human rights is the indispensable foundation for their fulfilment.

## FURTHER READING

AJ Harding, *Law Government and the Constitution in Malaysia* (Kuala Lumpur, Malayan Law Journal, 1996) chs 11–14.

Khairil Azmin Mokhtar (ed), *Constitutional Law and Human Rights in Malaysia: Topical Issues and Perspectives* (Petaling Jaya, Thomson Reuters, 2013).

HP Lee, 'Human Rights in Malaysia' in R Peerenboom, CJ Peterson and Albert HY Chen (eds), *Human Rights in Asia: A Comparative Study of Twelve Asian Jurisdictions, France and the USA* (London, Routledge, 2006).

Kevin YL Tan and Thio Li-ann, *Constitutional Law in Malaysia and Singapore* (3rd edn, Singapore, LexisNexis, 2010) chs 11–19.

# 8

# *The Judiciary and the Defence of Judicial Power*

Judicial Independence – Judicial Power – Constitutional Interpretation – Judicial Crisis – Lawyers' Walk for Justice

## I. INTRODUCTION

'Yang menang pulang menjalar, yang alah pulang merangkak'
(Those who win [at law] go home wriggling, while those who lose crawl home on their bellies)

THE MALAYSIAN JUDICIARY has frequently been placed in the eye of the constitutional storm, and judicial independence has been an arena, rather than simply a condition, for the defence or promotion of constitutionalism. The judiciary therefore holds a position that is undeniably difficult. On the one hand the executive power may well be uncomfortable with decisions that it cannot control. On the other hand, a lively, well-organised and idealistic Bar is ready to pounce on the slightest defect in judicial reasoning or the least shortcoming of the bench or adherence to the rule of law. For example, a decision concerning the deportation of more than 1200 Myanmar citizens in 2021 was met with de facto deportation by the Government, and protest from the Bar.[1]

The fact is that Malaysia has rapidly become a highly litigious society. Not only are the courts flooded with cases, but the cases themselves often relate to the most sensitive political issues, often having profound

---

[1] Bar Council press statement, 'Halt the Involuntary Repatriation of Myanmar Detainees Immediately', 22 February 2021, available at www.malaysianbar.org.my/article/news/press-statements/press-statements/press-comment-halt-the-involuntary-repatriation-of-myanmar-detainees-immediately.

ethnic, religious and human rights implications. They even have immediate implications for the survival of governments, as we saw in Chapters 2 and 5. In this chapter we will see, for example, the judiciary holding the ruling party an unlawful society, and finding a Prime Minister guilty of corruption on the widest imaginable scale. We will also see the judiciary subjected both to a dramatic coup by the executive, and interference with senior judicial appointments. In Chapter 7 we have seen the judiciary defending human rights, albeit not entirely consistently. In Chapter 9 we will see the judiciary defining the all-important role of religion in society. The issues at stake in this chapter are not only dramatically represented, but are also fundamental to the adherence to constitutional government. This chapter tells the story of continuing controversy concerning judicial power and independence, its long defence by the Bar, and its revival in recent years.

There are of course reasons for the centrality of the judiciary and litigation in the constitutional system. First, politics and legislation were so much dominated by the BN coalition for most of the last few decades that other venues for pursuing claims, such as Parliament or direct dealings with the executive, have usually been ineffective. The judiciary has tended to be both first and last resort. Second, Malaysia's powerful legal professional association, the Malaysian Bar Council, while never ceasing to criticise the actual performance of the judiciary, has leapt to its defence whenever its independence was threatened. What has been at stake here is not simply the fear of domination of the executive over the judicial branch, but the independence of the entire legal complex, including the Bar itself. As Harding and Whiting claim,

> Malaysian lawyers have developed and sustained a capacity to support and defend the core liberal legal values of the rule of law, the independence of the judiciary and the integrity of the constitution and of constitutional government, and to speak and act, sometimes vigorously, in defence of civil and political rights.[2]

In spite of the apparent unwillingness by the judiciary to act as an effective check on the executive power, at least until recent times, the Bar has succeeded in mobilising effectively, alongside the civil society, to defend constitutional values from repeated attacks by an authoritarian state. For example, judicial independence itself has in practice

---

[2] AJ Harding and A Whiting, '"Custodian of Civil Liberties and Justice in Malaysia": The Malaysian Bar and moderate state' in T Halliday, L Karpik and M Feeley (eds), *Fates of Political Liberalism in the Post-Colony: The Politics of the Legal Complex* (Cambridge, Cambridge University Press, 2012).

depended principally on the Bar. Consequently, the Bar has had to defend, successfully, its own autonomy in the face of attempts to interfere with its internal organisation.[3] Third, the Bar has, 'almost without exception, evidenced a cultural orientation typical of common lawyers towards "liberal legalism", rendering it passionate in its defence of constitutionalism, the rule of law, and human rights, for which judicial independence is regarded as an indispensable condition'.[4] In Chapter 7 we also saw how the fundamental-rights guarantees, restricted as they are, have given rise to extensive opportunities for constitutional litigation, highlighting the need for judicial independence. The executive has consistently attempted, but often, and increasingly, fails to control this kind of public discourse, as we also saw in Chapter 7. In some respects, although we in Chapter 2 how flagship government policies have not in general been litigated, the Constitution has acted as a mechanism for criticising the Government in a more general fashion, translating political debates into legal ones.

The judiciary itself, in spite of many criticisms and an executive-led onslaught, has nonetheless survived undermining events; sometimes reaching courageous decisions that defy cynicism, but often also weak decisions that confirm that cynicism. Thus, although many people have legitimate doubts about several aspects of the judiciary and its role, such doubts are not reflected in any unwillingness on the part of lawyers or their clients to go to court or to defend the judiciary as an institution when attacked. Indeed, on 26 September 2007 large numbers of lawyers, with the virtually unanimous support of their professional colleagues, turned out at Putrajaya in the pouring rain to 'march for justice', protesting interference with judicial appointments.

However judges are themselves judged or defended, the judiciary in Malaysia has, as we have noted, the power and duty of adjudicating claims of great importance. In performing its task it can review the constitutionality of legislation and the validity of executive or judicial acts, and has in its armoury a wide variety of weapons, in terms of legal doctrines and remedies, to give practical effect to judicial power. The most significant of these weapons is the Constitution itself, which, by providing for judicial review and judicial independence, reserves to the judiciary a prominent role in the constitutional process. For this very reason judicial independence and the nature of the judicial power that

---

[3] See *Malaysian Bar v Government of Malaysia* [1987] CLJ 185.
[4] Harding and Whiting (n 2) 271.

is thereby protected have been particularly fraught issues. In this chapter we will examine the judiciary crisis of 1988 and the way in which judicial independence has been defended and the judiciary revived as an institution of prime importance.

The judiciary, at least as far as the civil courts are concerned, is organised on the pattern of the common-law tradition. Its common law origins in Malaysia go back 200 years, and were consolidated by the Civil Law Act 1956.[5] The *Merdeka* Constitution elevated the judiciary to its present constitutional role as an independent branch. The last formal link with the English legal system was the final appeal to the Privy Council, which was abolished with effect from 1 January 1985. The Federal Court of Malaysia, master of its own judicial household for the first time, was renamed the Supreme Court, and then renamed the Federal Court again in 1994 with the setting up of a new Court of Appeal. For the reasons explained in Chapter 1, there are two High Courts – of Malaya and of Sabah and Sarawak – each with its own Chief Judge. The Federal Court has a Chief Justice, referred to until 1994 as the Lord President. The power of interpretation of the Constitution (for which see below) is in theory vested in any court, on the basis that the Constitution is supreme law and therefore must be given effect in any court. However, the Federal Court alone enjoys the power to decide on issues arising between the Federation and a State, or between States, and has a special advisory jurisdiction in relation to matters referred to it for its opinion by the Federal Government.[6] In relation to applications for judicial review, it is the High Courts that have jurisdiction.

In the initial stages after *Merdeka* the Malaysian judiciary was recognised to have achieved one of the highest standards of competence and independence in all of Asia. Not only did Malayans speedily replace expatriate judges on the bench without any noticeable decline in the quality of decision-making, but the local judiciary was also drawn from all ethnic groups and religions (although a large majority were and are Malay Muslim), and acted as a symbol of unity in a diverse nation.[7] When a prince of the royal house of Johor was sentenced more lightly than would have been the case with a commoner, the Federal Court,

---

[5] J Foong, *The Malaysian Judiciary: A Record from 1786 to 1993* (Singapore, Malayan Law Journal, 1994).
[6] Arts 128, 130.
[7] Tun Suffian, 'Four Decades in the Law – Looking Back' in FA Trindade and HP Lee (eds), *The Constitution of Malaysia: Further Perspectives and Developments* (Kuala Lumpur, Oxford University Press, 1986) 216.

asserting equality before the law, was unequivocal in its criticism of the Judge.[8] As we will see, the judiciary fell very far from these heights in subsequent years.

Some judges have achieved outstanding reputation both in Malaysia and abroad, which suggests a degree of social standing that is unusual; they have become, in some cases, household names in both judicial and non-judicial capacities. One former Lord President, Raja Azlan Shah (as he then was), became Sultan of Perak and then *Yang di-Pertuan Agong*.[9] Most Malaysian judges have been appointed from the government legal service and the magistracy, and fewer from the practising Bar, although in recent years appointments from the Bar and appointments of female judges and judges from ethnic minority groups have increased in number. The current Chief Justice is the first female Chief Justice and more than 30 per cent of judges at High Court level and above are female.

One other issue that has been controversial in relation to the judiciary is the relationship between the common law and Islamic law. This issue, one of transcendent importance, will be discussed in detail in Chapter 9. For now we can note that from time to time judicial and other personnel have raised the question whether the general law of Malaysia should diverge from the common law and be based on Islamic principles, which currently only apply to personal law and a limited and disputed range of criminal liability within the jurisdiction of the Syariah courts. This demand has been persistent over many years, but has never found favour with the Bar, who have repeatedly insisted on Malaysia's membership of the common-law family.[10]

## II. JUDICIAL INDEPENDENCE AND THE CONSTITUTION

'Besar kayu, besar bahan-nya'

(The tree may be great, but so is the work of cutting it up)

The Constitution attempts to secure judicial independence in several ways.

---

[8] *Public Prosecutor v Tungku Mahmood Iskandar* [1973] 1 MLJ 128; and see *Public Prosecutor v Tengku Mahmood Iskandar* [1977] 2 MLJ 123.

[9] See ch 5.

[10] See eg Bar Council Press Statement, 'Leave the Common Law Alone', 24 August 2007, quoted in AJ Harding and A Whiting, '"Custodian of Civil Liberties and Justice in Malaysia": The Malaysian Bar and Moderate State' in T Halliday, L Karpik and M Feeley (eds), *Fates of Political Liberalism in the Post-Colony: The Politics of the Legal Complex* (Cambridge, Cambridge University Press, 2012) 247.

First, superior judges are appointed by the *Yang di-Pertuan Agong*, acting on the advice of the Prime Minister, after consulting the Conference of Rulers, and (except for the Chief Justice's own appointment) the Chief Justice. The Prime Minister is also required to consult the Chief Justice and Chief Judges on appointments to the Federal Court; the President of the Court of Appeal on appointments to the Court of Appeal; and the Chief Judge of a High Court on appointments to that High Court. In the case of the appointment of the Chief Judge of a High Court, he must also consult the Chief Judges of both High Courts; and in the case of the appointment of a Chief Judge of the High Court of Sabah and Sarawak, he must consult the Chief Ministers of Sabah and Sarawak.[11]

In addition to these obligations to consult, the Judicial Appointments Commission (JAC) Act 2009 imposes a further requirement. The JAC is empowered to report to the Prime Minister with reasons the names of selected persons who merit appointment to the positions listed above, as well as the position of judicial commissioner: three persons in the case of an appointment to a High Court, and two persons in the case of an appointment to a higher court. The Prime Minister may require the JAC to request the selection of two further names for consideration, but is not able to substitute his own preferences. He is also under a statutory duty 'to uphold the continued independence of the judiciary' and 'must have regard to ... the need to defend that independence'.[12] These provisions were enacted due to concerns about interference with judicial appointments following the Royal Commission Report on the Lingam Tapes (see below). Article 123 restricts judicial appointment to a citizen who has for the preceding 10 years been an advocate of one of the High Courts or a member of the judicial and legal service of the Federation or of the legal service of a State. Appointment is to the age of 65, although the *Yang di-Pertuan Agong* government may extend that period by six months.[13]

The *Yang di-Pertuan Agong* acts on advice in the matter of judicial appointments. The Conference of Rulers, which is entitled to be consulted, has taken its role of being consulted seriously, rejecting one candidate proposed by the Prime Minister for a senior judicial appointment.[14]

---

[11] Art 122B.

[12] Judicial Appointments Commission Act 2009, s 2 and Part III.

[13] Art 125. See also *Bar Council Malaysia v Tun Dato' Seri Ariffin bin Zakaria & Ors* [2020] 4 MLJ 773, Fed Ct; and A Harding and others, *ICONnect-Clough Centre Global Review of Constitutional Law 2017*, available at https://papers.ssrn.com/sol3/papers.cfm?abstract_id=3215613.

[14] 'Malaysia's Sultans Seek to Get Their own Back', *Asia Sentinel*, 10 August 2007.

The Constitution also provides for security of judicial tenure. Judges' salaries are charged on the Consolidated Fund, and the salary of a judge and other terms of office, including pension rights, may not be altered to the judge's disadvantage after appointment. Furthermore, the conduct of a judge may only be discussed in Parliament on a substantive motion supported by one quarter of the total number of members.[15] However, the matter of dismissal of judges has been a highly controversial issue, and in the next section we will examine the judiciary crisis of 1988, which resulted in three judicial dismissals – this in spite of constitutional provision in Article 125 designed to secure their tenure. This Article provides that if the Prime Minister, or the Chief Justice after consulting the Prime Minister, represents to the *Yang di-Pertuan Agong* that a Judge of the Federal Court, Court of Appeal, or the High Court, ought to be removed on the ground of any breach of the Code of Ethics prescribed under Article 125(3A) (formerly the criterion was 'misbehaviour') or on the ground of inability, from infirmity of body or mind or any other cause, properly to discharge the functions of his office, the *Yang di-Pertuan Agong* (acting here again on advice) shall appoint a Tribunal and refer the representation to it; and may on the recommendation of the Tribunal remove the judge from office. The Tribunal must consist of not less than five persons who hold or have held high judicial office, or, if it appears to the *Yang di-Pertuan Agong* expedient to make such appointment, persons who hold or have held equivalent office in any other part of the Commonwealth; and must ordinarily be presided over by the Chief Justice.

The tribunal procedure laid out in Article 125 was inserted into the *Merdeka* Constitution at the insistence of the judiciary itself. The Reid Commission had recommended a method of dismissal similar to that pertaining in Britain, whereby an address of both Houses of Parliament is required: it was thought that judicial tenure should not be placed at the mercy of a parliamentary majority. Unfortunately, as we will see, this protection, when invoked, proved to be quite inadequate for the purpose.

The ethnic backgrounds of the judges are mixed. Since the early 1970s around 70 per cent of judges have been Malay. Currently,[16] the higher judiciary (the two high courts, the Court of Appeal and the Federal Court) comprises 98 judges and 40 Judicial Commissioners.

---

[15] Arts 125–27.

[16] As at November 2021; see the judiciary website, available at http://www.jac.gov.my/spk/en/commission/superior-court-judges.html.

The Federal Court comprises 11 Judges (of whom, seven are Malay, two are Chinese and two are Indian), and the Court of Appeal comprises 26 judges (of whom, 18 are Malay, four are Chinese, three are Indian and one is a Sarawak native). In the Federal Court seven, and in the Court of Appeal eight, judges are female. The increased diversity in judicial backgrounds, evident since the Judicial Appointments Act 2009, is welcome in itself, given the visibility of the judiciary and the need to reflect the composition of society; it has also resulted in an improvement in judicial decisions, as we see in this chapter and in Chapters 7 and 9.

## III. THE JUDICIAL POWER

'Bintang di-langit dapat di-bilang, arang di-muka tak sedar'

(He can count the stars in the heavens, but misses the smuts on his own face)

Of course the independence of the judiciary is only important if the judiciary itself has sufficient formal power and is willing and able to dispense justice in terms of the rule of law, fundamental rights, and in conformity with constitutional principles.[17] The extent of its formal power is partly determined by its willingness to protect judicial independence, and in this respect the Malaysian judiciary's powers are somewhat hobbled by two developments, both of which are related to the 1988 amendment of Article 121.

The first relates to Islamic law jurisdiction and is discussed in Chapter 9, where we will see that, although the ordinary civil courts retain the power to interpret Article 121(1A), which prevents the civil courts from exercising the jurisdiction of the Syariah Courts, they have done so in a way that has tended to defer to the Syariah Courts.

The second development relates to the separation of powers and is both fundamental and instructive with regard to the performance of the judiciary. Before it was amended in 1988, Article 121(1) vested the judicial power of the Federation in the High Courts and such inferior courts as might be provided by federal law. After the 1988 and subsequent amendments Article 121(1)–(2) merely provide for the jurisdiction of the High Courts, the Court of Appeal, and the Federal Court being determined by statute. This has the effect of reversing the decision in

---

[17] HP Lee, 'The Judicial Power and Constitutional Government: Convergence and divergence in the Australian and Malaysian Experience' (2005) 25 *Journal of Malaysian and Comparative Law* 1.

*Dato Yap Peng* – preventing the judiciary from protecting its own power by defining that power and isolating it from statutory intervention. In that case the Supreme Court used the concept of judicial power to strike down a controversial statutory provision (section 418A of the Criminal Procedure Code), which allowed the Attorney-General to withdraw a criminal case before a lower court, even after the court was seized of the case, and send it to the High Court. As Eusoffe Abdoolcader SCJ so graphically and prophetically put the matter, 'any other view would … result in relegating the provisions of Article 121 vesting judicial power in the curial entities specified to no more than a munificent bequest in a pauper's will'.[18] Thus in one aspect the amendment was designed in effect to limit and codify judicial powers, taking the power of defining them away from the judiciary itself and vesting it in the legislature. Whether it succeeded, however, in that objective remained unclear.

In *Sugumar Balakrishnan*, in 1998, Gopal Sri Ram JCA in the Court of Appeal was decisive in holding that Article 121(1) 'does not have the effect of taking away the judicial power from the High Court … [it] remains where it has always been, with the judiciary'.[19] In *Kok Wah Kuan* in 2007 the Court of Appeal, led again by Gopal Sri Ram JCA, faced with a statute providing that the sentencing of juveniles should be at the discretion of the executive power, not of the courts, struck down the statute as violating the separation of the judicial power. However, the Federal Court on appeal took an entirely different view, the majority holding that the Constitution does *not* recognise the separation of powers since this doctrine is not an express provision of the Malaysian Constitution, and therefore could not be inferred.[20] Richard Malanjum FCJ, however, dissenting, stoutly upheld the principle of the separation of powers,[21] and in *Semenyih Jaya*, in 2019, the Federal Court endorsed that dissent, holding that judicial independence is a basic feature of the Constitution.[22]

Interestingly enough, the Commission of Inquiry into the Lingam tape (discussed below) addressed this issue, recommending that Article 121(1) be re-amended back to its original form, and the Bar

---

[18] *Dato Yap Peng v Public Prosecutor* [1988] 1 MLJ 119.

[19] *Sugumar Balakrishnan v Pengarah Imigresen* [1998] 3 MLJ 289.

[20] *Public Prosecutor v Kok Wah Kuan* [2008] 1 MLJ 1.

[21] Ibid paras 33–34; see, further, R Foo, 'Malaysia: Death of a separate constitutional judicial power' [2010] *Singapore Journal of Legal Studies* 253.

[22] *Semenyih Jaya Sdn Bhd v Pentadbir Tanah Daerah Hulu Langat* [2017] 5 CLJ 526.

Council too has called for constitutional amendments to provide for a clear separation of powers.[23]

We see here a stark division between, on the one hand, judges unwilling to uphold a doctrine that seems very evident in the provisions of the Constitution, and very necessary in view of Malaysian experience, and on the other hand judges who are staunch in defending the judicial power and the Constitution.

## IV. CONSTITUTIONAL INTERPRETATION

When Malaysian judges are seized with a constitutional case, exercising the judicial power to uphold the Constitution, how do they set about the task of constitutional interpretation? What principles do they apply?

Principles of constitutional interpretation are not stated in the Constitution, and the judiciary is not necessarily consistent or predictable in its methods. Two main approaches can be discerned.

First, the Constitution must be interpreted within its own four walls. Thus, although the Malaysian Constitution may bear a family resemblance to other constitutions of similar provenance and vintage, its provisions must be considered in the light of the entire Constitution and the prevailing conditions in Malaysia. It follows that although authorities from other jurisdictions may interpret similar or identical provisions and offer some guidance, they cannot be regarded as in principle applicable. In general, English authorities have been found to be more persuasive than Indian authorities, even though the Malaysian Constitution is nearer in content and structure to the Indian Constitution than the British.[24] The Malaysian judiciary has found that, while Indian cases can be highly instructive or persuasive, there are sharp differences between the cases, which create difficulties in terms of using them as precedents.[25]

---

[23] 'Prove Commitment to an Independent Judiciary, Bar Council Tells Putrajaya', *The Malaysian Insider*, 9 September 2011, available at www.themalaysianinsider.com/mobile/malaysia/article/prove-commitment-to-independent-judiciary-bar-council-tells-putrajaya.

[24] See eg FJ Suffian in *Karam Singh v Minister for Home Affairs* [1969] 2 MLJ 129.

[25] As Ong Hock Thye CJ said in *Karam Singh*, 'Indian judges impress me as indefatigable idealists seeking valiantly to reconcile the irreconcilable whenever good conscience is pricked by an abuse of executive powers': [1969] 2 MLJ 129, 141; to similar effect is the discussion by Suffian LP in *Datuk Harun Idris* at [1977] 2 MLJ 155.

Second, it must be assumed that the constitution-makers intended their words to be of broad application. Thus Eusoffe Abdoolcader J said in *Datuk Harun Idris*:

> The court stands as arbiter in holding the balance between individuals and between the state and the individual and will not have the slightest hesitation to condemn or strike down any statutory shelter for bureaucratic discrimination, any legislative refuge for the exercise of naked arbitrary power in violation of any of the provisions of the Constitution and equally any executive action purported to be made thereunder.[26]

This broad approach has in some recent cases involved reference to persuasive international norms and conventions.

Principles adopted have often been contradictory even within the same case. Sometimes the Constitution is treated as if it were an ordinary statute and judicial review is seen as an aspect of administrative rather than constitutional law; while at other times the Constitution is given an expansive interpretation, referring to international law and precedents.[27] It has never been definitively resolved which approach is correct, and even recent cases point in different directions. For example, the High Court and Federal Court in *Public Prosecutor v Kok Wah Kuan* took a restrictive approach, while the Court of Appeal took an expansive approach.[28] In *Indira Gandhi v Pengarah Jabatan Agama Islam, Perak* the opposite occurred, the High Court and Federal Court taking an expansive view, based on international understandings of parental rights, while the Court of Appeal took a restrictive view.[29]

The other main issue affecting the scope of judicial interpretation is the doctrine of precedent, which is a fundamental aspect of judicial reasoning in common law jurisdictions. As elsewhere in the common law world, courts are bound by decisions of higher courts and the Court of Appeal is bound by its own decisions, subject to some exceptions.

Article 10 has given rise to recent examples that illustrate the principles. In *Sivarasa Rasiah v Badan Peguam Malaysia*,[30] in 2010, a lawyer who was elected to Parliament challenged a statute, section 46A of the Legal Profession Act 1976, which prevented MPs from holding

---

[26] *Public Prosecutor v Datuk Harun Idris* [1976] 2 MLJ 116, 124.
[27] Y Tew, *Constitutional Statecraft in Asian Courts* (Oxford, Oxford University Press, 2020), Part 1 (IV).
[28] *Public Prosecutor v Kok Wah Kuan* [2004] 5 MLJ 193, [2007] 5 MLJ 174, [2008] 1 MLJ 1.
[29] *Indira Gandhi v Pengarah Jabatan Agama Islam, Perak* [2013] 5 MLJ 552, [2016] 4 MLJ 455, [2018] 1 MLJ 545.
[30] *Sivarasa Rasiah v Badan Peguam Malaysia* [2010] 2 MLJ 333.

office in the Bar Council on the basis that his freedom of association had been infringed. The Federal Court held that it had not, because morality (a permissible restriction under Article 10) was not maintained by preventing conflicts of interest in the legal profession. However, in so holding the court adopted what it called a 'prismatic approach to interpretation', importing the notion of reasonableness into Article 10 on the basis also that restrictions on guaranteed rights must be read restrictively. In *Muhammad Hilman bin Idham*,[31] in 2011, the Court of Appeal by a majority struck down section 15(5) of the Universities and University Colleges Act 1971, which prevented students from expressing or doing anything which might reasonably be construed as expressing support for, sympathy with or opposition to any political party. The majority used the prismatic approach and concept of reasonableness in *Sivarasah Rasiah*, arguing that the statute was an unreasonable or even irrational restriction on freedom of expression which did not in fact serve public order, as was argued by the Government. However, in *Public Prosecutor v Azmi Sharom* the Federal Court reverted to a rigidly literal approach to Article 10, pointing out that reasonableness is not imported in to that article.

A similar bifurcation of views is evident with regard to the 'basic structure doctrine', under which courts can review the constitutionality of constitutional amendments on the basis of violation of the constitution's basic structure. Again recent cases indicate a bifurcation of view. In *Indira Gandhi* and *Semenyih Jaya* the Federal Court looked with favour on the doctrine's applicability to the Malaysian Constitution, but in the most recent cases the Court rejected it.[32]

## V. THE JUDICIAL CRISIS OF 1988

'Pedena tidak, terpelok sarang tebuan'

(What I grasped was not a jar of treasure but a hornet's nest)

We now turn to the most traumatic constitutional episode in Malaysian history: the judicial crisis of 1988. This episode, more than any other, has defined attitudes towards the judiciary and its independence. Despite this legacy of political interference with the judiciary, in *Semenyih Jaya*

---

[31] *Muhammad Hilman bin Idham* [2011] 6 MLJ 507.
[32] *Maria Chin Abdullah v Ketua Pengarah Imigresyen & Anor* [2021] 1 MLJ 750, *Rovin Joty a/l Kodeeswaran v Lembaga Pencegahan Janaya & Ors* [2021] 2 MLJ 822.

in 2019 the Federal Court asserted the separation and preservation of the judicial power. The 1988 crisis resonated internationally, defined a generation of lawyers, and destroyed overnight the strong reputation of the Malaysian judiciary. The story is a very complex one involving a concatenation of events in which the judiciary was caught in a perfect storm: involved in an intense conflict with the executive power it was then trapped in an internal conflict within the ruling party. It is both a tragic story and an instructive episode with regard to the protection of the constitutional value of judicial independence.[33]

## A.  Judicial Activism 1986–88

Following the abolition of the final appeal from the Malaysian courts to the Judicial Committee of the Privy Council from 1 January 1985, the Malaysian judiciary had taken a more activist line than previously in constitutional matters. According to the Lord President (equivalent of chief justice) at the time, Tun Mohamed Salleh Abas, the judges, now that they were master of their own household, felt that they had the responsibility to 'chart a new judicial course'.[34] It does not appear that they had any preconceived philosophy to be implemented, but simply a heightened sense of the importance of their role in a new situation in which they had final authority when it came to legal interpretation. It should be mentioned here that the judiciary had not sought to challenge the executive in crucial matters of Government policy. Still less did they have any political agenda. They were indeed accused by lawyers and others of being timid and of not protecting constitutional rights in the way the Constitution envisaged. While this was regrettable it had also probably lulled the executive, during 30 years of BN political hegemony, into a false sense of security and heightened expectation of deference.

During the ensuing period of about three years, a number of crucial judicial decisions were made. It is worth mentioning some of these decisions to indicate what kind of a new course was being charted during a period of intense political strife, especially within the dominant party,

---

[33] For a fuller discussion, see V Sinnadurai, 'The 1988 judiciary crisis and its aftermath' in AJ Harding and HP Lee (eds), *Constitutional Landmarks in Malaysia: The First 50 Years, 1957–2007* (Kuala Lumpur, LexisNexis, 2007).

[34] Tun Salleh Abas, John Galway Foster Memorial Lecture, University College London, 4 November 1988, reproduced in Tun Salleh Abas, *The Role of an Independent Judiciary* (Kuala Lumpur, Promarketing Publications, 1989). See also Tun Salleh Abas, 'Independence of the Judiciary' [1987] 1 MLJ xi.

UMNO, as Prime Minister Tun Mahathir tightened his grip on political power. It was during this period, let us note, that the power of the centralised state was seen at its most intolerant. The Government was no longer prepared to see mounting criticism from unionists, opposition parties and civil-society organisations, and in October 1987 it instituted the *Operasi Lalang* crackdown on political opponents and civil society activists. These detentions resulted in many habeas corpus cases coming before the courts in 1988. As many as 107 Opposition political leaders, unionists, students and social activists were detained under the Internal Security Act – some for two years – on the grounds that their activities inflamed racial tensions and threatened national security.[35]

In *Berthelsen*[36] the revocation of a foreign correspondent's employment pass on grounds of national security was quashed because he had not been given a hearing according to the principle of natural justice. A number of other important decisions worked against the perceived interests of the executive power. *Mamat Daud*,[37] discussed in Chapter 6, affirmed States' rights under Schedule 9 of the Constitution. *Dato Yap Peng*[38] employed the doctrine of judicial power to strike down the Government's choice of venue for a criminal trial. In the *UEM*[39] case, initially, the Leader of the Opposition Lim Kit Siang, was given standing to raise in court telling allegations of corruption against the Cabinet itself, although the decision was eventually reversed by the Supreme Court by the slimmest of majorities, overruling its own previous decisions in the very same matter. Most impressively of all, perhaps, the *Tun Mustapha* litigation arising out of a constitutional crisis in Sabah (for which see Chapter 6) was resolved against the result probably preferred by the Federal Government, the apex court rejecting the idea that the constitutionality of an appointment of a Chief Minister was an issue beyond judicial determination.[40]

These were not the only cases of significance decided around this time. However, the judiciary was not placing the Government in a judicial stranglehold: it should be noted that a number of critical cases at that time also went in the Government's favour.[41]

---

[35] See ch 4.

[36] *JP Berthelsen v Director-General of Immigration* [1987] 1 MLJ 134.

[37] *Mamat bin Daud v Public Prosecutor* [1988] 1 MLJ 119.

[38] *Dato Yap Peng v Public Prosecutor* (n 18).

[39] *Government of Malaysia v Lim Kit Siang* [1988] 2 MLJ 12.

[40] *Tun Datuk Haji Mahomed Adnan Robert v Tun Datu Haji Mustapha bin Datu Harun* [1987] I MLJ 471. And see ch 5, section IV.

[41] Eg *Theresa Lim Chin Chin v Inspector-General of Police* [1988] 1 MLJ 293; and see *Deputy Minister for Home Affairs v Cheow Siong Chin* [1988] 1 MLJ 432.

Several of the decisions struck down had been made by the Prime Minister Tun Mahathir himself, in his capacity as Minister of Home Affairs, or had been made by officials under his direction. He was clearly displeased by these decisions, because in several speeches he attacked the judiciary. The Leader of the Opposition cited him for contempt of court when he complained to Time Magazine about the obstructiveness of the judiciary. The Prime Minister's frustration was so graphically expressed that one might have sympathised with his plight but for the veiled threat with which he concluded:

> The Judiciary says, 'Although you passed a law with certain thing in mind, we think that your mind is wrong, and we want to give our interpretation.' If we disagree, the courts say, 'We will interpret your disagreement.' If we go along, we are going to lose our power of legislation. We know exactly what we want to do, but once we do it, it is interpreted in a different way, and we have no means to interpret it our way. If we find that a court always throws us out on its own interpretation, if it interprets contrary to why we made the law, then we will have to find a way of producing a law that will have to be interpreted according to our wish.[42]

The case was dismissed, but not before the courts had given the Prime Minister a lecture on the separation of powers.[43]

It was following these decisions that the constitutional amendment to Article 121 was passed, which as we have seen removed the term 'judicial power' from the Constitution. The Lord President replied to executive criticisms of the judiciary in speeches, and even from the bench. It was in this soured atmosphere that the most crucial case of all came to be decided.[44]

## B. The UMNO Election Case

In April 1987 UMNO held elections for the posts of party President and Deputy President. In eight successive Governments since *Merdeka* the holders of these posts had been the Prime Minister and the Deputy Prime Minister. This was the first occasion on which the UMNO leadership had been challenged from within the party. The elections were

---

[42] *Time Magazine*, 24 November 1986.
[43] *Lim Kit Siang v Datuk Seri Dr Mahathir Mohamad* [1987] 1 MLJ 383, 387.
[44] *Mohamed Noor bin Othman v Mohamed Yusoff Jaafar* [1988] 2 MLJ 129, affirmed on appeal sub nom *Mohamed Noor bin Othman v Haji Mohamed Ismail* [1988] 3 MLJ 82.

very hard fought, and the results were extremely close: the incumbents narrowly defeated the challengers, but 11 UMNO members filed a suit challenging the legality of the elections, and seeking orders for the holding of fresh elections. Their case was that, amongst other irregularities, the presence of delegates from 30 branches which had not been approved by the Registrar of Societies (enough the alter the result) made the elections invalid.

As a political party, UMNO was required to be registered under the Societies Act 1966, which applies to all societies (see Chapter 4). Under section 12 of the Act, 'where a registered society establishes a branch without the prior approval of the Registrar such registered society and the branch so established shall be deemed to be unlawful societies'. When the case was tried by Justice Harun Hashim in the High Court in Kuala Lumpur in February 1988, the defendant UMNO officials did not dispute the allegations of illegality, but argued that in any event the plaintiffs were not entitled to the relief sought because they had no enforceable interest in the matter, UMNO having become an unlawful society by operation of section 12. Paradoxically therefore, it was the *defendants* who argued that the party itself was an unlawful society, while the plaintiffs urged on the court a benevolent construction of the Act which would allow UMNO to remain lawful. The defendant incumbents were thus attempting to scuttle the party itself to avoid the possibility of an order for new elections.

The Judge held that from the first moment an unapproved branch was established, both UMNO and the branch became unlawful societies; the elections were therefore invalid. However, he also held that the plaintiffs could not have a remedy because they could not acquire any right which was founded upon that which was unlawful. Using a Malay proverb, he said that it was a case of *keris makan tuan*: the *keris* (a traditional curved Malay dagger) turning on its owner.

For the ruling party to be held unlawful is probably without precedent in the constitutional history of any country. The Prime Minister reassured the public that the Judge's decision would be accepted, but was quick to draw a distinction between his party and the Government, pointing to his majority support in Parliament. The illegality was, he said, a technical matter.[45]

---

[45] AJ Harding, 'The 1988 Constitutional Crisis in Malaysia' (1990) 39 *International and Comparative Law Quarterly* 57.

It was, however, the challengers who took the initiative. An 'UMNO Protem Committee' was set up with the Tunku himself, now 85 years old, as President, and the third Prime Minster (and son of UMNO's founder) Tun Hussein Onn, as Deputy President. It applied for the registration of 'UMNO Malaysia' – a new party. The application was rejected by the Registrar, who was under the Prime Minister's direction, on the ground that the old UMNO had not yet been deregistered, and the name of the new party was too similar to that of the old party. Just after deregistration occurred, the incumbents submitted a similar application, which was granted, to register a new party, UMNO Baru ('New UMNO'). The Prime Minister made it clear that his opponents would not be welcome in the new party. They proceeded to register a new party, Semangat '46 (Spirit of '46; 1946 marks UMNO's founding). UMNO Baru consolidated its position and Semangat '46 went into parliamentary opposition. In due course the word 'Baru' was in practice dropped. The general election of 1990 confirmed the continuance of the BN in Government. In the meantime the UMNO litigation continued, as the plaintiffs had appealed to the Supreme Court, which ordered that the appeal should be heard before nine judges, comprising the entire membership of the bench. In view of the settlement of the UMNO issue, it was clearly crucial from the Government's point of view that the settlement they had engineered should not be disturbed by the Supreme Court.[46]

## C. A Perfect Storm: The Judiciary Entangled

This was the very delicate political situation in mid-1988, at the time the judiciary crisis also reached its height. Following a meeting of the Kuala Lumpur judges on 25 March to discuss ways of resolving the tension between the judiciary and the executive, the Lord President was mandated to write to the *Yang di-Pertuan Agong*, asking him to intervene. The letter expressed disappointment with accusations made against the judiciary by the Prime Minister, and expressed the hope that they would be stopped. The *Yang di-Pertuan Agong* took exception to

---

[46] HP Lee, *Constitutional Conflicts in Contemporary Malaysia* (2nd edn, Oxford, Oxford University Press, 2017) ch 5; HP Lee, 'A fragile bastion under siege: The 1988 convulsion in the Malaysian judiciary' [1990] *Melbourne University Law Review* 38.

the letter, because he considered the Rulers would have been brought into conflict with the executive if he had acted on the letter's implied request to intervene, and communicated his disapproval to the Prime Minister. It should be noted that the Rulers had already come into serious conflict with the executive over the royal assent to legislation in 1983, as we saw in Chapter 5.

Subsequently the Prime Minister, acting under Article 125, represented to the *Yang di-Pertuan Agong* that the Lord President should be removed on grounds of misbehaviour and being unable to perform his functions as Lord President, and advised the appointment of a Tribunal and Tun Salleh's suspension pending the report of the Tribunal. This was agreed to by the *Yang di-Pertuan Agong* and, after an unsuccessful attempt to persuade Tun Salleh to retire quietly, put into effect.

Tun Salleh objected to the Tribunal on several grounds, including the ground that it was to be chaired by the Chief Justice of Malaya and Acting Lord President, Tan Sri Hamid Omar, who would succeed him if he was dismissed, so that the proceedings would breach the principles of natural justice. The Tribunal rejected his arguments and Tun Salleh applied to the High Court for an order of prohibition to prevent the Tribunal from proceeding, on grounds of its unconstitutionality.

Amid unprecedented scenes in Kuala Lumpur with lawyers and others protesting in the streets in large numbers, on 2 July 1988 the High Court postponed the hearing of Tun Salleh's application, refusing an interim order restraining the Tribunal, which was now sitting. Tun Salleh renewed his application for a stay before the Supreme Court the same day. Five Supreme Court Justices heard the case immediately, granting Tun Salleh an order restraining the Tribunal from submitting its report. Then, on 7 July, the five judges constituting the Supreme Court were themselves suspended and another Tribunal was convened under Article 125 to investigate charges of misbehaviour against them. They were charged principally with conspiring to hold an illegal sitting of the Supreme Court.

What followed had an air of inevitability. Tun Salleh's application for leave was dismissed by the High Court, and the Supreme Court lifted the stay on the Tribunal's proceedings, at the same time rejecting a number of applications and appeals by Tun Salleh. The reasoning was that the Supreme Court's order of 2 July was made without jurisdiction and that, as the Tribunal was only an investigative body, not a deciding body, to restrain it would be to restrain the *Yang di-Pertuan Agong* from receiving the Tribunal's report. Subsequently, the appeal in the UMNO Election case was unanimously dismissed by the Supreme Court,[47] the Tun Salleh Tribunal reported recommending his dismissal, and the Tribunal on the five Judges also reported.[48] The outcome was that Tun Salleh and two of the five Judges were removed from office.

Impartial observers have found that the tribunals were packed by the executive, and the charges against Tun Salleh were flimsy, the evidence failing to reveal any misbehaviour on the part of him or the other Judges. Signally, the Tribunal on Tun Salleh based its findings on uncontradicted evidence, Tun Salleh having refused to appear before them, and seemingly applied a civil rather than a criminal standard of proof; it also applied a very broad test of misbehaviour, failing to consider the attacks to which Tun Salleh had been subjected.[49]

## D. The Bar Responds

These events created a storm across Malaysia and internationally. They were an important issue in the 1990 general election. They resulted in a complete stand-off between the Government and the new Lord President, Tan Sri Hamid Omar, on the one hand, and the Bar on the other. The Bar, passing a motion of no-confidence in the Lord President and demanding his removal, sued him unsuccessfully for contempt of court, alleging obstruction of justice in the 1988 proceedings.[50] Thereupon the Government retaliated with a successful contempt prosecution against the Bar Council Secretary for scandalising the judiciary.[51] The Bar responded by avoiding the Lord President at social events. In Malaysia's very protocol-conscious society this move was highly confrontational. Many senior statesmen, lawyers, and other public figures, principally the

---

[47] Above n 44.

[48] *Report of the Tribunal Established under Article 125(3) and (4) of the Federal Constitution Re YAA Tun Dato Haji Mohamed Salleh Abas, Lord President, Malaysia* (Kuala Lumpur, Government Printer, 1988); [1988] 3 MLJ xxxiii; *Report of the Tribunal Established under Article 125(3) and (4) of the Federal Constitution Re YA Tan Sri Wan Suleiman bin Pawan Teh, Supreme Court Judge* [etc] (Kuala Lumpur, Government Printer, 1988); [1989] 1 MLJ lxxxix.

[49] Lee, *Constitutional Conflicts* (n 46) ch 5; FA Trindade, 'The Removal of the Malaysian Judges' (1990) 106 *Law Quarterly Review* 51; Lawyers' Committee for Human Rights, *Malaysia: Assault on the Judiciary* (New York, 1990); M Gillen and T McDorman, 'The Removal of the Three Judges of the Supreme Court of Malaysia' (1991) 25 *University of British Columbia Law Review* 171.

[50] *Malaysian Bar v Tan Sri Dato Abdul Hamid bin Omar* [1989] 2 MLJ 281.

[51] *Attorney-General of Malaysia v Manjeet Singh Dhillon* [1991] 1 MLJ 167.

Tunku and former Lord President Tun Suffian, weighed in with fierce criticism of the Government. The episode was correctly described as an unconstitutional interference with judicial independence. The decisions of the judiciary predictably reverted to an extreme timidity not even generally seen before 1985. The judiciary had never been at such a low ebb. Looking back on those events in 2006 the Bar Council President told the public: 'Those were the sickest hours of executive incursion into the judiciary ... those shameful events have left gaping wounds in the Malaysian society, from which we are yet to fully recover'.[52]

To the credit of the Malaysian Bar, for 20 years (1988–2008) the issue of the 1988 tribunals was never allowed to fade into history. A campaign was persistently pursued to reverse the result of the 1988 crisis. Eventually in 2008, five years after Dr Mahathir's retirement, an independent Panel of Eminent Persons cleared the judges of any wrongdoing, and financial compensation and public recognition (although no formal apology) was granted by the Government.[53]

The Bar and many commentators consider the 1988 judicial crisis a watershed in Malaysian constitutional history: before 1988, courts were independent and judges decided according to the rule of law; after 1988, both the appearance and the reality of judicial autonomy were compromised. Before the removal of the judges in 1988 there was no suspicion of corruption or actual bias, but soon afterwards abundant evidence began to appear of political and corporate interference in court processes and judicial appointments. The hornet's nest was now broken and the judiciary was to suffer even further.

## VI.  JUDICIAL INDEPENDENCE: A DOWNWARD SLIDE

'Di-lutu umpama tebuan sarang pechah'

(Blows raining down like hornets swarming from a broken nest)

If 1988 was an unmitigated disaster for the judiciary, it also heightened awareness of constitutional issues generally and in particular inculcated vigilance in relation to judicial appointments and performance, placing the Bar, which had been strong in defence of the judiciary, firmly in a position of civil-society leadership in relation to these issues. The

---

[52] Harding and Whiting (n 2) 275.

[53] *Report of the Panel of Eminent Persons to Review the 1988 Judicial Crisis in Malaysia* (Kuala Lumpur, Bar Council, 2008).

Bar established a standing committee to monitor the erosion of judicial independence, published a declaration of judicial independence for the benefit of the public, and conducted public talks across the nation to explain the basis of constitutionalism, and how the concept of judicial independence was essential to constitutional democracy.

However, matters got worse rather than better; the judiciary became not simply neutered in public law matters, but mired in corruption allegations in relation to private law matters. In a string of commercial and defamation cases throughout the 1990s it seemed that some judges were not deciding cases according to the law, but in order to please powerful business interests. In the *Ayer Molek* litigation, it was held on appeal that the first instance decision gave 'the impression to right-thinking people that litigants can choose the judge before whom they wish to appear'; 'there is something rotten in the state of Denmark', said one of the Judges in the Court of Appeal[54] (there was a sub-text: the special applications and appeals division of the High Court was located, along with the Danish Embassy, in Denmark House). A well-known businessman, Vincent Tan, was also involved in a number of defamation cases where his activities had been questioned.[55] Although the defamation cases were private actions, they had a chilling effect on journalists and lawyers commenting on judicial matters, with the damages running to extraordinarily large figures.

By 1996 the judiciary had reached an ebb probably even lower than that of 1988. An anonymous 33-page 'poison-pen' letter was circulated at the annual judges' conference. It detailed extensive accusations of judicial corruption and incompetence, naming judges and itemising instances. These allegations seemed plausible to many observers, but even before he had commenced a formal investigation, the Attorney-General characterised them as 'vile, insidious, devious and scurrilous', designed to 'ridicule, abuse and insult the judiciary'. He then authorised an investigation by the police and the Anti-Corruption Agency – not into the substance of the allegations, but into their *authorship*.[56] Later the

---

[54] *Ayer Molek Rubber Company Berhad v Insas Berhad* [1995] 2 MLJ 734 (Court of Appeal, describing the conduct of the plaintiff's lawyer as an abuse of process, criticising severely while reversing the High Court).

[55] See eg *Ling Wah Press (M) Sdn Bhd v Vincent Tan Chee Yioun* [2000] 4 MLJ 77; *MGG Pillai v Tan Sri Dato' Vincent Tan Chee Yioun* [2002] 2 MLJ 673.

[56] CV Das (ed), *Justice Through Law: Fifty Years of the Bar Council of Malaysia, 1947–1997, A Pictorial Biography of the Legal Profession* (Kuala Lumpur, Bar Council of Malaysia, 1997) 89–90.

Attorney-General announced that the allegations were baseless, and that the author (popularly believed to be a certain High Court Judge) had voluntarily resigned and therefore he would not be prosecuted.[57] Indeed it was the legal profession that was blamed: even before the formal investigation had commenced, the Attorney-General stated that he believed some lawyers were plotting to 'undermine the integrity of the judiciary and the administration of this country'.[58] As a result the allegations were not properly investigated, and the evidence of corruption was never brought into the open.

The Bar Council was prominent in a demand to set up a Judicial Appointments Commission, which would insulate judicial appointments from political interference; and a Royal Commission of Investigation into the administration of justice, to investigate thoroughly allegations of such interference. The Bar Council's defence of the principle of judicial integrity was, however, met with accusations such as that of Tun Mahathir himself when he accused the Bar of 'always oppos[ing] Government decisions' and behaving 'like an opposition party'; and he challenged it to form a political party instead of 'hiding behind the shield of a professional body'.[59]

From 1998 to 2004, as *reformasi* supporters rallied around deposed Deputy Prime Minister Anwar Ibrahim, Anwar was tried and sentenced for the crimes of sodomy and corruption in a judicial process condemned by Malaysian and international observers as hopelessly flawed.[60] Ultimately Anwar was cleared: by 2004, after the end of Tun Mahathir's first premiership, one conviction was struck down, while on another Anwar received a pardon. Judicial deference to the Government during these trials, and intimidation of Anwar's lawyers, raised further concerns about the separation of powers and the administration of justice.[61] In addition the Government attempted to intimidate defence lawyers involved in the case. For example, former Bar Council President, Zainur Zakaria, was sentenced to three months' imprisonment for contempt of court when he accused prosecutors of fabrication, fraud and blackmail.[62]

---

[57] Ibid 92.
[58] *New Straits Times*, 17 March 1996.
[59] *New Straits Times*, 17 October 1996.
[60] Eg Amnesty International, *Sodomy Verdicts a Major Setback for Human Rights*, AI Index ASA 28/009/2000 (8 August 2000).
[61] Wu Min Aun, 'The Saga of Anwar Ibrahim' in Harding and Lee (n 42); and for background on the Mahathir/Anwar conflict, Tey Tsun Hang, 'Malaysia: The fierce politico-legal backlash' (1999) 3 *Singapore Journal of International and Comparative Law* 1.
[62] *Re Zainur Zakaria* [1999] 3 CLJ 696; however, this was reversed on appeal, see *Zainur Zakaria v Public Prosecutor* [2001] 3 CLJ 673.

In 2000 allegations supported by photographs and receipts appeared to show that the Chief Justice Eusoff Chin had taken a holiday with defamation lawyer VK Lingam in 1994. This raised considerable concern at possible collusion between the country's highest judge and a prominent lawyer representing particular business interests.

This time the response was more positive, and an ameliorative process at last commenced. The de facto law minister, Datuk Seri Rais Yatim, criticised the Chief Justice for his actions, recognising public concern about judicial corruption, adding that change would have to come 'largely from within the legal community' in the absence of political will.[63] By this time even the largely Government-owned newspapers were commenting adversely upon the administration of justice.

In 2001, a new Chief Justice, Tun Mohamed Dzaiddin Abdullah, replacing Eusoff Chin who had retired, attempted reconciliation, but this was roundly rejected by the Bar. Moreover, the Court of Appeal, in the course of protracted litigation by a rogue member of the Bar seeking to prevent the Bar from engaging with these judicial issues by calling EGMs and passing motions,[64] interpreted Article 125 of the Constitution as actually prohibiting *any and all public discussion* of the administration of justice unless it took place in Parliament. This decision clearly elevated judicial independence over freedom of speech.[65]

## VII. A SCANDAL LEADS TO BETTER OUTCOMES: THE LAWYERS' WALK FOR JUSTICE

'Puchot yang layu di-siram hujan'

(The shoot that was withering was revived by the rain)

It was indeed in the pouring rain on 26 September 2007 that the Malaysian judiciary turned the corner and began to hope for better days.

Earlier that month, Anwar Ibrahim released on the internet the first part of a secret videotape (known as the 'Lingam Tape') dating from 2002, showing VK Lingam speaking on the phone with a person who appeared to be the then Chief Judge of the High Court of Malaya, and later Chief Justice, Ahmad Fairuz Abdul Halim. The tape indicated a

---

[63] *New Straits Times*, 8 June 2000.

[64] For the extended *Raja Segaran* litigation, see Harding and Whiting (n 2).

[65] *Majlis Peguam Malaysia v Raja Segaran a/l Krishnan* [2005] 1 MLJ 15; and see Harding and Whiting (n 2).

conspiracy to use defamation suits to crush lawyers and journalists criticising Vincent Tan and to broker senior judicial appointments. It also contained evidence that a senior judge had decided an election petition against an opposition MP for political reasons.[66] Anwar claimed that the tape proved 'a political conspiracy of the highest level and corruption of the highest judicial office', and that many court proceedings, including his own trials, had to be viewed as tainted and unreliable.[67]

Later, Anwar released two other parts of the tape, raising further similar concerns, and as a result the Bar organised the 'Lawyers' Walk for Justice' to Putrajaya. The Bar Council called on its members to march to the Palace of Justice and then to the Prime Minister's office to present two memoranda calling for a royal commission of inquiry into the judiciary and a permanent judicial appointments commission to oversee a non-political appointment process for judges:

> [F]or too long we have watched the judicial appointment process become unfathomable and shrouded in secrecy. For too long we have cried out for reform, but the authorities have not heeded our pleas. Malaysians cannot afford to stand by and watch any longer. The time has come for us to act decisively.[68]

Harding and Whiting report on the march as follows:

> In order to dramatise that their actions were motivated by justice, not politics, many lawyers donned formal court attire when on 26 September 2007 about 1500 of them, accompanied by 500 civil society activists, marched in pouring rain under the watchful eyes of the riot police. The event was reported extensively on the internet. In defiance of a police road block and instructions that their march was illegal, the protesters presented the Bar's two demands at the Prime Minister's Office.[69]

The Government had already responded to public concerns by establishing a three-person independent panel of eminent persons, under the chairmanship of a former Chief Judge of the High Court of Malaya, to look into the scandal. This panel reported a few weeks later recommending a royal commission of inquiry. The Government acted on this and the Commission reported in May 2008. The Report found that the tape was indeed authentic, and expressed concern about interference in judicial appointments organised by some judges and lawyers, some members of

---

[66] See www.youtube.com/watch?v=CeDX78s3Rl0.
[67] Harding and Whiting (n 2) 286; *Malaysiakini*, 17 September 2007.
[68] Ibid.
[69] Ibid.

the government, and some businessmen. This 'had the effect of seriously undermining and eroding the independence and integrity of the judiciary as a whole'.[70] Accordingly the Commission agreed that a judicial appointments commission was necessary.[71]

The Judicial Appointments Commission Act (discussed above) was passed in 2009, although the Attorney-General decided to take no criminal action against any individual as a result of the Commission's Report, a decision that outraged the Bar.[72] The post-2009 dispensation concerning judicial appointments probably still leaves something to be desired. In particular the executive still controls the process, and being consulted or offering advice or names is not the same thing as being able to ensure judicial independence. In November 2007 Chief Justice Ahmad Fairuz retired, and following the general election in March 2008 an UMNO minister implicated in the affair was dropped from the Cabinet.

In June 2008 a High Court Judge made extensive and shocking allegations from the bench concerning Government interference in the judiciary; these included an allegation that he himself and selected judges had been threatened by Tun Mahathir and 'packed off to a boot camp [in] 1997 where there was an attempt to indoctrinate them with the view "that the government interest was more important than all else"'.[73] No action was taken on these allegations, and the Judge himself resigned.

As a result of all these events, and especially the post-2009 position on judicial appointments, the contemporary judiciary looks much more secure and enjoys a higher reputation than as recently as 2008.

## VIII. CONCLUSION

'Tak boleh tandok, telinga di-pulaskan'

(If he cannot twist the horn, he twists the ear)

In 1979 in *Teh Cheng Poh* the Privy Council made its most notable decision on the Malaysian Constitution when it struck down the notorious Emergency (Security Cases) Regulations 1975. It held that once Parliament had sat, the Government could not by delegated power make

---

[70] *Report of the Commission of Enquiry on the Video Clip Recording of Images of a Person Purported to Be an Advocate and Solicitor, etc*, 9 May 2008.

[71] Ibid 37, 77–78, 175.

[72] *The Malaysian Insider*, 26 February 2009.

[73] 'Justice Ian Chin Tells of Threats and Indoctrination Attempt', *The Star*, 11 June 2008.

law that it could not now make under primary emergency legislation; the Cabinet could not, said the Court, pull itself up by its own bootstraps.[74]

Shortly after this, moves were commenced to abolish the final appeal from Malaysia to the Privy Council. This proved to be a turning point. For the first 30 years of its post-*Merdeka* existence the Malaysian judiciary had proceeded along a smooth path, upholding a somewhat thin version of the rule of law and the Constitution, while allowing scope for executive power to operate its most important policies without what the Tunku had called 'too much legality'. Even the emergence of a highly centralised state did not change the position unduly. Following the abolition of the Privy Council appeal, the Malaysian judiciary's reputation was more obviously at stake compared to pre-1985; but so was Tun Mahathir's control over the important levers of state. In asserting this control he found that in many respects the existing constitutional order placed obstacles in his path: political opposition, civil society, human rights, the Bar, Parliament, and even the internal democratic processes of his party. Added to this, from 1985 was the increasingly confident and activist judiciary of the Salleh court that gave impetus to all of those aspects of the constitutional order that obstructed the Government's notion of development.

The cataclysm that followed shook the nation and its constitutional order to its very foundations. The judiciary was tamed and trained to serve the needs of the executive power, as if it were a department of the Federal Government answerable to the Prime Minister rather than the law. The decline of a once-proud institution into servility and corruption was dramatically precipitate. As Tun Mahathir's first premiership came to an end, the Bar's tenacity and solidarity finally began to reverse the order of events. Distancing themselves from the unconscionable actions of the 1980 and 1990s, Tun Mahathir's successors recognised a national interest in rescuing the judiciary. The acquittal of Anwar Ibrahim in January 2012, in the case that has come to be known as *Sodomy II*, created a new sense of optimism either that judicial independence had survived, or that the Government was in effect compelled by events to sustain it at some level.[75] It will now take more than a recklessly ambitious government at any future time to bring the judiciary back to where

---

[74] *Teh Cheng Poh* [1979] 1 MLJ 50; [1980] AC 458.
[75] T Thomas, 'Why was Anwar Ibrahim acquitted?', *The Malaysian Insider*, 19 January 2012, available at www.malaysianbar.org.my/article/news/legal-and-general-news/members-opinions/why-was-anwar-ibrahim-acquitted-tommy-thomas.

it was after 1988. Cause for some hope in this regard may be found in the Federal Court decisions on judicial power in *Semenyih Jaya*[76] and the Constitution's basic structure in *Indira Gandhi*;[77] and in the conviction on corruption charges of the country's one-time highest executive official, Prime Minister Najib Razak, in 2020.[78]

## FURTHER READING

AJ Harding and A Whiting, '"Custodian of Civil Liberties and Justice in Malaysia": The Malaysian Bar and Moderate State' in T Halliday, L Karpik and M Feeley (eds), *Fates of Political Liberalism in the Post-Colony: The Politics of the Legal Complex* (Cambridge, Cambridge University Press, 2012).

HP Lee, *Constitutional Conflicts in Contemporary Malaysia* (2nd edn, Oxford, Oxford University Press, 2017).

J Neo and H Whalen-Bridge, 'A Judicial Code of Ethics: Regulating Judges and Restoring Public Confidence in Malaysia' in R Devlin and A Dodek (eds), *Regulating Judges: Beyond Independence and Accountability* (Cheltenham, Edward Elgar, 2016).

V Sinnadurai, 'The 1988 Judiciary Crisis and its Aftermath' in AJ Harding and HP Lee (eds), *Constitutional Landmarks in Malaysia: The First 50 Years, 1957–2007* (Kuala Lumpur, LexisNexis, 2007).

Y Tew, *Constitutional Statecraft in Asian Courts* (Oxford, Oxford University Press, 2020).

---

[76] *Semenyih Jaya* (n 22).
[77] *Indira Gandhi* (n 29).
[78] *Pendakwa Raya v Dato' Seri Mohd Najib bin Hj Abd Razak* [2020] MLJU 1254.

# 9

# Religion and the Constitution

Islam in Constitutional History – An Islamic State? – Religion of the
Federation – Religious Freedom – Sites of Conflict – Syariah Courts and
Jurisdiction

## I. INTRODUCTION

'Lain lubok, lain ikan-nya'
(Different pools, different fish)

MALAYSIA'S PLURALISTIC SOCIETY has been seen in this book
as the crucial factor guiding all analysis of contemporary
constitutional issues. It is also the factor that makes the
attempts to deal with pluralism in a constitutional fashion a matter of
comparative interest in a world where the exclusively secular nature of
states is no longer taken for granted, and religious pluralism is almost
universal. There is in Malaysia, as we have seen, a profound even if
not completely commensurate relationship between ethnicity and religion, particularly given that virtually all Malays are Muslim: indeed
the definition of 'Malay' in the Constitution includes being Muslim.[1]
Muslims comprise about 61 per cent of the total population of 33 million; Buddhists 19 per cent; Christians 9 per cent; Hindus 6 per cent;
Confucian/Taoists 3 per cent; Sikhs 2 per cent; and others 1 per cent.
In recent years religion has played a larger role even than ethnicity in
defining identity and interest in this complex and contested polity.[2]

---

[1] Art 160(2). However, not all Muslims are Malay; they include Indian Muslims and
Chinese, Indian and Sabah/Sarawak native converts.
[2] AJ Harding, 'Constitutionalism, Islam, and National Identity in Malaysia' in
R Grote and T Rode (eds), *Constitutionalism in Islamic Countries: Between Upheaval and
Continuity* (Oxford, Oxford University Press, 2012); D Shah, *Constitutions, Religion and
Politics in Asia: Indonesia, Malaysia and Sri Lanka* (Cambridge, Cambridge University
Press, 2017).

In this chapter, this book, unlike other books in this series, singles out for attention the constitutional treatment of religion as an element of great constitutional significance. Accordingly we will examine not just the actual official religious structures, but also the debates around religion and the Constitution, which have intensified significantly since the millennium. In particular we will consider the debate concerning Malaysia as an 'Islamic state'; conflict over the jurisdiction of the civil and Syariah courts; and the related issue of religious freedom. In this sense consideration of religion is offered not merely by way of completeness of coverage, but because it is fundamental to an understanding of the constitution as a whole.

## II.  LAW AND RELIGION: HISTORY AND CONTEXT

'Adat yang kawi, Shara' yang lazim'

(Custom is the real law, Syariah is the ideal law)

To understand the constitutional consequences and importance of religion, and the contemporary debates around it, it is necessary to trace the place of religion through history.

The royal houses of the Malay states are derived from the Malacca Empire, which splintered following its destruction by the Portuguese in 1514. In these states the Malay Rajas (later usually styled 'Sultan') linked themselves symbolically with the Arab mainstream Islamic tradition, attempting in general to base their laws and governments on a combination of Islamic principles and *adat*. Sabah and Sarawak were originally parts of the Brunei sultanate which was also culturally related to the states of Malaya. Hence Islam was invariably the State religion and the Ruler was also the Head of Islam. Indeed, as a result of the treaties with Britain (discussed in Chapter 1 and below), this remained the case throughout the period of colonial rule, and up until today.[3]

Although the nineteenth-century legal systems of Malaya are described as Islamic, they were often very far in practice from any particular Islamic ideal, the position varying according to the power and the inclination of the Ruler, as well as the extent of local adherence to *adat*.[4]

---

[3] In Penang, Malacca and Sarawak, however, Islam is not the State religion, and the *Yang di-Pertuan Agong* serves as the Head of Islam.

[4] MB Hooker, *Adat Laws in Modern Malaysia* (Kuala Lumpur, Oxford University Press, 1972); MG Peletz, *Islamic Modern: Religious Courts and Cultural Politics in Malaysia* (Princeton, Princeton University Press, 2002) ch 1.

As we saw in Chapter 1, the 1874 Pangkor Engagement between the Crown and the Sultan of Kedah provided a precedent ultimately followed without variation in all the Malay states. This Treaty required the Sultan to follow the British Resident's advice in all matters except those relating to Islam and Malay custom.[5] In so providing, the treaties reserved the special and official nature of Islam as the religion of the State, but also laid a foundation for the secularisation of the general law and legislation. The mention of 'advice' was clearly a legal fig-leaf to cover the reality of colonial ambitions in the context of indirect rule in these protected states.[6] However, the reservation of Islam and Malay custom represented a genuine form of jurisdiction which the British had no interest in exercising. This arrangement also, of course, acted as a legal fig-leaf to cover the reality of creeping federalisation.

The extension of British power over Malaya during the late nineteenth and early twentieth centuries also entailed the introduction of increasing numbers of adherents of non-Muslim religions, as well as the common law and its typical institutions. The latter was achieved at first gradually, by stealth, via judicial decisions, and eventually decisively by the use of legislative power, so that the outcome was the adoption of the common law as the general law. The resulting subordination of Islamic law created a grievance which is now expressed in terms of proposals variously to base the general law of Malaysia on Islamic principles; to mix common law and Islamic law; or to raise the level of the Syariah courts to that of equality with the civil (ie common law) courts.[7] Fundamental rights were not enshrined in law until the *Merdeka* Constitution, but the plural nature of Malayan society was such that legislation interfering with religion was practically impossible and clearly undesirable; indeed, the increasing exercise of indirect power by the British in Malaya tended to result in statutory entrenchment and harmonisation of Islamic law alongside recognition of other forms of customary or religious law.[8] As a result, freedom of religion and mutual toleration was a necessary and

---

[5] I Hussain, 'The Pursuit of the Perak Regalia: Islam, Law, and the Politics of Authority in the Colonial State' (2007) 32(3) *Law and Social Inquiry* 759.

[6] R Emerson, *Malaysia: A Study in Direct and Indirect Rule* (New York, Macmillan, 1942).

[7] D Horowitz, 'The Qur'an and the Common Law: Islamic Law Reform and the Theory of Legal Change' XLII 2 and 3 *American Journal of Comparative Law* 233, 543; Farid Sufian Shuaib, *Powers and Jurisdiction of Syariah Courts in Malaysia* (Kuala Lumpur, Malayan Law Journal, 2003); M Peletz, *Sharia Transformations Cultural Politics and the Rebranding of an Islamic Judiciary* (Oakland, University of California Press, 2020).

[8] Mohamed Azam Mohamed Adil, 'Law of Apostasy and Freedom of Religion in Malaysia' (2007) 2(1) *Asian Journal of Comparative Law*, art 6.

pervasive social fact rather than a legally guaranteed right or obligation, although the primacy of Islam was also a necessary consequence of the treaties and the system of indirect rule. By the time the legal 'reception' of the common law and equity was consolidated throughout the Federation by the Civil Law Act 1956,[9] the distinction between common-law based public and general private law, on the one hand, and Islamic personal law on the other hand, was firmly entrenched in legislation and legal practice. It was then further entrenched by the *Merdeka* Constitution. The failure to create a unitary state in 1946 and the adoption of federalism in 1948 were largely due, as we saw in Chapter 1, to the unwillingness of the Malays to accept the dissolution of their State traditions. Part of their cultural attachment to these traditions was the association of the States and their Rulers with religion. This meant that religion as a *State* matter was of necessity preserved by the constitutional settlements of 1948, 1957 and 1963, despite the simultaneous enshrining of Islam, under Article 3 of the Constitution, as the official religion of the *Federation*. The debates around this issue were discussed in Chapter 1.[10]

The position was hardly different in the other territories which ultimately formed modern Malaysia in 1963. In the Straits Settlements colony (Penang, Malacca and Singapore), as a result of royal charters, the common law was the general law from the early nineteenth century; Islamic law was recognised, as in the Malay States, but only as personal law for Muslims. Sarawak was under the rule of the White Rajahs for a century from 1841–1941: their policy, as also with British policy in the colony of North Borneo (Sabah) was to preserve native customs.[11] In these two territories Islam was recognised but was not associated with the States, until they became subject to the Malaysian Constitution in 1963, and then only in the case of Sabah.[12]

Concerning the role of Islam, the Constitution therefore essentially entrenched the position which had applied under British rule in the Malay States. It was clear that an Islamic state as such was not contemplated and there was no proposal that the matter of religion be taken any further than Article 3. This dispensation regarding the official religion has become increasingly contested in various ways, as we shall see.

---

[9] Civil Law Act 1956 (Act 67), ss 3, 5.

[10] See, further, Shah (n 2) ch 2.

[11] A Harding, 'Legal pluralism and the constitutional position of East Malaysia's indigenous peoples: The view from the longhouse' in G Bell (ed), *Pluralism, Transnationalism and Culture in Asian Law: A Book in Honour of MB Hooker* (Singapore, ISEAS, 2017).

[12] J Chin, 'Federal-East Malaysia relations: Primus-inter-pares?' in A Harding and J Chin (eds), *50 Years of Malaysia: Federalism Revisited* (Singapore, Marshall Cavendish, 2014).

III. ISLAMICISATION AND THE ISLAMIC STATE

'Let there be no compulsion in religion'
(The Holy Quran, verse 256 of Sura al-Baqara)

The constitutional changes of 1971, which revised the social contract (see Chapter 3) did not affect the issue of religion, which had been settled in 1957. However, during the 1980s, Malaysian society experienced a resurgence of Islam in the wake of the Iranian revolution of 1979. This is referred to as the '*dakwah* movement'. During this period, the Islamic Party PAS made specifically legal claims at the boundaries where Islam and the common law met, working for the establishment of an Islamic state.[13] At the end of the 1970s for a short period PAS took over the State Government of traditionally Islamic Kelantan. During PAS' tenure of the State Government at that time, and again from 1990 until today, PAS adopted a policy of Islamicisation so far as was consistent with State powers. It did so again, briefly, in Terengganu between 1999 and 2004. These measures involved, for example, regulation of public entertainments, the sale of alcohol, and gambling. Furthermore, a controversial attempt in both States to introduce *hudud* (Islamic criminal) law led to demands for an expansion of the Syariah Courts' criminal jurisdiction.[14]

In response to the passing of the Syariah Criminal Code Enactment by the Kelantan State Legislative Assembly in 1993[15] there was a chorus of dismay, not just from lawyers, non-Muslim groups and political parties, but also Muslim groups such as Sisters in Islam, who objected vigorously to the discriminatory effect against women of several provisions, and its inconsistency with the concept of fundamental rights in the Constitution.[16] The Federal Government refused to enforce this law on the grounds that it was an unconstitutional exercise of States' powers – criminal law being reserved under Schedule 9 to the Federation. This has

---

[13] Shah (n 2) ch 3.

[14] In 2017 the Federal Government declined to table amendments to the Syariah Courts (Criminal Jurisdiction) Act 1965 that would have increased the powers of Syariah courts. See J Neo and D Shah, 'Hudud and the struggle for Malaysia's constitutional soul', *Constitutionnet*, 25 June 2015, available at https://constitutionnet.org/news/hudud-and-struggle-malaysias-constitutional-soul; A Harding and others, *ICONnect-Clough Centre Global Review of Constitutional Law 2016*, available at https://papers.ssrn.com/sol3/papers.cfm?abstract_id=3014378.

[15] Mohammad Hashim Kamali, *Punishment in Islamic Law: An Enquiry into the Hudud Bill of Kelantan* (Kuala Lumpur, Institut Kajian Dasar, 1995).

[16] Rose Ismail (ed), *Hudud in Malaysia: The Issues at Stake* (Kuala Lumpur, SIS Forum, 1995).

recently been affirmed in the case of *Iki Putra bin Mubarrak v Kerajaan Negeri Selangor* in which the Federal Court struck down a State enactment creating the Islamic offence of *liwat* (unnatural sex) on the ground that the subject matter fell within the federal legislative power over criminal law.[17] The *hudud* law therefore remains a political project rather than effective law, which would require a constitutional amendment providing for its validity. It seems unlikely, given current and prospective political alignments, that an appropriate constitutional amendment would receive the necessary two-thirds majorities in both houses.

With the aim of undercutting PAS' Islamist appeal, the BN Government from the early 1980s mounted its own programme of Islamicisation, for example in education and finance.[18] With regard to the legal system, it pursued the harmonisation of Islamic law (family law and the law of evidence, for example) and institutional reform (the Syariah Courts and Islamic legal profession, and the religious bureaucracy). In 1988 Article 121 of the Constitution was amended, as we saw in Chapter 8, to divide the Syariah Courts from the civil courts by providing that the civil courts could not exercise jurisdiction in any case falling under the Syariah Courts' jurisdiction. Article 121 has proved highly problematical in terms of religious freedom, as discussed in detail below.

The electoral successes of PAS and its legislative proposals created a new and controversial environment for the discussion of the role of Islamic law in more general terms. In recent years, for example, there has been public debate about the concept of an Islamic state,[19] which started in 1999 and intensified following an announcement by Prime Minister Mahathir in June 2002 that Malaysia was an 'Islamic state'. He went even further to say (with obvious exaggeration) that Malaysia was a 'fundamentalist, not a moderate Islamic state', and was also a 'model Islamic state'.[20] These statements sparked great controversy.[21] Catholic bishops and non-Muslim parties, for example, denounced them as creating a

---

[17] *Iki Putra bin Mubarrak v Kerajaan Negeri Selangor* [2021] 2 MLJ 323.

[18] Joseph Chinyong Liow, *Piety and Politics: Islamism in Contemporary Malaysia* (Oxford, Oxford University Press, 2009).

[19] AJ Harding, 'The Keris, the Crescent and the Blind Goddess: The State, Islam and the Constitution in Malaysia' (2002) 6 *Singapore Journal of International and Comparative Law* 154.

[20] 'Malaysia a fundamentalist Islamic country, says PM', Malaysiakini, 17 June 2002, available at https://www.malaysiakini.com/news/11804.

[21] T Thomas, 'Is Malaysia an Islamic State?' [2006] 4 *MLJ* xv; see, further, Tamir Moustafa, 'Liberal rights versus Islamic law: The construction of a binary in Malaysian politics' (2013) 47(4) *Law and Society Review* 771.

climate of fear and discrimination in a society that has always embraced religious and ethnic pluralism, and as being factually and legally incorrect. A similar response greeted a remark by Najib Tun Razak, when he was Deputy Prime Minister in 2007 that Malaysia 'has never been a secular state'. In this issue the Bar became increasingly vocal, basing its view that Malaysia is a secular state on the Constitution and the social contract.[22] It responded even more angrily when confronted with the then Chief Justice's view that the common law system should be brought into conformity with Islamic law, stating that 'any attempt to dismantle the common law system is a direct attack on our Federal Constitution ... and violates the social contract'.[23]

PAS, however, while adhering to the concept of an Islamic state, was forced to reach political accommodation with other opposition parties (DAP and PKR), and their PR coalition obtained success in the 2008 elections. In the lead up to the 2018 election and the creation of the PH coalition PAS split, its dissidents becoming the Parti Amanah, which allied with PH. PAS ultimately turned to supporting UMNO, with which it shares the idea of Malay supremacy and the dominant role of Islam. It has refrained from making clear what an Islamic state would look like, and accepts that its proposals need to be negotiated in terms of the existing Constitution and political process. Its publication 'The Islamic State Document'[24] has been described as doing 'little more than state general principles drawn from classical Islamic sources and identify areas of government policies that need to reflect these principles'.[25]

We have seen here and in Chapter 1 how Islam came to be adopted as the official religion of the Federation despite the absence of any recommendation in this regard by the Reid Commission, and despite the continuance of Islam as a State matter, as guaranteed by Schedule 9. Given the lack of any current political project, let alone consensus, to amend the Constitution on the matter of religion, which we can safely attribute to its continuing sensitivity, the interpretation of the

[22] Bar Council Press Statement, 'Malaysia is a Secular State', 18 July 2007.

[23] Bar Council Press Statement, 'Leave the Common Law Alone', 24 August 2007, quoted in AJ Harding and A Whiting, '"Custodian of Civil Liberties and Justice in Malaysia": The Malaysian Bar and Moderate State' in T Halliday, L Karpik and M Feeley (eds), *Fates of Political Liberalism in the Post-Colony: The Politics of the Legal Complex* (Cambridge, Cambridge University Press, 2012) 247.

[24] Issued in 2003: see kurzman.unc.edu/files/2011/06/pas-islamic-state-2003.pdf.

[25] Nazish Ansari, 'Malaysia: Limitations of the human rights discourse and the deployment of rights in a religious identity debate' (2004) 1(1) *Muslim World Journal of Human Rights* 14.

Constitution as it is has become the weapon of choice in a fierce struggle over the constitutional position regarding religion. As we shall see, the role of the courts has become crucial in this respect.[26]

## IV. ISLAM AS THE OFFICIAL RELIGION

'Ai ka-lagi-lagi, bagai Belanda minta tanah'

(More, more! Like a Dutchman asking for land – a Perak proverb)

The last two decades have seen a plethora of legislation intended to harmonise Islamic law across 13 State jurisdictions and one Federal jurisdiction, and improve the position of the Syariah Courts with respect to the civil courts.[27] A considerable religious bureaucracy has emerged at both State and Federal levels. In each State the Ruler has retained his function as Head of Islam and is advised by the Religious Council (usually called the *Majlis Agama Islam dan Adat Melayu*[28]), which is chaired by a *Mufti* and is competent to promulgate *fatwas*[29] which are binding on Muslims.[30] Departments for Religious Affairs are responsible for the Syariah Courts and other Syariah matters; for the appointment of judges; and for the enforcement of Islamic law in general, including some policing functions. As part of extensive reforms from 1984, the Syariah Courts were separated from the Departments for Religious Affairs, and the practice of Islamic law placed on a professional footing equivalent to that for ordinary lawyers. The Syariah Courts in each State are now divided into the Syariah Subordinate Court, the Syariah High Court, and the Syariah Court of Appeal, as a result of legislation in all States during 1984–91.[31] The judges are appointed by the *Yang di-Pertuan Agong* on the advice of the minister after consulting with the Majlis Agama (Religious Council). In 2010 the first two female Syariah Court judges were appointed.[32]

---

[26] Shah (n 2) ch 6.

[27] Sharifah Zaleha Syed Hassan and Sven Cederroth, 'Institutionalization of the Syariah in Malaysia' in *Managing Marital Disputes in Malaysia* (NIAS, Copenhagen, 1997).

[28] Literally, Council of the Religion of Islam and Malay Custom.

[29] MB Hooker, 'Fatwa in Malaysia 1960–1985: Third Coulson Memorial Lecture' (1993) 8 *Arab Law Quarterly* 93.

[30] See eg Administration of Islamic Law (Federal Territories) Act 1993, s 34.

[31] Horowitz (n 7) 260. Non-Muslims, even if otherwise qualified, are not allowed to practise before the Syariah Courts: *Majlis Agama Islam Wilayah Persekutuan v Victoria Jayaseele Martin* [2016] MLJU 40.

[32] 'A First for Women Syariah Judges', *Malaysian Bar*, 4 July 2010, available at www. malaysianbar.org.my/legal/general_news/a_first_for_women_syariah_judges.html.

The State (or, for federal territories, the Federal) Government is responsible for Islam, which is defined exhaustively in Schedule 9 to include most aspects of personal and family law for Muslims; places of worship and charitable and religious endowments; creation and punishment of offences by Muslims against religious precepts; the Syariah Courts; control of propagating doctrines and beliefs among Muslims; and the determination of matters of Islamic law and doctrine and Malay custom.

Despite this articulation of Islam as a State matter, the Federal Government has established a federal bureaucracy, under the Prime Minister's department, for Islamic affairs (JAKIM), which has expanded considerably in recent years, now employing 3,000 staff and a RM800 million budget. Its functions are to centralise matters relating to religion, which includes licensing of preachers as well as vetting of sermons and banning of un-Islamic materials. It remains a question whether such a bureaucracy can be regarded as consistent with the Constitution.[33]

Beyond this structure of religious jurisdiction, Article 3, while enshrining Islam as the religion of the Federation, adds that 'other religions may be practised in peace and harmony'. To understand Article 3 further we need to refer also to Article 11, which guarantees freedom of religion and is discussed further in the next section. Under Article 11: 'Every person has the right to profess and practice his religion and, subject to Clause (4), to propagate it.' Clause (4) provides: 'State law and in respect of the Federal Territories … federal law may control or restrict the propagation of any religious doctrine or belief among persons professing the religion of Islam.' Article 11 also attaches religious freedom to religious communities by guaranteeing the rights of religious communities to manage their own affairs.[34] Under Article 12, discrimination against any citizen on the grounds of religion is prohibited in relation to the administration of public education, and every religious group has the right to establish and maintain institutions for educating children in its own religion. It is, however, lawful under Article 12 for the Federal and State Governments to maintain Islamic institutions. However, no person shall be required to receive instruction in or to take part in any ceremony or act of worship of a religion other than his own.[35]

---

[33] Shah (n 2) 86ff; Tamir Moustafa, 'Judging in God's name: State power, secularism, and the politics of Islamic law in Malaysia' (2013) *Oxford Journal of Law and Religion* 1.

[34] Art 11(3); see also Art 12(2).

[35] The provisions are Arts 12(1), (2) and (3) respectively.

These provisions, balancing the primacy of Islam with religious freedom, have in practice raised a number of problems. What are the consequences, if any, of an official religion, especially under a federal system? Does Article 3 indeed make the State Islamic, as has been argued, and if so, in what sense? To what extent do adherents of religions other than Islam enjoy freedom of religion when the State does not treat Islam equally with other religions? How does this impact on, for example, religious offences, conversion and parental rights? These questions will now be explored.

First, the enshrinement of Islam as the religion of the Federation clearly means at least that the Federation exercises over federal territories jurisdiction equivalent to those of the States. Other than this, it appears that Islam is essentially confined to a ceremonial role. In the constitution-making process of 1956–57 it was repeatedly stated that Article 3 would not imply that the State was not secular. Article 3(2) also heavily implies that in providing Islam to be the religion of the Federation, only 'acts, observances and ceremonies' are affected, and 'all the rights, privileges, prerogatives and powers' of the Rulers as Heads of Islam 'are unaffected and unimpaired'. Moreover Article 3(4) provides that '[n]othing in this Article derogates from any other provision of this Constitution'; this would be an obstacle for those who argue that Article 3 has some kind of supervening importance with regard to constitutional interpretation. In practice Article 3(1) is observed by, for example, the *doa* (Muslim prayers) and *halal* food at official events. Any other federal role for Islam would undermine the powers of the States and their Rulers: a concern of the Rulers that was met with assurances when Article 3 was introduced that this would not be the case (hence the provision in Article 3(2) that their powers are not affected). It would also undermine freedom of religion, to which we turn in the next section, and upon which assurances were also given to non-Muslims, set out in Articles 3, 11 and 12.

This position was recognised by the Supreme Court in *Che Omar bin Che Soh v Public Prosecutor* in 1988.[36] It was argued in this case that the death penalty for drug-trafficking was contrary to Islam and therefore prohibited by Article 3. The Court, rejecting the idea that legislation could be struck down as being contrary to Islam, pointed out that, although Islam is a complete way of life covering all fields of human activity, Article 3 did not make Malaysia into an Islamic state, but merely provided for its ritualistic and ceremonial role. In doing so, the Court

---

[36] *Che Omar bin Che Soh v Public Prosecutor* [1988] 2 MLJ 55.

indicated that the Constitution draws a distinction between public and private (Islamic personal) law.[37] However, this position remains in doubt in the light of more recent cases, which have acknowledged a much larger than ceremonial significance of Article 3, establishing Islam as having primacy over other religions.[38]

## V. RELIGIOUS FREEDOM

'Kalau ayer tenang, jangan di-sangkakan ta'ada buaya'

(Still water does not mean there are no crocodiles)

The constitutional provisions relating to religious freedom were set out in the last section, where it was noted that Article 11, while providing for freedom of religion, draws a distinction between the *profession and practice* of religion on the one hand, and its *propagation* on the other hand. There are indeed relevant laws in 10 States prohibiting propagation of religions other than Islam amongst Muslims,[39] so that the Constitution both restricts freedom of religion and discriminates in favour of Islam in the way it restricts that freedom. In a society where religion is of great importance and there is fierce competition for adherents, naturally the position regarding propagation and conversion is objected to by non-Muslim religious groups. As a result, non-Muslim religions have organised themselves to secure religious freedom: the Malaysian Consultative Council of Buddhism, Christianity, Hinduism, Sikhism and Taoism was set up in 1983, although Muslim groups declined to join this organisation. While it can be seen that, in the Malaysian context, attempts to proselytise amongst Muslims might be incendiary, it is hard to see why this would not also be true for proselytisation amongst non-Muslims. In *Minister for Home Affairs v Jamaluddin bin Othman* the Supreme Court struck down a detention order issued under the Internal Security Act against a Malay convert to Christianity who had converted several Muslims to Christianity, reasoning that even national security could not prevail over freedom of religion.[40]

---

[37] See further, Mohamed Azam (n 8) 10–11.

[38] *Meor Atiqulrahman bin Ishak v Fatimah binte Sihi* [2000] 5 MLJ 375.

[39] See, further, Mohamed Azam (n 8). These laws, passed between 1980 and 1991 are, however, rarely enforced in practice.

[40] *Minister for Home Affairs v Jamaluddin bin Othman* [1989] 1 MLJ 418.

The constitutional provisions raise acutely the question of how far religious freedom is in practice guaranteed. Whilst actual religious observance of all kinds can be seen throughout Malaysia, and holy days of all major religions are observed as public holidays, religious freedom as such is clearly restricted in several respects.[41] For example, Article 11(5) allows legislative restrictions on religious freedom on the basis of maintaining public order, public health or morality. An example of this is the case of *Halimatussaadiah v Public Service Commission*, in which the court upheld on the basis of public order a prohibition on a public servant from wearing a *tudung* (headscarf) that covered her face while on duty. However, in so finding the court took into account the evidence of the Mufti that this form of dress was not mandated by Islam.[42] This can be contrasted with *Meor Atiqulrahman v Fatimah binte Sihi*, in which the High Court overturned the dismissal from school of three Muslim boys for wearing a *serban* (turban) rather than a *songkok* (black cap) as required by the school authorities. In this case no issue of public order of morality arose.[43] The following issues which have arisen in recent years illustrate the problem of religious conversion and its effect on religious freedom.

In 2009 objections were made about a Catholic publication, the *Herald*, which in its Malay edition (there are Malay-speaking Catholics, especially in East Malaysia) used the word 'Allah' to indicate the Christian God. The Minister for Home Affairs, using his powers under the Publications and Printing Presses Act 1984, banned the publication. The Catholic Archbishop of Kuala Lumpur, the publisher of the *Herald*, applied for judicial review, and the High Court issued a powerful judgment striking down the Minister's ban on the ground that it violated the right to practise religion 'in peace and harmony' under Article 3(1), and the right of freedom of expression under Article 10. The Government appealed the decision successfully, and an application by the Archbishop for leave to appeal to the Federal Court was unsuccessful, as was an attempt to secure revision of the refusal of leave.[44]

---

[41] Jaclyn Ling-Chien Neo, 'Malay Nationalism, Islamic Supremacy and the Constitutional Bargain in the Multi-ethnic Composition of Malaysia' (2006) 13 *International Journal of Minority and Group Rights* 95.

[42] *Halimatussaadiah v Public Service Commission* [1992] 1 MLJ 513.

[43] *Meor Atiqulrahman v Fatimah binte Sihi* [2000] 5 MLJ 375; and see Abdul Aziz Bari, 'Islam in the Federal Constitution: A commentary on the decision of *Meor Atiqulrahman*' (2000) 2 MLJ cxli; Thio Li-ann and J Neo, 'Religious dress in schools: The serban controversy in Malaysia' (2006) 55 *International and Comparative Law Quarterly* 671.

[44] *Menteri Dalam Negeri & Ors v Titular Roman Catholic Archbishop of Kuala Lumpur* [2013] 6 MLJ 468; *Titular Roman Catholic Archbishop of Kuala Lumpur v Menteri Dalam Negeri & Ors* [2014] 6 CLJ 541.

Several aspects of the appeal court rulings are problematical.[45] The publication in question had used the word 'Allah' for the Christian God for many years without any public order issues, and such usage was shown to have existed since the seventeenth century. Moreover, the propriety of the appeal courts' process was brought into question by the fact that the Federal Court's judgment refusing leave was a split decision occupying more than 100 pages, indicating clearly that the appeal was at least highly arguable. The notion advanced in the Court of Appeal that the concept of practising other religions in 'peace and harmony' meant that other religions must not disturb the practice of Islam appears to defy the language and intention of Article 3. And the approach taken to religious freedom, applying the concept only to elements of religious practice that are essential to the religion in question, seems to deny the essence of religious freedom rather than enforcing it. On the other hand, by the time the case reached the appeal level it had indeed become a highly divisive matter, and the Cabinet proceeded to issue a letter stating its policy on religious freedom. The situation was also addressed by the Conference of Rulers, which issued a statement expressing 'sadness' over the use of the word 'Allah', emphasising the role of the Rulers in protecting Islam 'without neglecting the rights and religious freedoms of the other races [sic]', and deploring attacks which had taken place on places of worship.[46] On this last point it is noted that inter-religious violence has been unusual in Malaysia, and has been directed mainly to property.

Other divisive matters have included raids on churches by the religious police, and regulatory measures against Malay-language Bibles.

The restrictions on religious freedom, it is important to note, extend to Muslims as well as non-Muslims. The religious and other State authorities in Malaysia, an orthodox Sunni country, are highly suspicious of what are regarded as deviant forms of Islamic doctrine and observance. For example, in 1994, the Darul Arqam movement, an apparently harmless neo-Sufist, anti-State Muslim community, was declared deviant by the National Fatwa Council and ordered to disband. It was later declared an unlawful society under the Societies Act 1966, and its leaders were detained under the Internal Security Act and forced to confess on television their deviance from Islamic teachings.[47]

---

[45] J Neo, 'What's in a name? Malaysia's "Allah" controversy and the judicial intertwining of Islam with ethnic identity' (2014) 12(3) *International Journal of Constitutional Law* 751; see also *Rosliza bt Ibrahim v Kerajaan Negeri Selangor* [2021] 2 MLJ 281, Fed Ct.

[46] Shah (n 2) 118.

[47] Abdullahi An-Na'im, 'The Cultural Mediation of Human Rights Implementation: Al-Arqam Case in Malaysia' in J Bauer and D Bell (eds), *Human Rights in East Asia* (New York, Cambridge University Press, 1999).

What seems conspicuously lacking in these episodes is any constitutionally mandated process whereby the various religious communities can negotiate a mutually acceptable solution to issues such as proselytisation, conversion, burials, doctrinal schisms, naming of illegitimate children, and the use of religious texts. Litigation and media wars seem to encourage paranoia rather than tolerance. Fears of mass conversion of Muslims and undermining of Islam's position are clearly unfounded.[48]

Where issues of actual as opposed to feared apostasy or conversion are concerned, the legal rights and interests of individuals are potentially deeply affected. It is in this area that conflict between the two legal systems, civil and Syariah, is most evident, and it has taken the form of litigation over the Syariah Courts' jurisdiction. The implications of this extend beyond immediate family law issues, profoundly affecting Malaysia's constitutional architecture.

## VI. CONVERSION AND THE COURTS

'Katuk bawah tempurong'

(A frog under a coconut shell)

In 1988 the controversial constitutional amendment mentioned earlier introducing Article 121(1A) provided that the High Courts 'shall have no jurisdiction in respect of any matter within the jurisdiction of the Syariah Courts'. The ostensible reason for this was that the civil courts had on occasion reversed a decision of the Syariah Court, even though the civil judges, as common lawyers, are not required to be qualified in Islamic law. This amendment ultimately raised issues of public concern in the area of conversion and religious freedom, and at a higher level the proper place of religion in the polity.[49]

The case law on Article 121(1A) reached a critical juncture with the 2007 decision of the Federal Court in the problematical case of *Lina Joy v Federal Territory Islamic Council*, which related to an attempt by a

---

[48] Mohamed Azam (n 8).

[49] Tamir Moustafa, *Constituting Religion: Islam, Liberal Rights, and the Malaysian State* (Cambridge, Cambridge University Press, 2018). For dealing with issues of Islamic finance in relation to these matters, see *JRI Resources v Kuwait Finance House (President of Association of Islamic Banking Institutions Malaysia) & Anor, Interveners* [2019] 3 MLJ 561, Fed Ct; A Harding and others, *ICONnect-Clough Centre Global Review of Constitutional Law 2019*, available at https://papers.ssrn.com/sol3/papers.cfm?abstract_id=3736382.

Muslim woman to change her religion.[50] Lina Joy was brought up as a Muslim, but as an adult she converted to Christianity. When requested to change her National Identity Card to show a new name and religion, the National Registration Department (NRD) refused to accept her declaration that she was now a Christian, saying that she should obtain a statement of apostasy from the Syariah Court. This she was unwilling to do, relying on her freedom of religion under Article 11. The application for judicial review of the NRD's decision continuously preoccupied and inflamed public opinion as it proceeded through the courts during 2004–07. A majority of the Federal Court (two to one) ultimately rejected the application, deciding that the NRD had acted lawfully.

The majority judgment proceeded on the basis that if a Muslim wanted to leave Islam, this was a question of Islamic law which had its own jurisprudence on apostasy. Article 3 was stated to 'have a far wider and meaningful purpose than a mere fixation of the official religion'. Article 11, despite providing for freedom of religion, was interpreted as meaning that Islamic law determined the method of converting into and out of Islam; under Article 121(1A) apostasy, as a matter relating to Islamic law, was within the jurisdiction only of the Syariah Court. By so deciding the court had, in effect, by reference to Article 121(1A) elevated the official religion above freedom to choose one's religion, and given a practical effect to Article 3, as opposed to Article 11, in determining the rights of citizens. However a passionate dissent was registered by Justice Richard Malanjum, who was the only non-Muslim judge hearing the appeal, and was later the Chief Justice; he was also the only one of the three judges to render his judgment in English. The majority view fails to grasp that the jurisdiction of Islamic law itself depends on the freedom of an individual's choice of religion.

Subsequently there were three much-discussed child-custody cases involving Hindu women – Shamala's case,[51] Subashini's case[52] and

---

[50] *Lina Joy v Majlis Agama Islam Wilayah Persekutuan* [2007] 4 MLJ 585; and see the contrary decision in *Azmi Mohamad Azam v Director of Jabatan Agama Islam Sarawak and Others* [2016] 6 CLJ 562. Commentary on this issue can be found in Thio Li-ann, 'Jurisdictional imbroglio: Civil and religious courts, turf wars and Article 121(1A) of the Federal Constitution' in A Harding and HP Lee (ed), *Constitutional Landmarks in Malaysia: The First 50 years, 1957–2007* (Kuala Lumpur, LexisNexis, 2007); Dian AH Shah and Kevin YL Tan, 'Indigenous interactions: Syariah and administrative law in Malaysia' in S Jhaveri and M Ramsden (eds), *Judicial Review in the Common Law World* (Cambridge, Cambridge University Press, 2021).

[51] *Shamala a/p Sathiyaseelan v Dr Jeyaganesh a/l C Mogarajah* [2004] 2 MLJ 648.

[52] *Subashini a/p Rajasingam v Saravanan a/l Thangathoray* [2007] 4 MLJ 97. For discussion of these cases see A Whiting, 'Desecularising Malaysian Law?' in P Nicholson and S Biddulph (eds) *Examining Practice, Interrogating Theory: Comparative Legal Studies in*

Indira Gandhi's case[53] – all related to children whose Hindu father had converted them to Islam when he himself converted, with the divorced wife and mother of the children remaining Hindu. The civil courts interpreted Article 121(1A) in these cases in such a fashion as to deny a remedy to the mothers seeking custody, who as a result fell into a gap between the respective jurisdictions of the civil courts and the Syariah Courts. The civil courts held that only the Syariah Courts could decide if the children were converted, but the Syariah Courts could not entertain any application by the mothers as they were not Muslims. The case of Indira Gandhi became particularly problematical when there were conflicting custody orders. Eventually the Federal court ruled in Indira Gandhi's favour, holding that the right to determine a child's religion lies with both parents, not one, even though Article 11 refers to 'parent'.

In doing this the Federal Court, in one of the most important judicial decisions ever made in Malaysia's superior courts, went two stages further. First, it defined the relationship between the civil courts and the Syariah Courts as analogous to that between an administrative tribunal and the courts, which is to say that the courts can review a decision of the Syariah Court only for jurisdictional error, not for an error in the application of Islamic law. This is a happy compromise in that it establishes the civil courts in a position of superiority without allowing them to overturn substantive decisions in an area of law with which they are not required to be familiar. Secondly, the Federal Court accepted the applicability in Malaysia of the basic structure doctrine, which would act as a limitation on the enactment of constitutional amendments. This position was also set out in *Semenyih Jaya*, as we saw in Chapter 8.

## VII. CONCLUSION

'Ada-kah duri di-pertajam?'

(Does one sharpen thorns?)

The Malaysian Government's efforts over the years towards inter-ethnic reconciliation, social stability and economic development for all Malaysians have to be recognised. However, the historical basis and

---

*Asia* (Martinus Nijhoff, Leiden, 2008); D Shah, 'Religion, conversions and custody: Battles in the Malaysian appellate courts' in A Harding and D Shah (eds), *Law and Society in Malaysia: Pluralism, Religion and Ethnicity* (Abingdon, Routledge, 2017).

[53] *Indira Gandhi a/p Mutho v Pengara Jabatan Agama Islam Perak* [2018] 1 MLJ 545.

practical consequences of this reconciliation seem not to be accepted by newer generations of Malaysians. For centuries Malaysian society has embraced a culture of mutual tolerance, and the principle of mutual non-interference in religious affairs is culturally entrenched. Pluralism has been a characteristic of many Islamic societies, but Malaysia is in this respect an outstanding present-day example because the country lies in a part of the world – Southeast Asia – where pluralism is a penetrating fact that deeply influences Islam along with other social phenomena. Development, education and urbanisation have also brought about closer proximity between those following different religions, more religious conversions, and larger numbers of inter-religious mixed marriages, especially in East Malaysia, where inter-marriage has been endemic. The position of Islamic law in relation to national law and the Constitution has become a matter of intense political conflict. The issue of the religious nature of the state has re-emerged in the form of a struggle waged in the courts to define the respective jurisdictions of the civil and Syariah Courts. These decisions, prior to *Indira Gandhi*, tended to undermine the jurisdiction of the civil courts to enforce the fundamental right of freedom of religion.

The liberal-democratic order implied in the Constitution has been partially maintained, not least due to its dogged defence by the legal profession as we saw in Chapter 8,[54] but at the expense of restrictions on religious freedom, and the privileging of Islam over other religions. The religious dispensation presently obtaining has been hotly disputed, and not just in the context of *Lina Joy* and *Indira Gandhi*. For example, in 2007 unprecedented and widespread protests by Malaysia's Hindu minority, referred to the 'HINDRAF' (Hindu Rights Action Force) protests, based on religious and socio-economic discrimination, were suppressed by the Government.[55] Non-Muslim groups cite instances where places of worship have been bulldozed by the authorities, or permission has not been given for construction of places of worship in predominantly Muslim areas.[56] In one ugly incident Muslim protesters placed a cow's head at the gate of a State Government building in Selangor in protest against the construction of a Hindu temple; they were convicted and fined under the Sedition Act.[57]

---

[54] And see A Whiting, 'Secularism, the Islamic State and the Malaysian Legal Profession' (2010) 5(1) *Asian Journal of Comparative Law*.
[55] Aliran Press Statement, 'Aliran AGM Deplores High-handed Police Action at Hindraf Assembly', 25 November 2007.
[56] Shah (n 2) 93.
[57] Ibid 118.

A syncretic, creative and peaceful solution to the problem of religion and the Constitution is by no means impossible. At present, however, it seems as though the path which could lead to such an ideal outcome is fraught with ever-changing political controversy, a good deal of intellectual confusion, and little in the way of actual legal reform. Even quite practical issues such as the failure of relief for plaintiffs caught between the conflicting demands of two legal systems, and the increased incidence of child marriages, have failed to result in meaningful reform. Nonetheless, we should not ignore the fact of historically peaceful cohabitation of Islam and other conceptions of state and law in Malaysia over several centuries The apparent contemporary polarisation along religious lines, rendered complex by the new two-coalition politics of the period post-2008, should not obscure this history. There have been and continue to be significant skirmishes conducted principally in terms of legal struggles over jurisdiction. These skirmishes, given the extent of public anger on both sides, are clearly far more than lawyers' turf wars. They even at times seem likely to veer towards more intense forms of conflict. There are, however, far-reaching compromises on both sides: Islam largely concedes, in practice and for the time being, that Islamic law is not the fundamental basis of the constitutional and legal order, while the constitutional order itself concedes that strict equality for Muslims and non-Muslims will not apply in some circumstances.

The Malaysian example is certainly one of inter-religious conflict, but this conflict is largely expressed in terms of the media and litigation. Although feelings have run high, violence is a very rare. The Constitution and the institutions of the common law have provided the means whereby accommodation between two fundamentally contradictory conceptions of legality, one secular, the other religious, has been achieved. Whether this will continue to be so remains, of course, to be seen.

### FURTHER READING

AJ Harding, '"Sharia" and national law in Malaysia' in JM Otto (ed), *Sharia Incorporated: A Comparative Overview of the Legal Systems of Twelve Muslim Countries in Past and Present* (Leiden, Leiden University Press, 2010).

Tamir Moustafa, *Constituting Religion: Islam, Liberal Rights, and the Malaysian State* (Cambridge, Cambridge University Press, 2018).

Tamir Moustafa, 'Judging in God's name: State power, secularism, and the politics of Islamic law in Malaysia' (2014) 3(1) *Oxford Journal of Law and Religion* 152.

J Neo, 'Competing imperatives: Conflicts and convergences in state and Islam in pluralist Malaysia' (2015) 4 *Oxford Journal of Law and Religion* 1.

D Shah, *Constitutions, Religion and Politics in Asia: Indonesia, Malaysia and Sri Lanka* (Cambridge, Cambridge University Press, 2017).

# Conclusion

'Jahit sudah, kelindan putus'
(The sewing is done, the thread is snapped)

W E HAVE SEEN in this book a number of important, albeit sometimes contradictory, trends in the working out of Malaysian constitutionalism, twenty-first century style. In particular, 2008 seems to have been a watershed in many ways, and many of the most prominent changes have occurred and long-standing positions debated since the political landscape changed with the 2008 elections. May 2018 provided another milestone with a smooth, constitutional change of government; the first change of government since independence. This indicates a high level of constitutional maturity. Unfortunately, this was reversed undemocratically with the change of government without an election in March 2020, bringing to an end a creative if somewhat inchoate period of reform. Nonetheless GE14 laid down a clear lesson that government is only with the consent of the electorate, and no government has an inherent right to govern.

Undeniably, the state looks more Islamic than it did in 1957, due to, for example, the effect of Article 121(1A), but inter-religious conflict, although more intense, has been kept within the bounds of reasonable discourse. If there is, as many fear, a serious threat to religious freedom, it is also true that many elements in Malaysian society are in favour of more democracy and a tolerant, open society.

We have seen recognition of the injustice of the 1988 sacking of the judges. Several judicial decisions following the enactment of the Judicial Appointments Commission Act 2009 have renewed the confidence in the judiciary that was lost in 1988. Civil society and elements of many political parties continue to demand constitutional and governance reforms. The Bar has remained as steadfast and as solid as ever in its defence of the Constitution, the rule of law and human rights. Minorities, ethnic and religious, have stood up for their rights in spite of the social contract, while the social contract itself has come under question from some quarters, in spite of its sensitivity. The courts have advanced the claims of indigenous people. Malaysians are willing to protest against unconstitutional actions and employ new media in doing so, to an unprecedented degree. Interest in and writing about and debating the constitution has never been more extensive.

For its part, the Government has to some extent redesigned the social contract in ways that make it less significant than it was, and twice embarked on a process of reform, albeit short-lived in both cases, in 2011–12, when the emergency laws were revoked, and in 2018–20. Both Government and Opposition coalitions have shown how a consociational approach can work, thereby offering the electorate a genuine choice and forcing parties to satisfy voters of different communities in their search for power. This has, in conjunction with greater electoral change, intensified political competition and thrown into relief the powers of the Rulers.

Changes of government at the State level have rendered quite normal the cohabitation of State Governments opposed politically to the Federal Government, and this has reinforced federalism as lived constitutional practice. A strong demand for more meaningful federalism has grown in East Malaysia. The Government has fitfully undertaken a process of removing or restricting some parts of the apparatus of the authoritarian, centralised state. Reforms have also raised the bar in terms of public expectations of the conditions of democracy and governance.

These developments can be stated in counterpoint to some negative developments. However most of these can be called incidents rather than trends. The most marked trend here is the escalation of inter-religious struggle, which lies at the root of more incidents and more wars of words than ever before. Human rights abuses still often go uncorrected in many instances. Disappearances of non-mainstream religious figures are especially troubling, and remain unresolved in spite of official inquiries.[1] There are still concerns about the impartiality and independence of the judiciary, even though improvements can be seen. Many highly repressive and unjustifiable laws remain on the statute book, even if they are not routinely enforced. The Sedition Act has had a particularly chequered history. The fact is that if present trends are the beginning of an uncertain and haphazard reform process there is a great deal to do, and it will take a long time to decide basic directions and assumptions and work through the maze of issues that require to be addressed in such a process. But a start that cannot be erased from public consciousness has been made during 2018–20, has raised expectations and possibilities.

---

[1] D Landau, 'Abusive constitutionalism' (2013) 47 *University of California, Davis Law Review* 189.

Having said all this, it remains the case that Malaysia is well placed to advance the rule of law and democracy because it has the benefit of long-established traditions of constitutional government. The Constitution has been subjected to more than 600 textual changes since *Merdeka*, although the process of textual change appears to have ground to a halt, with the end of two-thirds majorities since 2008 making constitutional amendments especially difficult to achieve unless there is a broad consensus, as with the lowering of the voting age to 18. In this sense the substance of the Constitution is probably safe from deleterious amendment. In these terms it seems as if the Constitution's basic structure and significance have been spared the erosion that has afflicted much of its detail. It remains uncertain, however, whether the judiciary will entrench the 'basic structure' doctrine to prevent 'abusive constitutionalism' in future.

Following the PH's unexpected victory in 2018 there was a palpable wish that constitutional and broader governance reforms had been discussed more seriously and more practically than had been the case. An institutional reform committee was hastily assembled and reported equally hastily. Sadly, the Government did not choose to reveal what was in the committee's report. It would have been useful to know what was in their minds in terms of reform. But the fact is that such preparatory work ought to have been undertaken in advance, and ought to have involved a broad range of perspectives.

However that may be, it seems that constitutional change, whether one sees it as reform or not, has happened anyway, mainly via the judiciary, even without a concerted holistic discussion. The events of 2020–21, however, appear to many to constitute democratic backsliding on a disturbing scale. In particular, it is disturbing to witness the avoidance of parliamentary accountability by a Government whose majority had never been clearly demonstrated. It seems safe to say, nonetheless, that the events of 2020 are not the end of this story. Political fragmentation might indeed afford an opportunity for different actors and processes at different levels (at the State level, for example, or in civil society organisations, or in inter-religious discourse) to discuss or implement different aspects of reform; and one lasting legacy of 2018–20 might be that at least the discussion of reform was iterated seriously even if not followed through very extensively. In September 2021, following the appointment of Ismail Sabri Yaakob as Prime Minister, the Government and the Opposition concluded an unprecedented memorandum of understanding designed to ensure political stability and parliamentary reforms – a promising development for Malaysian constitutionalism.[2] This book began with a hymn to the diversity of Malaysian society expressed in Malacca's history and culture. Whatever changes are in store for it, there is little reason to think that in this defining characteristic at least – its kaleidoscopic and often baffling diversity – Malaysia will change, and who knows if this will not prove in the long run a very great asset?

---

[2] '5 key takeaways from bipartisan cooperation MOU between Malaysian government and Pakatan Harapan opposition', *Channelnewsasia*, 14 September 2021, available at www.channelnewsasia.com/asia/malaysia-mou-bipartisan-cooperation-government-pakatan-harapan-political-stability-reforms-2176266.

# Index

## Introductory Note

References such as '178–79' indicate (not necessarily continuous) discussion of a topic across a range of pages. Wherever possible in the case of topics with many references, these have either been divided into sub-topics or only the most significant discussions of the topic are listed. Because the entire work is about the 'Constitution of Malaysia', the use of this term (and certain others which occur constantly throughout the book) as entry points has been restricted. Information will be found under the corresponding detailed topics.

www.ingramcontent.com/pod-product-compliance
Lightning Source LLC
Chambersburg PA
CBHW061142220326
41599CB00025B/4322